J.W.ORR N.Y.

UNIV. OF MICH.

NOBLE DEEDS

OF

AMERICAN WOMEN.

EDITED BY J. CLEMENT.

WITH AN INTRODUCTION

BY

MRS. L. H. SIGOURNEY.

ILLUSTRATED.

BOSTON:
LEE AND SHEPARD.
1869.

The compiler rather ignores Mrs. Ellet & Conklin yet quotes when necessary

Editor's Preface.

This work was suggested by one of similar character, entitled "Noble Deeds of Woman," an English work, which contains but three references to American Women, two of which are of but very little importance. Only one article is the same in both works, and that is the letter written by Mrs. Sigourney to the women of Greece, in 1828, in behalf of the ladies of Hartford.

This failure to do justice to American women, may have been an oversight; be that as it may, a work of the kind here presented, seemed to be needed, and we regret that its preparation had not been assigned to an abler pen. Multitudes of works have been consulted, and such anecdotes gleaned as it is thought will have a salutary influence on the mind and heart. Should the records of female courage and virtue herein presented to the daughters of the land, encourage, even in the slightest degree, a laudable spirit of emulation, our humble labors will not have been put forth in vain.

Facts are more sublime than fictions; and American women have actually performed all the good, and grand, and glorious deeds which the honest and judicious novelist dares ascribe to the female sex; hence we have found no occasion, in striving to make this work interesting, to deviate from the path of historical truth.

The sources whence our materials have been derived, are largely indicated in the body of the work. Possibly, however, we may have failed, in some instances, to indicate our indebtedness to historians and biographers where such reference was justly demanded; suffice it to say, therefore, once for all, that, although something like two hundred of these pages are in our own language, we deserve but little credit for originality, and would prefer to be regarded as an unpretending compiler, rather than as an aspirant to the title of author. J. C.

NOTE TO THE REVISED EDITION.

The fact that eight thousand copies of this work have been published in less than a year after its appearance, indicates a degree of popularity which was not anticipated. In this edition we have thrown out a few pages of the old matter, and substituted, in most instances, fresher anecdotes; and this revision, with the illustrations which the liberal-minded publishers have added, will, it is hoped, render the work still more acceptable. J. C

CONTENTS.

INTRODUCTION.

The advantages of Biography are obvious and great. To the weight of precept, it adds the force and efficacy of example. It presents correct and beautiful models, and awakens the impulse to imitate what we admire. Other sciences strengthen the intellect, this influences and amends the heart. Other subjects interest the imagination, this modifies conduct and character. By the recorded actions of the great and good, we regulate our own course, and steer, star-guided, over life's trackless ocean.

In remote ages, the department of Female Biography was almost a void. Here and there on the pages of the Sacred Volume, a lineament, or a form, is sketched with graphic power, either as a warning, or bright with the hues of heaven. Yet uninspired history, though she continued to utter "her dark sayings upon the harp," was wont to relapse into silence at the name of woman. Classic antiquity scarcely presents aught that might be cited as a sustained example. In the annals of ancient Greece, the wife of one of its philosophers has obtained a place, but only through the varied trials, by which she contributed to perfect his patience. Rome but slightly lifts the household veil from the mother of the Gracchi, as she exultingly exhibits her heart's jewels. Cleopatra, with her royal barge, casts a dazzling gleam over the Cydnus, but her fame is like the poison of the reptile that destroyed her. Boadicea rushes for a moment in her rude chariot over the battle field, but the fasces and the chains of Rome close the scene.

Modern Paganism disclosed a still deeper abyss of degradation for woman. The aboriginal lord of the American forests lays the burden on the shoulder of his weaker companion, and stalks on in unbowed majesty, with his quiver and his tomahawk. Beneath the sultry skies of Africa she crouches to drink the poison water before her judges, having no better test of her innocence than the deliverer, Death. In India, we see her plunging into the Ganges her female infants, that they may escape her lot of misery, or wrapped in the flames of the burning pile, turn into ashes with the corpse of her husband. Under the sway of the Moslem, her highest condition is a life-long incarceration, her best treatment, that of a gilded toy—a soulless slave. Throughout the whole heathen world, woman may be characterized, as Humanity, in Central Asia has been, by an elegant French writer, as "always remaining anonymous,—indifferent to herself,—not believing in her liberty, having none,—and leaving no trace of her passage upon earth."

Christianity has changed the scene. Wherever her pure and pitying spirit prevails, the sway of brute force is softened, and the "weaker vessel" upheld. Bearing in her hand the blessed Gospel, "a light to lighten the Gentiles, and the glory of the people Israel," she adds to the literature of the world a new volume, the History of Woman.

She spreads a page, for which the long, slow ages had neither looked, nor inquired,— neither waited for, nor imagined, the page of female biography.

So liberal have been our own immediate times in supplying fitting materials, that an extensive and valuable library might readily be selected in this department alone. Since knowledge has shed her baptism upon the head of woman, her legitimate sphere of duty has become extended, and enriched by incident. We see her not only brought forward as a teacher, but entering unrebuked the fields of science and literature ; we see her amid the hardships of colonial life, displaying a martyr's courage, or ascending the deck of the mission ship to take her part in "perils among the heathen."

The venerable moralist of Barley Wood, who so perseveringly encouraged her sex to reflect, to discriminate, to choose the good and refuse the evil, who, after attaining the age of sixty years, presented them with eleven new and instructive volumes, has not long laid down her pen, for the rest and reward of the righteous. That high souled apostle of erring, suffering humanity, to whose dauntless benevolence crowned heads did honor, whose melodious voice I almost fancy that I again hear, as in the plain garb of her order, she stood as a tutelary being among the convicts at Newgate,— she has but recently arisen to that congenial society of the just made perfect, who rejoice over "one sinner that repenteth."

And the harp of that tuneful one, so recently exchanged for a purer harmony, still breathes upon our hearts the echoes of her varied lay, as when touched by her hand it warbled—

Fame hath a voice, whose thrilling tone
  Can bid the life pulse beat,
As when a trumpet's note hath blown,
  Warning the hosts to meet;
But ah! let mine, a woman's breast,
With words of home-born love be bless'd."

She, too, who sleeps beneath the hopia-tree in Burmah, whose courage and constancy no hero has transcended, how rapidly has she been followed in the same self denying path, by others who "counted not their lives dear unto them," if they might bear to the perishing heathen the name and love of a Redeemer.

And one still lives, the wonderful Scandinavian maiden, whose melody now holds our own land in enchantment, and who exhibits, on a scale hitherto unknown in the world's history, rare endowments, boundless liberality, and deep humility; God's grace held in subservience to the good of her fellow creatures. Through the power of song, which, as the compeer of the nightingale, she possesses, and with a singular freedom from vanity and selfishness, she charms and elevates, while with the harvest of her toils she feeds the hungry, clothes the naked, comforts the desolate, aids the hallowed temple to uplift its spire, and the school to spread its brooding wing over the children of future generations.

One there lives, who doth inherit
Angel gifts with angel spirit,
Bidding streams of gladness flow
Through the realms of want and woe,
'Mid lone age and misery's lot,
Kindling pleasures long forgot,
Seeking minds oppress'd with night,
And on darkness shedding light;
She the seraph's speech doth know,
She hath learn'd their deeds below

So, when o'er this misty strand,
She shall clasp their waiting hand,
They will fold her to their breast,
More a sister than a guest.

If all true greatness should be estimated by its tendencies, and by the good it performs, it is peculiarly desirable that woman's claims to distinction should be thus judged and awarded. In this young western world, especially in New England, her agency has been admitted, and her capacity tested, of mingling a healthful leaven with the elements of a nation's character. Here, her presence has been acknowledged, and her aid faithfully rendered. from the beginning. There is a beautiful tradition, that the first foot which pressed the snow clad rock of Plymouth was that of Mary Chilton, a fair young maiden, and that the last survivor of those heroic pioneers was Mary Allerton, who lived to see the planting of twelve out of the thirteen colonies, which formed the nucleus of these United States.

In the May Flower, eighteen wives accompanied their husbands to a waste land and uninhabited, save by the wily and vengeful savage. On the unfloored hut, she who had been nurtured amid the rich carpets and curtains of the mother land, rocked her new born babe, and complained not. She, who in the home of her youth had arranged the gorgeous shades of embroidery, or, perchance, had compounded the rich venison pasty as her share in the housekeeping, now pounded the coarse Indian corn for her children's bread, and bade them ask God's blessing, ere they took their scanty portion. When the snows sifted through their miserable roof-trees upon her little ones, she gathered them closer to her bosom; she taught them the Bible, and the catechism, and the holy hymn, though the war-whoop of the Indian rang through the wild. Amid the untold hardships of colonial life, she infused new strength into her husband by her firmness, and solaced his weary hours by her love. She was to him,

> "An undergoing spirit, to bear up
> Against whate'er ensued."

During the struggle of our Revolution, the privations sustained, and the efforts made by women, were neither few nor of short duration. Many of them are delineated in the present volume, and in other interesting ones of the same class, which have found favor with the public.

Yet innumerable instances of faithful toil, and patient endurance, must have been covered with oblivion. In how many a lone home, whence the father was long sundered by a soldier's destiny, did the Mother labor to perform to their little ones both his duties and her own, having no witness of the extent of her heavy burdens, and sleepless anxieties, save the Hearer of Prayer.

A good and hoary headed man, who had passed the limits of fourscore, once said to me, "my father was in the army during the whole eight years of the Revolutionary war, at first as a common soldier, afterwards as an officer. My mother had the sole charge of us, four little ones. Our house was a poor one, and far from neighbors. I have a keen remembrance of the terrible cold of some of these winters. The snow lay so deep and long, that it was difficult to cut or draw fuel from the woods, and to get our corn to mill, when we had any. My mother was the possessor of a coffee mill. In that she ground wheat, and made coarse bread, which we ate, and were thankful. It was not always that we could be allowed as much, even of this, as our keen appetites craved. Many is the time that we have gone to bed, with only a drink of water for our supper, in which a little molasses had been mingled. We patiently received it, for we knew our mother did as well for us as she could, and hoped to have something better in the morning. She was never heard to repine; and young as we were, we tried to make her loving spirit and heavenly trust, our example.

"When my father was permitted to come home, his stay was short, and he had not much to leave us, for the pay of those who achieved our liberties was slight, and irregularly rendered. Yet when he went, my mother ever bade him farewell with a cheerful face, and not to be anxious about his children, for she would watch over them night and day, and God would take care of the families of those who went forth to defend the righteous cause of their country. Sometimes we wondered that she did not mention the cold weather, or our short meals, or her hard work, that we little ones might be clothed, and fed, and taught. But she would not weaken his hands, or sadden his heart, for she said a soldier's lot was harder than all. We saw that she never complained, but always kept in her heart a sweet hope, like a well of living water. Every night ere we slept, and every morning when we arose, we lifted our little hands for God's blessing on our absent father, and our endangered country."

How deeply the prayers from such solitary homes, and faithful hearts, were mingled with the infant liberties of our dear native land, we may not know until we enter where we see no more "through a glass darkly, but face to face."

Incidents repeatedly occurred during this contest of eight years, between the feeble colonies and the strong mother land, of a courage that ancient Sparta would have applauded.

In a thinly settled part of Virginia, the quiet of the Sabbath eve was once broken by the loud, hurried roll of the drum. Volunteers were invoked to go forth and prevent the British troops, under the pitiless Tarleton, from forcing their way through an important mountain pass. In an old fort resided a family, all of whose elder sons were absent with our army, which at the North opposed the foe. The father lay enfeebled and sick. Around his bedside the Mother called their three sons, of the ages of thirteen, fifteen, and seventeen.

"Go forth, children," said she, "to the defence of your native clime. Go, each and all of you. I spare not my youngest, my fair-haired boy, the light of my declining years.

"Go forth, my sons. Repel the foot of the invader, or see my face no more."

It has been recorded in the annals of other climes, as well as our own, that Woman, under the pressure of unusual circumstances, has revealed unwonted and unexpected energies. It is fitting that she should prove herself equal to every emergency, nor shrink from any duty that dangers or reverses may impose.

Still, her best happiness and true glory are doubtless found in her own peculiar sphere. Rescued, as she has been, from long darkness, by the precepts of the religion of Jesus, brought forth into the broad sunlight of knowledge and responsibility, she is naturally anxious to know how to discharge her debt to the age, and to her own land. Her patriotism is, to labor in the sanctuary of home, and in every allotted department of education, to form and train a race that shall bless their country, and serve their God.

There has been sometimes claimed for her, under the name of "*rights*," a wider participation in the pursuits, exposures, and honors appertaining to men. Were these somewhat indefinite claims conceded, would the change promote her welfare? Would she be a gainer by any added power or sounding title, which should require the sacrifice of that delicacy which is the life-blood of her sex?

Would it be better for man to have no exercise for those energies, which the state of a gentle, trustful being calls forth; those protecting energies which reveal his peculiar strength, and liken him to a god-like nature? Would it add either to her attractions or his happiness, to confront her in the arena of political strife, or enable her to bear her part in fierce collision with the bold and unprincipled? Might it not endanger or obliterate that enthusiasm of love, which she so much prizes, to meet the tutelary spirit of his home delights, on the steep unsheltered heights of ambition, as a competitor or a rival?

Would it be as well for the rising generation, who are given into the arms of Woman for their earliest guidance, that the ardor of her nature should be drawn into different and contradictory channels? When a traveler in those lands where she goes forth to manual toil in the fields, I have mourned to see her neglected little ones, deprived of maternal care, unsoftened by the blandishments of its tenderness, growing up like animals, groveling, unimpressible, unconscientious. Whatever detaches her thoughts or divides her heart from home duties and affections, is especially a loss to the young plants that depend on her nurture and supervision.

If, therefore, the proposed change should profit neither man, woman, nor the rising race, how can it benefit the world at large? Is it not the province of true wisdom to select such measures as promote the greatest good of the greatest number?

A moralist has well said, that "in contentions for power, both the philosophy and poetry of life are dropped and trodden down." A still heavier loss would accrue to domestic happiness, and the interests of well balanced society, should the innate delicacy and prerogative of woman, *as woman,* be sacrificed or transmuted.

"I have given her as a help-meet," said the Voice that cannot err, when it spake unto Adam "in the cool of the day," amid the trees of Paradise. Not as a slave, a clog, a toy, a wrestler, a prize-fighter, a ruler. No. A *helper,* such as was meet for man to desire, and for her to become.

If the unerring Creator has assigned different spheres of action to the sexes, it is to be presumed that some adaptation exists to their respective sphere, that there is work enough in each to employ them, and that the faithful performance of that work will be for the welfare of both. If He hath constituted one as the priestess of the "inner temple," committing to her charge its veiled shrine and sacred harmonies, why should she covet to rage amid the warfare at its gates, or to ride on the whirlwind that may rock its turrets? Rushing, uncalled, to the strife, or the tumult, or the conflict, will there not linger in her heart the updraiding question, "with whom didst thou leave thy few sheep in the wilderness?" Why need she be again tempted by pride, or curiosity, or glozing words, to forfeit her own Eden?

The true nobility of Woman is to keep her own sphere,

and adorn it, not as the comet, daunting and perplexing other systems, but like the star, which is the first to light the day and the last to leave it. If she win not the laurel of the conqueror and the blood-shedder, her noble deeds may leave "footprints on the sands of time," and her good works, "such as become those that profess godliness," find record in the Book of Life.

Sisters, are not our rights sufficiently comprehensive, the sanctuary of home, the throne of the heart, the moulding of the whole mass of mind, in its first formation? Have we not power enough in all realms of sorrow and suffering, over all forms of want and ignorance, amid all ministries of love, from the cradle-dream to the sealing of the sepulchre?

Let us be content and faithful, aye, more, — grateful and joyful, — making this brief life a hymn of praise, until admitted to that choir which knows no discord, and where melody is eternal.

L. HUNTLEY SIGOURNEY.

HARTFORD, Conn..

THE MOTHER OF WASHINGTON

As the "mother" of our nation's "chief," it seems appropriate that Mary Washington should stand at the head of American females whose deeds are herein recorded. Her life was one unbroken series of praiseworthy actions—a drama of many scenes, none blood-chilling, none tragic, but all noble, all inspiring, and many even magnanimous. She was uniformly so gentle, so amiable, so dignified, that it is difficult to fix the eye on any one act more strikingly grand than the rest. Stretching the eye along a series of mountain peaks, all, seemingly, of the same height, a solitary one cannot be singled out and called more sublime than the others.

It is impossible to contemplate any one trait of her character without admiration. In republican simplicity, as her life will show, she was a model; and her piety was of such an exalted nature that the daughters of the land might make it their study. Though proud of her son, as we may suppose she must have been, she was sensible enough not to be betrayed into weakness and folly on that account. The honors that clustered around her name as associated with his, only humbled her and made her apparently more devout. She never forgot that she was a Christian mother, and that her son, herself, and, in perilous times especially, her country, needed her prayers. She was wholly destitute of aristocratic feelings, which are degrading to human beings; and never believed that sounding titles and high honors could confer lasting distinctions, without moral worth. The greatness which Byron, with so much justness and beauty, ascribes to Washington, was one portion of the inestimable riches which the son inherited from the mother:

> "Where may the weary eye repose,
>   When gazing on the great,
> Where neither guilty glory glows,
>   Nor despicable state?
> Yes, one—the first—the last—the best—
> The Cincinnatus of the West,
>   Whom envy dared not hate—
> Bequeathed the name of Washington,
> To make men blush there was but one."

Moulding, as she did, to a large extent, the character of the great Hero, Statesman and Sage of the Western World; instilling into his young heart the virtues that warmed her own, and fitting him to become the man of unbending integrity and heroic courage, and the father of a great and expanding republic, she may well claim the veneration, not of the lovers of freedom merely, but of all who can appreciate moral beauty and thereby estimate the true wealth of woman's heart. A few data and incidents of such a person's life should be treasured in every American mind.

The maiden name of Mrs. Washington was Mary Bell. She was born in the Colony of Virginia, which is fertile in great names, towards the close of the year 1706. She became the second wife of Mr. Augustine Washington, a planter of the "Old Dominion," on the sixth of March, 1730. He was at that time a resident of Westmoreland county. There, two years after this union, George, their oldest child, was born. While the "father of his country" was an infant, the parents removed to Stafford county, on the Rappahannoc river, opposite Fredericksburg.

Mrs. Washington had five more children, and lost the youngest in its infancy. Soon after this affliction, she was visited, in 1743, with a greater — the death of her husband. Thus, at the age of thirty-seven, Mrs. Washington became a widow, with five small children. Fortunately, her husband left a valuable property for their maintenance. It was mostly in land, and each son inherited a plantation. The one daughter was also suitably provided for. "It was thus," writes Mr Sparks, "that Augustine Washington, although suddenly cut off in the vigor of manhood, left all his children in a state of comparative independence. Confiding in the prudence of the mother, he directed that the proceeds of all the property of her children should be at her disposal, till they should respectively come of age."

The same writer adds that, "this weighty charge of five young children, the eldest of whom was eleven years old, the superintendence of their education, and the management of complicated affairs, demanded no common share of resolution, resource of mind, and strength of character. In these important duties Mrs. Washington acquitted herself with fidelity to her trust, and with entire success. Her good sense, assiduity, tenderness and vigilance, overcame every obstacle; and, as the richest reward of a mother's solicitude and toil, she had the happiness of seeing all her children come forward with a fair promise into life, filling the sphere allotted to them in a manner equally honorable to themselves, and to the parent who had been the only guide of their principles, conduct and habits. She lived to witness the noble career of her eldest son, till, by his own rare merits, he was raised to the head of a nation, and applauded and revered by the whole world."

Two years after the death of his father, George Washington obtained a midshipman's warrant, and had not his mother opposed the plan, he would have entered the naval service, been removed from her influence, acted a different part on the theatre of life, and possibly changed the subsequent aspect of American affairs.

Just before Washington's departure to the north, to assume the command of the American army, he persuaded his mother to leave her country residence, and assisted in effecting her removal to Fredericksburg. There she took up a permanent abode, and there died of a lingering and painful disease, a cancer in the breast, on the twenty-fifth of August, 1789.

A few of the many lovely traits of Mrs. Washington's character, are happily exhibited in two or three incidents in her long, but not remarkably eventful life.

She who looked to God in hours of darkness for light, in her country's peril, for Divine succor, was equally as ready to acknowledge the hand and to see the smiles of the "God of battles" in the victories that crowned our arms; hence, when she was informed of the surrender of Cornwallis, her heart instantly filled with gratitude, and raising her hands, with reverence and pious fervor, she exclaimed: "Thank God! wa1 will now be ended, and peace, independence and happiness bless our country!"

When she received the news of her son's successful passage of the Delaware — December 7th, 1776 — with much self-possession she expressed her joy that the prospects of the country were brightening; but when she came to those portions of the dispatches which were panegyrical of her son, she modestly and coolly observed to the bearers of the good tidings, that "George appeared to have deserved well of his country for such signal services. But, my good sirs," she added, "here is too much flattery!—Still, *George will not forget the lessons I have taught him*—he will not forget *himself*, though he is the subject of so much praise."

In like manner, when, on the return of the combined armies from Yorktown, Washington visited her at Fredericksburg, she inquired after his health and talked long and with much warmth of feeling of the scenes of former years, of early and mutual friends, of all, in short, that the past hallows; but to the theme of the ransomed millions of the land, the theme that for three quarters of a century has, in all lands, prompted the highest flights of eloquence, and awakened the noblest strains of song, to the deathless fame of her son, she made not the slightest allusion.

In the fall of 1784, just before returning to his native land, General Lafayette went to Fredericksburg, "to pay his parting respects" to Mrs. Washington. "Conducted by one of her grandsons, he approached the house, when the young gentleman observed: 'There, sir, is my grandmother!' Lafayette beheld—working in the garden, clad in domestic-made clothes, and her gray head covered with a plain straw hat—the mother of 'his hero, his friend and a country's preserver!' The lady saluted him kindly, observing: 'Ah, Marquis! you see an old woman; but come, I can make you welcome to my poor dwelling without the parade of changing my dress.'" During the interview, Lafayette, referring to her son, could not withhold his encomiums, which drew from the mother this beautifully simple remark: "I am not surprised at what George has done, for he was always a good boy."

The remains of Mrs. Washington were interred at Fredericksburg. On the seventh of May, 1833, the corner-stone of a monument to her memory was laid under the direction of a Committee who represented the citizens of Virginia. General Jackson, then President of the United States, very appropriately took the leading and most honorable part in the ceremony. With the following extracts from the closing part of his chaste and elegant Address, our humble sketch may fittingly close:

"In tracing the few recollections which can be gathered, of her principles and conduct, it is impossible to avoid the conviction, that these were closely interwoven with the destiny of her son. The great points of his character are before the world. He who runs may read them in his whole career, as a citizen, a soldier, a magistrate. He possessed unerring judgment, if that term can be applied to human nature; great probity of purpose, high moral principles, perfect self-possession, untiring application, and an inquiring mind, seeking information from every quarter, and arriving at its conclusions with a full knowledge of the subject; and he added to these an inflexibility of resolution, which nothing could change but a conviction of error. Look back at the life and conduct of his mother, and at her domestic government, as they have this day been delineated by the Chairman of the Monumental Committee, and as they were known to her contemporaries, and have been described by them, and they will be found admirably adapted to form and develop, the elements of such a character The power of greatness was there; but had it not been guided and directed by maternal solicitude and judgment, its possessor, instead of presenting to the world examples of virtue, patriotism and wisdom, which will be precious in all succeeding ages, might have added to the number of those master-spirits, whose fame rests upon the faculties they have abused, and the injuries they have committed. . . . . . .

"Fellow citizens, at your request, and in your name, I now deposit this plate in the spot destined for it; and when the American pilgrim shall, in after ages, come up to this high and holy place, and lay his hand upon this sacred column, may he recall the virtues of her who sleeps beneath, and depart with his affections purified, and his piety strengthened, while he invokes blessings upon the Mother of Washington."

THE WIFE OF WASHINGTON.

A woman's noblest station is retreat:
Her fairest virtues fly from public sight;
Domestic worth — that shuns too strong a light.
LORD LYTTLETON.

The drying up a single tear has more
Of honest fame than shedding seas of gore.
BYRON.

Woman may possess an equal share of the elements of greatness with man, but she has not an equal opportunity to display them in such a manner as to call forth the admiration and applause of the world. She was not made to pour the tide of eloquence in the Senate chamber, or lead on to victory the brave and heroic spirits of the land. Her course leads mainly through the quiet valley of domestic retirement, where the stream can rarely leap from dizzy heights with a thundering plunge, whose echoes shall go booming on to fill the ear of coming generations: her movements and influence are more like those of springs, which, flowing noiselessly and unseen, are widely scattered, and every where diffuse incalculable blessings.

The wife of Washington could not be the hero of a seven-years' war, or the chief magistrate of a republic; but, as the companion of such a man, she could shine, in her own proper sphere, with a lustre as mild, as steady, as serene, as his. And thus she did. Prompt to obey the calls of duty, when the voice of humanity beckoned her to the camp, she hastened away, at the sacrifice of ease and comfort, to relieve the wants of the suffering; and when forced to leave her "paradise" at Mount Vernon, to preside, as the matron of the nation, at the President's house, she did it with a dignity and propriety perhaps never equalled, certainly never excelled. But let us not anticipate.

Martha Dandridge was born in New Kent county, Virginia, in May, 1732. She was endowed with good sense, a strong mind, sound ideas of feminine proprieties, and correct views of woman's practical duties: and these had to answer measurably as a substitute for the discipline of female seminaries, which were rare in the "Old Dominion," and in the Colonies generally, in her younger days. The advantages to be derived from domestic instruction, she enjoyed, and those only. They, however, were cut off at the age of seventeen, by her union in marriage with Colonel Daniel P. Custis, a gentleman of many excellent parts. They settled on his plantation in her native county. Beautiful, lovely in disposition, and fascinating in manners, the young wife was warmly admired by her neighbors and all with whom she came in contact; and her residence, known as the "*White House*," was the centre of strong attractions, and the scene of much genuine or — which is the same thing — *Virginian*, hospitality. Colonel Custis became the father of three children, and then died. Previous to this solemn event, however, the White House had been veiled in weeds for the loss of his oldest child.

With two small children, a son and daughter, Mrs. Custis early found herself a widow, with the disposition and management of all pecuniary interests left by her confiding husband, at her control. As sole executrix, it is said that she "managed the extensive landed and pecuniary concerns of the estate with surprising ability, making loans on mortgages, of money, and through her stewards and agents, conducting the sales or exportation of the crops to the best possible advantage."

But from the cares of an extensive estate she was shortly relieved. On the sixth of January, 1759, she gave her hand, with upwards of a hundred thousand dollars, to Colonel George Washington, another planter of her native Colony. At the same time, she relinquished into his hands the guardianship of her children — the son six, and the daughter four years old — together with the care of their property. From the White House, Mrs. Washington now removed to Mount Vernon, which remained her home till her death, and became the final resting place of her remains.

In her new home, as in the White House, she superintended the affairs of the household, exercising continual control over all culinary matters; carefully educating her offspring, and aiming to rear them up for usefulness. These duties she discharged with the utmost assiduity and faithfulness, in spite of the many social obligations which a woman in her position must necessarily encounter.* Nor did the demands of courtesy and of her family debar her from habitual and systematic charities, dispensed in her neighborhood, or from those most important of all daily duties, the calls of the "closet." In the language of Miss Conkling, in her Memoir: "It is recorded of this devout Christian, that never during her life, whether in prosperity or in adversity, did she omit that daily self-communion and self-examination, and those private devotional exercises, which would best prepare her for the self-control and self-denial by which she was, for more than half a century, so eminently distinguished. It was her habit to retire to her own apartment every morning after breakfast, there to devote an hour to solitary prayer and meditation."

In 1770, she lost a child of many prayers, of bright hopes, and of much promise, her blooming daughter. She looked upon this affliction as a visitation from Him who doeth all things well, and bore it with becoming resignation, which the Christian only is prepared to do.

During the Revolution, Mrs. Washington was accustomed to pass the winters with her husband at the head quarters of the army and the summers at Mount Vernon; and it was in the camp that she shone with the lustre of the true woman. "She was at Valley

* We have the authority of Mr. Sparks for asserting that while Washington's pursuits were those of a retired planter, he seldom passed a day when at home without the company of friends or strangers, frequently persons of great celebrity, and demanding much attention from the lady of the house.

Forge in that dreadful winter of 1777–8, her presence and submission to privation strengthening the fortitude of those who might have complained, and giving hope and confidence to the desponding. She soothed the distresses of many sufferers, seeking out the poor and afflicted with benevolent kindness, extending relief wherever it was in her power, and with graceful deportment presiding in the Chief's humble dwelling."*

In 1781, she lost her last surviving child, John Custis, aged twenty seven. Her widowed daughter-in-law and the four children, she took to her own home, and thenceforward they were the objects of her untiring solicitude.

The life of Mrs. Washington, after her husband took the Presidential chair, was marked by no striking incidents, and affords scanty material of the nature marked out for this work. During the eight years that he was Chief Magistrate, she presided in his mansion with the same unaffected ease, equanimity and dignified simplicity that had marked her previous course in more retired circles. Visitors were received on all days *except the Sabbath*, and, irrespective of rank, shared in her courtesies and hospitalities. A portion of each summer, at that period, was passed in the quiet and seclusion of Mount Vernon, she rarely, if ever, accompanying her husband on his tours through the land. She expressed regret when he was chosen President, because she

* Mrs. Washington, in writing to Mrs. Warren, says, "The General's apartment is very small; he has had a log cabin built to dine in, which has made our quarters more tolerable than at first."

preferred "to grow old" with him "in solitude and tranquillity;" hence it is not surprising that she found a luxury in retiring for a season from the scenes of public life, and in attending to the education of her grand-children and to other self-imposed tasks and important duties, in the performance of which she could bless her friends and honor God.

After the death of her illustrious companion, which occurred in December, 1799, she remained at Mount Vernon; where she spent seventeen months mourning her loss; receiving the visits of the great from all parts of our land, and from various parts of the earth; attending, as heretofore, to her domestic concerns; perfecting in the Christian graces, and ripening for the joys of a holier state of being. On the twenty-second of May, 1801, she who, while on earth, could be placed in no station which she did not dignify and honor, was welcomed to the glories of another world.

THE WIFE OF JOHN ADAMS.

The mother in her office holds the key
Of the soul; and she it is who stamps the coin
Of character, and makes the being who would be a savage,
But for her gentle cares, a Christian man.

OLD PLAY

———— O we will walk this world,
Yoked in all exercise of noble aim.

TENNYSON.

Abigail Smith was a daughter of the Rev. William Smith, a Congregational minister of Weymouth, Massachusetts, where she was born on the eleventh of November, 1744, O. S. "It was fashionable to ridicule female learning," in her day; and she says of herself in one of her letters, "I was never sent to any school." She adds, "I was always sick. Female education, in the best families, went no further than writing and arithmetic." But notwithstanding her educational disadvantages, she read and studied in private, and kept up a brisk correspondence with relatives, and by these means expanded and fed her mind, and cultivated an easy and graceful style of writing.

On the twenty-fifth of October, 1764, Miss Smith became the wife of John Adams, a lawyer of Braintree.*

*The part of the town in which he lived was afterwards called Quincy in honor of Mrs. Adams's maternal grandfather.

Her grandson, Charles Francis Adams, to whose Memoir of her we are indebted for these statistics, says, that "the ten years immediately following, present little that is worth recording."

Prior to 1778, Mr. and Mrs. Adams had been separated at sundry times, in all, more than three years, which was a severe trial to her fortitude. The strength of her conjugal affection may be gathered from an extract from one of her letters: "I very well remember," she writes, "when the eastern circuits of the courts, which lasted a month, were thought an age, and an absence of three months, intolerable; but we are carried from step to step, and from one degree to another, to endure that which at first we think impossible." Thus she was schooled for separation from her husband, when, in 1778, he went to France as a joint commissioner. While he was absent from his country on that occasion, faithful to the calls of duty, she remained at home, and managed, as she had done before, the affairs of the household and farm. And *there* let the reader look at her and see a picture of a true mother of the Revolution. "She is a farmer cultivating the land, and discussing the weather and crops; a merchant reporting prices-current and the rates of exchange, and directing the making up of invoices; a politician, speculating upon the probabilities of peace or war; and a mother, writing the most exalted sentiments to her son."

What nobler deed could the mother, thus situated, do with her son, John Quincy Adams, in a foreign land, than to write to him in a tone like that of the extracts which follow, and which are taken from letters dated 1778–80:

"'T is almost four months since you left your native land, and embarked upon the mighty waters, in quest of a foreign country. Although I have not particularly written to you since, yet you may be assured you have constantly been upon my heart and mind.

"It is a very difficult task, my dear son, for a tender parent to bring her mind to part with a child of your years going to a distant land; nor could I have acquiesced in such a separation under any other care than that of the most excellent parent and guardian who accompanied you. You have arrived at years capable of improving under the advantages you will be likely to have, if you do but properly attend to them. They are talents put into your hands, of which an account will be required of you hereafter; and being possessed of one, two, or four, see to it that you double your numbers.

"The most amiable and most useful disposition in a young mind is diffidence of itself; and this should lead you to seek advice and instruction from him, who is your natural guardian, and will always counsel and direct you in the best manner, both for your present and future happiness. You are in possession of a natural good understanding, and of spirits unbroken by adversity and untamed with care. Improve your understanding by acquiring useful knowledge and virtue, such as will render you an ornament to society, an honor to your country, and a blessing to your parents. Great learning and superior abilities, should you ever possess them, will be of little value and small estimation, unless virtue, honor, truth, and integrity are added to them. Adhere to those religious sentiments and principles which were early instilled into your mind, and remember that you are accountable to your Maker for all your words and actions.

"Let me enjoin it upon you to attend constantly and steadfastly to the precepts and instructions of your father, as you value the happiness of your mother and your own welfare. His care and attention to you render many things unnecessary for me to write, which I might otherwise do; but the inadvertency and heedlessness of youth require line upon line and precept upon precept, and, when enforced by the joint efforts of both parents, will, I hope, have a due influence upon your conduct; for, dear as you are to me, I would much rather you should have found your grave in the ocean you have crossed, or that any untimely death crop you in your infant years, than see you an immoral, profligate, or graceless child.

"You have entered early in life upon the great theatre of the world, which is full of temptations and vice of every kind. You are not wholly unacquainted with history, in which you have read of crimes which your inexperienced mind could scarcely believe credible. You have been taught to think of them with horror, and to view vice as

'a monster of so frightful mien,
That, to be hated, needs but to be seen.'

"Yet you must keep a strict guard upon yourself, or the odious monster will soon lose its terror by becoming familiar to you. The modern history of our own times, furnishes as black a list of crimes, as can be paralleled in ancient times, even if we go back to Nero, Caligula, or Cæsar Borgia. Young as you are, the cruel war into which we have been compelled by the haughty tyrant of Britain and the bloody emissaries of his vengeance, may stamp upon your mind this certain truth, that the welfare and prosperity of all countries, communities, and, I may add, individuals, depend upon their morals. That nation to which we were once united, as it has departed from justice, eluded and subverted the wise laws which formerly governed it, and suffered the worst of crimes to go unpunished, has lost its valor, wisdom and humanity, and, from being the dread and terror of Europe, has sunk into derision and infamy. . . . .

"Some author, that I have met with, compares a judicious traveler to a river, that increases its stream the further it flows from its source; or to certain springs, which, running through rich veins of minerals, improve their qualities as they pass along. It will be expected of you, my son, that, as you are favored with superior advantages under the instructive eye of a tender parent, your improvement should bear some proportion to your advantages. Nothing is wanting with you but attention, diligence, and steady application. Nature has not been deficient.

"These are times in which a genius would wish to live. It is not in the still calm of life, or the repose of a pacific station, that great characters are formed. Would Cicero have shone so distinguished an orator if he had not been roused, kindled, and inflamed by the tyranny of Catiline, Verres, and Mark Anthony? The habits of a vigorous mind are formed in contending with difficulties. All history will convince you of this, and that wisdom and penetration are the fruit of experience, not the lessons of retirement and leisure. Great necessities call out great virtues. When a mind is raised and animated by scenes that engage the heart, then those qualities, which would otherwise lie dormant, wake into life and form the character of the hero and the statesman. War, tyranny, and desolation are the scourges of the Almighty, and ought no doubt to be deprecated. Yet it is your lot, my son, to be an eye witness of these calamities in your own native land, and, at the same time, to owe your existence among a people who have made a glorious defence of their invaded liberties, and who, aided by a generous and powerful ally, with the blessing of Heaven, will transmit this inheritance to ages yet unborn.

"Nor ought it to be one of the least of your incitements towards exerting every power and faculty of your mind, that you have a parent who has taken so large and active a share in this contest, and discharged the trust reposed in him with so much satisfaction as to be honored with the important embassy which at present calls him abroad.

"The strict and inviolable regard you have ever paid to truth, gives me pleasing hopes that you will not swerve from her dictates, but add justice, fortitude, and every manly virtue which can adorn a good citizen, do honor to your country, and render your parents supremely happy, particularly your ever affectionate mother.

. . . "The only sure and permanent foundation of virtue is religion. Let this important truth be engraven upon your heart. And also, that the foundation of religion is the belief of the one only God, and a just sense of his attributes, as a being infinitely wise, just, and good, to whom you owe the highest reverence, gratitude, and adoration; who superintends and governs all nature, even to clothing the lilies of the field, and hearing the young ravens when they cry; but more particularly regards man, whom he created after his own image, and breathed into him an immortal spirit, capable of a happiness beyond the grave; for the attainment of which he is bound to the performance of certain duties, which all tend to the happiness and welfare of society, and are comprised in one short sentence, expressive of universal benevolence, 'Thou shalt love thy neighbor as thyself.' . . . .

"Justice, humanity, and benevolence, are the duties you owe to society in general. To your country the same duties are incumbent upon you, with the additional obligation of sacrificing ease, pleasure, wealth, and life itself for its defence and security. To your parents you owe love, reverence, and obedience to all just and equitable commands. To yourself, — here, indeed, is a wide field to expatiate upon. To become what you ought to be, and what a fond mother wishes to see you, attend to some precepts and instructions from the pen of one, who can have no motive but your welfare and happiness, and who wishes in this way to supply to you the personal watchfulness and care, which a separation from you deprived you of at a period of life, when habits are easiest acquired and fixed; and though the advice may not be new, yet suffer it to obtain a place in your memory, for occasions may offer, and perhaps some concurring circumstances unite, to give it weight and force.

"Suffer me to recommend to you one of the most useful lessons of life, the knowledge and study of yourself. There you run the greatest hazard of being deceived. Self-love and partiality cast a mist before the eyes, and there is no knowledge so hard to be acquired, nor of more benefit when once thoroughly understood. Ungoverned passions have aptly been compared to the boisterous ocean, which is known to produce the most terrible effects. 'Passions are the elements of life,' but elements which are subject to the control of reason. Whoever will candidly examine themselves, will find some degree of passion, peevishness, or obstinacy in their natural tempers. You will seldom find these disagreeable ingredients all united in one; but the uncontrolled indulgence of either is sufficient to render the possessor unhappy in himself, and disagreeable to all who are so unhappy as to be witnesses of it, or suffer from its effects.

"You, my dear son, are formed with a constitution feelingly alive; your passions are strong and impetuous; and, though I have sometimes seen them hurry you into excesses, yet with pleasure I have observed a frankness and generosity accompany your efforts to govern and subdue them. Few persons are so subject to passion, but that they can command themselves, when they have a motive sufficiently strong; and those who are most apt to transgress will restrain themselves through respect and reverence to superiors, and even, where they wish to recommend themselves, to their equals. The due government of the passions, has been considered in all ages as a most valuable acquisition. Hence an inspired writer observes, 'He that is slow to anger is better than the mighty; and he that ruleth his spirit, than he that taketh a city.' This passion, coöperating with power, and unrestrained by reason, has produced the subversion of cities, the desolation of countries, the massacre of nations, and filled the world with injustice and oppression. Behold your own country, your native land, suffering from the effects of lawless power and malignant passions, and learn betimes, from your own observation and experience, to govern and control yourself. Having once obtained this self-government, you will find a foundation laid for happiness to yourself and usefulness to mankind. 'Virtue alone is happiness below;' and consists in cultivating and improving every good inclination, and in checking and subduing every propensity to evil. I have been particular upon the passion of anger, as it is generally the most predominant passion at your age, the soonest excited, and the least pains are taken to subdue it;

——'what composes man, can man destroy.'"

With such a mother to counsel him, one is led to ask, how could John Quincy Adams *help* becoming a noble-minded and great man? Who wonders that, with good natural endowments and his excellent privileges, coupled with maternal training, he fitted himself to fill the highest office in the gift of a free people?

In June, 1784, Mrs. Adams sailed for London to join her husband, who was then our Minister at the Court of St. James. While absent, she visited France and Netherlands; resided for a time in the former country; and returned with her knowledge of human nature, of men, manners, &c., enlarged; disgusted with the splendor and sophistications of royalty, and well prepared to appreciate the republican simplicity and frankness of which she was herself a model. While Mr. Adams was Vice-President and President, she never laid aside her singleness of heart, and that sincerity and unaffected dignity which had won for her many friends before her elevation, and which, in spite of national animosity, conquered the prejudices and gained the hearts of the aristocracy of Great Britain. But her crowning virtue was her Christian humility, which is beautifully exemplified in a letter which she wrote to Mr. Adams, on the 8th of February, 1797, "the day on which the votes for President were counted, and Mr. Adams, as Vice-President, was required by law to announce himself the President elect for the ensuing term:"

"'The sun is dressed in brightest beams,
To give thy honors to the day.'

"And may it prove an auspicious prelude to each

ensuing season. You have this day to declare yourself head of a nation. 'And now, O Lord, my God, thou hast made thy servant ruler over the people. Give unto him an understanding heart, that he may know how to go out and come in before this great people; that he may discern between good and bad. For who is able to judge this thy so great a people?' were the words of a royal sovereign; and not less applicable to him who is invested with the chief magistracy of a nation, though he wear not a crown, nor the robes of royalty.

"My thoughts and my meditations are with you, though personally absent; and my petitions to Heaven are, that 'the things which make for peace may not be hidden from your eyes.' My feelings are not those of pride or ostentation, upon the occasion. They are solemnized by a sense of the obligations, the important trusts, and numerous duties connected with it. That you may be enabled to discharge them with honor to yourself, with justice and impartiality to your country, and with satisfaction to this great people, shall be the daily prayer of your "A. A."

From her husband's retirement from the Presidency, in 1801, to the close of her life, in 1818, Mrs. Adams remained constantly at Quincy. Cheerful, contented, and happy, she devoted her last years, in that rural seclusion, to the reciprocities of friendship and love, to offices of kindness and charity, and, in short, to all those duties which tend to ripen the Christian for an exchange of worlds.

But it would be doing injustice to her character

and leaving one of her noblest deeds unrecorded, to close without mentioning the influence for good which she exerted over Mr. Adams, and her part in the work of making him what he was. That he was sensible of the benignant influence of wives, may be gathered from the following letter which was addressed to Mrs. Adams from Philadelphia, on the eleventh of August, 1777:

"I think I have some times observed to you in conversation, that upon examining the biography of illustrious men, you will generally find some female about them, in the relation of mother, or wife, or sister, to whose instigation a great part of their merit is to be ascribed. You will find a curious example of this in the case of Aspasia, the wife of Pericles She was a woman of the greatest beauty, and the first genius. She taught him, it is said, his refined maxims of policy, his lofty imperial eloquence, nay, even composed the speeches on which so great a share of his reputation was founded.

"I wish some of our great men had such wives. By the account in your last letter, it seems the women in Boston begin to think themselves able to serve their country. What a pity it is that our generals in the northern districts had not Aspasias to their wives.

"I believe the two Howes have not very great women to their wives. If they had, we should suffer more from their exertions than we do. This is our good fortune. A smart wife would have put Howe in possession of Philadelphia a long time ago."

While Mr. Adams was wishing that some of our great men had such wives as Aspasia, he had such a wife, was himself such a man, and owed half his greatness to *his* Aspasia. The exalted patriotism and the cheerful piety infused into the letters she addressed to him during the long night of political uncertainty that hung over these Colonies, strengthened his courage, fired his nobler feelings, nerved his higher purposes and, doubtless, greatly contributed to make him the right hand man of Washington.

The diligent and faithful Andromaches, the gifted and patriotic *Aspasias* of the Revolution, did their portion of the great work silently and unseen. Secretly they urged their husbands and sons to the battle-field, secretly spoke to them by letter in the camp or convention, and secretly prayed for wisdom to guide our statesmen and victory to crown our arms. Thus privately acting, how little of their labor or their worth is known. How few of their names are treasured in our annals. With rare exceptions, like the builders of the pyramids, their initials are lost. Then, while we have the name and the noble example of Mrs. Adams, with a few of her patriotic compeers, let us pledge our unswerving devotion to Freedom over the *unknown* names of the wives and mothers who secretly assisted in nerving the arm that broke the sceptre of British dominion on these shores, and gave the eagle of Liberty a safe and abiding home on our mountain tops.

ANN H. JUDSON.

God has a bright example made of thee,
To show that womankind may be
Above that sex which her superior seems.

COWLEY.

About the commencement of the present century, a new field was opened for the display of Christian heroism. The despairing wail of the pagan millions of the East, had reached the ears of a few of the most devoted people of God on these Western shores, and the question arisen, Who shall lead the way to heathen realms, who among us first encounter the perils of an attempt to plant the standard of the Cross beside the pagodas of Buddhism? He who would then go forth, must leave his native land with the parting benediction of but few friends; must be accompanied with few and faint prayers; must make his own path through the tiger-haunted jungles, and face alone the untried dangers of a dubious assault on the strong-holds of pagan superstition. But, notwithstanding the discouragements inwoven with the contemplation of the undertaking, and the great peril that must attend its completion, it was magnanimous and sublime, and there were hearts in the land philanthropic enough to embark in it and brave enough to face its terrors without fainting.

Among the foremost Americans who offered their services in this work, were the Rev. Adoniram Judson and his wife. They embarked from Salem, Massachusetts, for Calcutta, with Samuel Newell and lady, on the nineteenth of February, 1812: and five days afterwards Messrs. Hall and Nott, with their wives, and Mr. Rice, sailed from Philadelphia for the same place. The names of these pioneer missionaries are sacred to the memory of all living Christians, and, being embodied in the history of the grandest enterprise of the age, are to be handed down to all future generations.

While all the female portion of this little band, exhibited many excellent traits of character, and worked well while their day lasted, no other one endured so many and so great hardships and trials, encountered such fearful perils, and had such an opportunity to test the strength of the higher virtues, as Mrs. Judson.

Ann Hasseltine was born at Bradford, in Essex county, Massachusetts, on the twenty-second day of December, 1789. She was an active and enthusiastic child; of a gay disposition, yet thoughtful at times; and before she was seventeen, gave religion that attention which its importance demands.

She became acquainted with Mr. Judson in 1810. He was then a student in the Andover Theological Seminary, preparing for the work of foreign missions. A mutual and strong attachment sprang up, and they were married in February, 1812, two weeks before their embarkation for India.

Mr. and Mrs. Judson first halted at Serampore. There, soon after their arrival, they were immersed by an English missionary, having changed their views of the ordinance of baptism on the long voyage across the Atlantic and Indian oceans. From that place they were soon driven by the Directors and Agents of the British East India Company, who were at that time opposed to the introduction of the Christian religion into those parts. They sailed from Madras for Rangoon, on the twenty-second of June, 1813, and settled at the latter place.

From the commencement of missionary toil, Mrs. Judson had many inconveniencies to encounter, but they were met with patience and served to strengthen that energy which, it will be seen, was afterwards so much needed and so strikingly displayed. Four or five years after settling at Rangoon, Mr. Judson went to Chittagong, in a neighboring province, to secure help, some Arracanese converts being there, who spoke the Burman language. He expected to return within three months. "At the expiration of this period, however, when his return was daily expected, a vessel from Chittagong arrived at Rangoon, bringing the distressing intelligence that neither he nor the vessel in which he had embarked had been heard of at that port. Similar tidings were also contained in letters which Mrs. Judson received from Bengal.

"While the missionaries were in this state of fear

ful suspense, an incident occurred which was well calculated to increase the perplexity and dismay in which they were plunged. Mr. Hough,* who had continued quietly studying the language at the mission house, was suddenly summoned to appear immediately at the court house, and it was rumored among the affrighted domestics and neighbors who followed the officers that came for Mr. Hough, that the king had issued a decree for the banishment of all the foreign teachers. It was late in the afternoon when he made his appearance before the despotic tribunal that was charged with the execution of the imperial decree, and he was merely required to give security for his appearance the following morning; when, as the unfeeling magistrates declared, 'if he did not tell all the truth relative to his situation in the country, they would write with his heart's blood.' Mr. Hough was detained from day to day on the most flimsy pretences, himself unable to speak the language, and with no one near him who would attempt to explain his situation or vindicate his objects and his conduct. The viceroy whom Mr. and Mrs. Judson had known, had recently been recalled to Ava, and he who now held the reins of the government was a stranger, and, as his family were not with him, Mrs. Judson, according to the etiquette of the court, could not be admitted to his presence. The order which had led to the arrest was found to relate to some Portuguese priests whom the king had

* Mr Hough was a printer in the employment of the Baptist Board. AUTHOR.

banished, and Mr. Hough was at first summoned to give assurance that he was not one of the number, and then detained by the officers in order to extort money for his ransom. He was at length released by order of the viceroy, to whom Mrs. Judson boldly carried the cause and presented a petition which she had caused her teacher to draw up for the purpose.

"The anxiety occasioned by this arrest and its train of petty annoyances, and still more by the protracted and mysterious absence of Mr. Judson, was at this time greatly increased by rumors which reached Rangoon, of an impending war between the English and the Burman governments. There were but few English vessels lying in the river, and the English traders who were in the country were closing their business and preparing to hasten away, at any new indications of hostilities that should be presented. The condition of the missionaries was rendered still more distressing by the ravages of the cholera, which now, for the first time made its appearance in Burmah, and was sending its terrors throughout the empire. The poor people of Rangoon fell in hundreds before its frightful progress. The dismal death-drum continually gave forth its warning sound as new names were added to the melancholy list of victims to the desolating malady. In these gloomy circumstances, they saw ship after ship leave the river, bearing away all the foreigners who were in the province, until at length the only one remaining was on the eve of sailing. Harassed with doubts concerning the uncertain fate of Mr. Judson, and surrounded with perils, they saw before them what appeared the last opportunity of leaving the country, before the threatened hostilities should begin, and they should be exposed to all the merciless cruelties of barbarian warfare.

"Mr. and Mrs. Hough decided to go on board and escape to Bengal, while escape was still in their power, and they urged Mrs. Judson to accompany them. She at length reluctantly yielded to their advice, and with a heart burdened with sorrows she embarked with her companions, on the fifth of July, in the only ship that remained to carry them from the country. The ship, however, was delayed for several days in the river, and was likely to be subjected to still further detention. Mrs. Judson, who had gone on board rather in obedience to the entreaties of her associates, and the dictates of prudence, than from the suggestions of that truer instinct which often serves to guide the noblest natures in great emergencies, now decided to leave the ship and return alone to the mission house, there to await either the return of her husband, or the confirmation of her worst fears respecting his fate. It was a noble exhibiton of heroic courage, and gave assurance of all the distinguished qualities which, at a later period and amid dangers still more appalling, shone with unfailing brightness around the character of this remarkable woman. The event justified her determination; and, within a week after her decision was taken, Mr. Judson arrived at Rangoon, having been driven from place to place by contrary winds, and having entirely failed of the object for which he undertook the voyage." *

In the summer of 1820, Mrs. Judson's health had become so far undermined by the deleterious influences of the climate, that it was deemed necessary that she should go to Calcutta for medical advice, better physicians being located there than in Rangoon. She was so feeble that her husband was obliged to accompany her. She was soon removed to Serampore, where were eminently skillful physicians and a purer atmosphere. Her health so improved in six months that she returned with her husband to Rangoon. The malady which had afflicted her was the chronic liver complaint. It was not entirely removed at Serampore, and a few months after her return, it began to distress her more than ever. It was now thought that nothing but a visit to her native land could save her. Accordingly, on the twenty-first of August, 1821, she started for Calcutta, where, after some delay, she found a ship bound to England, by which route she returned, reaching New York on the twenty-fifth of September, 1822.

She remained in this country nine months. During that short period, aside from paying a visit to her relations, she attended the Triennial Convention at Washington, held in May, 1823; visited the larger cities North and South; attended numerous meetings of female associations; and prepared a history of

* Gammell's History of American Baptist Missions.

the Burman mission which was so ably written that even the London Quarterly Review, and, if we mistake not, other English periodicals of high critical character, noticed it in commendatory terms.

The following extracts from letters written to Dr. Wayland while in this country, show the interest she took in the affairs of Burmah while absent from that land of her adoption. Under date of "Baltimore, January twenty-second, 1823," she says, "I want the Baptists throughout the United States to feel, that Burmah *must be converted* through their instrumentality. They must do more than they have ever yet done. They must *pray* more, they must *give* more, and make greater efforts to prevent the Missionary flame from becoming extinct. Every Christian in the United States should feel as deeply impressed with the importance of making continual efforts for the salvation of the heathen, as though their conversion depended solely on himself. Every individual Christian should feel himself guilty if he has not done and does not continue to do *all* in his power for the spread of the gospel and the enlightening of the heathen world. But I need not write thus to you. You see, you feel the misery of the heathen world. Try to awaken Christians around you. Preach frequently on the subject of Missions. I have remarked it to be the case, when a minister feels *much* engaged for the heathen, his people generaly partake of his spirit."

Writing from Washington in the following March, she says, "I long to be in Rangoon, and am anxiously hoping to get away in the spring. Do make inquiries relative to the sailing of ships from Boston and Salem. I must not miss one good opportunity."

With her health much improved though not fully restored, she sailed for her Burman home on the twenty-second of June, 1823, and reached Rangoon on the fifth of the following December. She found the work of the mission prospering. The next year, however, a war broke out between the Burman government and the English in Bengal, and, not only suspended the operations of the missionaries, but jeopardised their lives. They were supposed to be spies employed by the English government. Mr. and Mrs. Judson, with Dr. Price, another of the mission aries, were at that time at Ava, where the imperial government of the Burman Empire had just been removed.

"It was on the eighth of June, 1824, that a company of Burmans, headed by an officer, and attended by a 'spotted-faced son of the prison,' came to the mission house, and, in the presence of Mrs. Judson seized her husband and Dr. Price, and after binding them tight with cords, drove them away to the court house. From this place they were hurried, by order of the king, without examination, to a loathsome dungeon, known as 'the death prison,' where along with the other foreigners they were confined, each loaded with three pairs of fetters and fastened to a long pole, so as to be incapable of moving. Meanwhile, Mrs. Judson was shut up in her house, deprived of her furniture and of most of her articles of property, and watched for several days by an unfeeling guard, to whose rapacious extortions and brutal annoyances she was constantly exposed, without being able to make any exertion for the liberation of the prisoners, or the mitigation of their cruel sentence. She however, at length succeeded in addressing a petition to the governor of the city, who had the prisoners in charge. By a present of one hundred dollars to his subordinate officer, their condition was somewhat meliorated, and by the unwearied perseverance of Mrs. Judson, and her affecting appeals to the sympathies of the governor, he was induced to grant her occasional permission to go to the prison, and at length to build for herself a bamboo shed in the prison yard, where she took up her abode, in order that she might prepare food for the prisoners, and otherwise minister to their necessities.

"At the end of nine months they were suddenly removed from Ava to Amarapura, and thence to a wretched place several miles beyond, called Oung-pen-la, where it was arranged that they should be put to death in presence of the pakah-woon, as a kind of sacrifice in honor of his taking command of a new army of fifty thousand men about to march against the English. This sanguinary chief had been raised from a low condition to the rank of woongyee; but in the height of his power, just as he was about to march at the head of the army he had mustered, he fell into disgrace, was charged with treason, and executed, at an hour's notice, with the unqualified approbation of all classes of people at Ava. His timely execution saved the missionaries from the fate which hung over them, and they were left uncared for in the miserable cells of Oung-pen-la, till the near approach of the English to the capitol induced the king to send for Mr. Judson, to accompany the embassy that was about to start for the English camp, for the purpose of averting the destruction that now threatened the Golden City.

"During this period of a year and a half Mrs. Judson followed them from prison to prison, beneath the darkness of night and the burning sun of noonday, bearing in her arms her infant daughter, — the child of sorrow and misfortune, who was born after the imprisonment of its father, — procuring for them food which Burman policy never supplies to prisoners, and perpetually interceding for them with their successive keepers, with the governor of the city, with the kinsmen of the monarch, and the members of the royal household. More than once the queen's brother gave orders that they should be privately put to death; but such was the influence which Mrs. Judson possessed over the mind of the governor, that he evaded the order each time it was given, and assured her that for her sake he would not execute her husband, even though he was obliged to execute all the others. And when at last they were to be taken from his jurisdiction and driven to the horid prison-house of Oung-pen-la, at the command of the pakah-woon, the old man humanely summoned Mrs. Judson from the prison where he had permitted her to go and sit with her husband, in order that she might be spared the pangs of a separation which he had not the power to prevent. Her own pen has traced, in lines that will never be forgotten by those who read them, the affecting history of the dismal lays and nights of her husband's captivity. We follow her alike with admiration and the deepest sympathy as she takes her solitary way from Ava, at first in a boat upon the river, and then in a Burman cart, in search of the unknown place to which the prisoners have been carried. At length, overcome with fatigue, with exposure, and the bitter pangs of hope deferred, we see her in a comfortless cabin, prostrate with disease and brought to the very gates of death, — while her infant is carried about the village by its father in the hours of his occasional liberation, to be nourished by such Burman mothers as might have compassion on its helpless necessities.

"Such is a single scene from this melancholy record of missionary suffering. History has not recorded; poetry itself has seldom portrayed, a more affecting exhibition of Christian fortitude, of female heroism, and all the noble and generous qualities which constitute the dignity and glory of woman. In the midst of sickness and danger, and every calamity which can crush the human heart, she presented a character equal to the sternest trial, and an address and fertility of resources which gave her an ascendency over the minds of her most cruel enemies, and alone saved the missionaries and their fellow captives from the terrible doom which constantly awaited them. Day after day and amid the lonely hours of night was she employed in conciliating the favor of their keepers, and in devising plans for their release, or the alleviation of their captivity. Sometimes, she confesses, her thoughts would wander for a brief interval to America and the beloved friends of her better days; 'but for nearly a year and a half, so entirely engrossed was every thought with present scenes and sufferings, that she seldom reflected on a single occurrence of her former life, or recollected that she had a friend in existence out of Ava.' "*

When peace was declared between the two powers, by the terms of negotiation, the European prisoners were all released; and thus closed the long and brutal incarceration of the missionaries. Mr. and Mrs. Judson immediately departed for Rangoon. They soon removed to Amherst, a new town on the Salwen or Martaban river. After having established a mission there, Mr. Judson had occasion to visit Ava. He started on the fifth of July, 1826, leaving his wife and infant daughter in the care of kind friends. He was detained at the Capital longer than he had anticipated; and before he returned he received the painful intelligence that his wife was dead. "A remittent fever had settled on her constitution, already enfeebled by suffering and disease, and she died on the twenty-fourth of October, 1826, amid the universal sorrow, alike of the English residents

* Gammell.

at Amherst and of the native Christians who had gathered around her at her new home. Her infant daughter died a few weeks afterwards, and side by side they were laid to rest, under a large hopia tree a few rods from the house where she had resided. Two marble stones, procured by the contributions of several female friends in her native land, are the humble memorial that marks the spot where sleeps one whose "name will be remembered in the churches of Burmah, in future times, when the pagodas of Gaudama shall have fallen; when the spires of Christian temples shall gleam along the waters of the Irrawaddy and the Salwen: and when the 'Golden City' shall have lifted up her gates to let the King of Glory in."

A CHRISTIAN WOMAN IN THE HOUR OF DANGER.

O rainbow of the battle-storm!
  Methinks thou 'rt gleaming on my sight;
I see thy fair and fragile form
  Amid the thick cloud of the fight.

SARA J. CLARKE.

One grain of incense with devotion offered,
Is beyond all perfumes or Sabæan spices.

MASSINGER.

The following incident, we are informed by Mrs. Ellet, was communicated to a minister—Rev. J. H. Saye—by two officers in the Revolutionary war. One of them was in the skirmish referred to; the other lived near the scene of action; hence, it may be relied on as authentic. The name of the heroine is unknown, which is greatly to be regretted:

"Early in the war, the inhabitants on the frontier of Burke county, North Carolina, being apprehensive of an attack by the Indians, it was determined to seek protection in a fort in a more densely populated neighborhood in an interior settlement. A party of soldiers was sent to protect them on their retreat. The families assembled, the line of march was taken towards their place of destination, and they proceeded some miles unmolested—the soldiers marching in a hollow square, with the refugee families in the centre. The Indians who had watched these movements, had laid a plan for their destruction. The road to be traveled lay through a dense forest in the fork of a river, where the Indians concealed themselves, and waited till the travelers were in the desired spot. Suddenly the war-whoop sounded in front, and on either side; a large body of painted warriors rushed in, filling the gap by which the whites had entered, and an appalling crash of fire-arms followed. The soldiers, however, were prepared; such as chanced to be near the trees darted behind them, and began to ply the deadly rifle; the others prostrated themselves upon the earth, among the tall grass, and crawled to trees. The families screened themselves as best they could. The onset was long and fiercely urged; ever and anon amid the din and smoke, the warriors would rush, tomahawk in hand, towards the centre; but they were repulsed by the cool intrepidity of the back-woods riflemen. Still they fought on, determined on the destruction of the victims who offered such desperate resistance. All at once an appalling sound greeted the ears of the women and children in the centre; it was a cry from their defenders—a cry for powder! 'Our powder is giving out,' they exclaimed. 'Have you any? Bring us some, or we can fight no longer!' A woman of the party had a good supply. She spread her apron on the ground, poured her powder into it, and going round, from soldier to soldier, as they stood behind the trees, bade each who needed powder put down his hat, and poured a quantity upon it. Thus she went round the line of defence, till her whole stock, and all she could obtain from others, was distributed. At last the savages gave way, and, pressed by their foes, were driven off the ground. The victorious whites returned to those for whose safety they had ventured into the wilderness. Inquiries were made as to who had been killed, and one running up, cried, 'Where is the woman that gave us the powder? I want to see her!' 'Yes!—yes!—let us see her!' responded another and another; 'without her we should have been all lost!' The soldiers ran about among the women and children, looking for her and making inquiries. Directly came in others from the pursuit, one of whom observing the commotion, asked the cause, and was told. 'You are looking in the wrong place,' he replied. 'Is she killed? Ah, we were afraid of that!' exclaimed many voices. 'Not when I saw her,' answered the soldier. 'When the Indians ran off, she was *on her knees in prayer* at the root of yonder tree, and there I left her.' There was a simultaneous rush to the tree—and there, to their great joy, they found the woman safe, and still on her knees in prayer. Thinking not of herself, she received their applause without manifesting any other feeling than gratitude to Heaven for their great deliverance."

HUMANITY OF HARTFORD LADIES.

As the rivers farthest flowing,
  In the highest hills have birth;
As the banyan broadest growing,
  Oftenest bows its head to earth,
So the noblest minds press onward,
  Channels far of good to trace;
So the largest hearts bend downward,
  Circling all the human race.

MRS. HALE.

The sympathies of a free people are always aroused when a nation is struggling for freedom. Hence the war between the Turks and Greeks not only called forth the eloquence of American orators, but the mothers and daughters of the land, reminded of the long struggle of their husbands and fathers for liberty, were alive to the interests, and prayed much for the ransom of the latter people. Nor was this all; the sufferings to which the war reduced the Greeks, so much moved the hearts of females that, in one instance at least, they made a demonstration of their sympathy worthy of record. The ladies of Hartford, Connecticut, sent out a ship to the women of Greece, containing money, and articles of wearing apparel, wrought by themselves expressly for an offering to suffering humanity. Mrs. Sigourney, the Secretary of the Ladies' Committee, wrote the following letter to accompany the contribution:

"*United States of America, March 12th*, 1828.
The Ladies of Hartford, in Connecticut, to the Ladies of Greece.

"Sisters and Friends,—From the years of childhood your native clime has been the theme of our admiration: together with our brothers and our husbands, we early learned to love the country of Homer, of Aristides, of Solon, and of Socrates. That enthusiasm which the glory of ancient Greece enkindled in our bosoms, has preserved a fervent friendship for her descendants: we have beheld with deep sympathy the horrors of Turkish domination, and the struggles so long and nobly sustained by them for existence and for liberty.

"The communications of Dr. Howe, since his return from your land, have made us more intimately acquainted with your personal sufferings. He has presented many of you to us in his vivid descriptions, as seeking refuge in caves, and, under the branches of olive trees, listening for the footsteps of the destroyer, and mourning over your dearest ones slain in battle.

"Sisters and friends, our hearts bleed for you. Deprived of your protectors by the fortune of war, and continually in fear of evils worse than death, our prayers are with you, in all your wanderings, your wants and your griefs. In this vessel (which may God send in safety to your shores!) you will receive a portion of that bounty wherewith He hath blessed us. The poor among us have given according to their ability, and our little children have cheerfully aided, that some of you and your children might have bread to eat and raiment to put on. Could you but behold the faces of our little ones brighten, and their eyes sparkle with joy, while they give up their holidays, that they might work with their needles for Greece; could you see those females who earn a subsistence by labor, gladly casting their mite into our treasury, and taking hours from their repose that an additional garment might be furnished for you; could you witness the active spirit that pervades all classes of our community, it would cheer for a moment the darkness and misery of your lot.

"We are the inhabitants of a part of one of the smallest of the United States, and our donations must therefore, of necessity, be more limited than those from the larger and more wealthy cities; yet such as we have, we give in the name of our dear Saviour, with our blessings and our prayers.

"We know the value of sympathy—how it arms the heart to endure—how it plucks the sting from sorrow—therefore we have written these few lines to assure you, that in the remoter parts of our country, as well as in her high places, you are remembered with pity and with affection.

"Sisters and friends, we extend across the ocean our hands to you in the fellowship of Christ. We pray that His Cross and the banner of your land may rise together over the Crescent and the Minaret—that your sons may hail the freedom of ancient Greece restored, and build again the waste places which the oppressor hath trodden down; and that you, admitted once more to the felicities of home, may gather from past perils and adversities a brighter wreath for the kingdom of Heaven.

"Lydia H. Sigourney,

"*Secretary of the Greek Committee of Hartford, Connecticut.*"

"MOTHER BAILEY."

No braver dames had Sparta,
No nobler matrons Rome.
W. D. Gallagher.

Anna Warner was born in Groton, Connecticut, on the eleventh of October, 1758, and married Captain Elijah Bailey of the same town, in 1774. He participated in the hardships and dangers, and she in the trials of the struggle for Independence. He is dead; she is still living.*

She was a witness of the terrible massacre at Fort Griswold, in Groton, on the sixth of September; and the following morning she hurried off to the scene of carnage, a distance of three miles, to search for an uncle who was among the brave defenders. She found him among the fatally wounded: at his request that he might see his wife and child before he died, she ran home, caught and saddled a horse for the feeble mother, and taking the child in her arms, carried it the whole distance, that it might receive the kisses and benediction of its dying father!

* We are informed by the Postmaster of Groton, in a letter dated the tenth of December, 1850, that Mrs. B. is still living, and that her mind is somewhat impaired. She is now in her ninety-third year.

In the month of July, 1813 a blockading fleet appeared off the harbor of New London; and on the thirteenth, demonstrations were noticed of an intention to attack the place. Intense excitement now prevailed not only in New London, but in all the adjacent towns. Fort Griswold was once more occupied; small cannon -- all to be had — were planted, and every preparation possible was made for a vigorous defence. The greatest deficiency was in flannel for cartridges; and in the emergency a messenger was dispatched to the village to consult with Mrs. Bailey on the most expeditious method of obtaining a supply. She promptly offered to see that each family was visited, and the wants of the soldiery made known. This was done, and each individual in the neighborhood cheerfully presented her and her co-laborers whatever of the desired articles could be spared, some in garments and some in the raw material. When these were delivered to the messenger, and there was still found a deficiency, she slyly slipped an under garment from her own person and charged him to give *that* to the British. As the enemy did not deem it expedient to make an attack, it is difficult to tell what aid that garment rendered; nor does it matter: its patriotic surrender showed the noble spirit which has always actuated "mother Bailey," and was an appropriation for her country which never caused her a blush. *

* The editor of the Democratic Review, to whom we are indebted for a portion of these facts, visited the heroine of Groton in the fall

of 1846, in the number of his periodical for the January following spoke of her as a remarkable woman, physically, as well as mentally and patriotically. She was then eighty-eight years old, yet as agile as a girl of eighteen, and neither sight nor hearing had began to fail. "Such then," he adds, "is Mother Bailey. Had she lived in the palmy days of ancient Roman glory, no matron of the mighty empire would have been more highly honored." In the same article Mrs. B. is spoken of as the Postmistress of Groton, an office, which the present Postmaster assures us, she never held.

Since the above was originally stereotyped, Mrs. Bailey has died. Her demise occurred in the winter of 1850–1.

ELIZABETH HEARD.

Kindness has resistless charms.

ROCHESTER.

Why should'st thou faint? Heaven smiles above,
Though storm and vapor intervene.

PARK BENJAMIN.

Mrs. Elizabeth Heard, "a widow of good estate, a mother of many children and a daughter of Mr. Hull, a revered minister formerly living at Pisquataqua," was among the sufferers from captivity by the Indians in the latter part of the seventeenth century. She was taken at the destruction of Major Waldron's garrison in Dover, New Hampshire, about 1689. She was permitted to escape on account of a favor which she had shown a young Indian thirteen years before—she having secreted him in her house on the "calamitous day," in 1676, when four hundred savages were surprised in Dover.*

Having been suffered to escape, writes the Rev. John Pike, minister at Dover, to Dr. Cotton Mather, "she soon after safely arrived at Captain Gerish's

* Drake's Indian Captivities.

garrison, where she found a refuge from the storm. Here she also had the satisfaction to understand that her own garrison, though one of the first that was assaulted, had been bravely defended and successfully maintained against the enemy. This gentlewoman's garrison was on the most extreme frontier of the province, and more obnoxious than any other, and therefore incapable of being relieved. Nevertheless, by her presence and courage it held out all the war, even for ten years together; and the persons in it have enjoyed very eminent preservations. It would have been deserted if she had accepted offers that were made her by her friends to abandon it and retire to Portsmouth among them, which would have been a damage to the town and land."

THE LADIES OF PHILADELPHIA IN 1780.

I have not shut mine ears to their demands,
Nor posted off their suits with slow delays.
SHAKSPEARE.

During the long war which resulted in the Independence of the American Colonies, the women all over the land were warmly interested in the condition of the soldiers, and prompt to relieve their wants when suffering. There was, at times, a sad deficiency of wearing apparel; and many are the instances in which a noble sacrifice of ease and a liberal expenditure of time and strength, were made by the ladies that this comfort might be restored to the self-sacrificing soldiers.

In 1780, the ladies of Philadelphia city and county, learning that the soldiers were in great need of clothing, sold their jewelry and converted *other* trinkets into something more serviceable; collected by solicitation large sums of money; purchased the raw material, plied the needle "with all diligence;" and in a short time the aggregate amount of their contributions was $7,500.*

* This sum was raised in and immediately around Philadelphia.

The number of shirts made by the ladies of Philadelphia during that patriotic movement, was twenty-two hundred! These were cut out at the house of Mrs. Sarah Bache, daughter of Dr. Franklin. This lady writing to a Mrs. Meredith, of Trenton, New Jersey, at that time, says, "I am happy to have it in my power to tell you that the sums given by the good women of Philadelphia for the benefit of the army, have been much greater than could be expected, and given with so much cheerfulness and so many blessings, that it was rather a pleasing than a painful task to call for them. I write to claim you as a Philadelphian, and shall think myself honored in your donation."

The efforts of the ladies were not, however, limited to their own neighborhood. They addressed circulars to the adjoining counties and states, and the response of New Jersey and Maryland was truly generous.

THE WIFE OF PRESIDENT REED.*

Mightier far
Than strength of nerve or sinew, or the sway
Of magic potent over sun and star,
Is love, though oft to agony distrest,
And though his favorite seat be feeble woman's breast.
WORDSWORTH

Undaunted by the tempest, wild and chill,
That pours its restless and disastrous roll,
O'er all that blooms below.
SANDS' YAMOYDEN.

Prominent among the ladies of Philadelphia who, in the summer and fall of 1780, were active in assisting the sufferers in the American army, was Esther Reed, the wife of President Reed. She stood at the head of the Association till her death, which occurred on the eighteenth of September of that year. She was succeeded by Mrs. Sarah Bache, Mrs. Francis, Mrs. Clarkson, Mrs. Blair and Mrs. Hillegas, who were constituted an Executive Committee.

---

* The facts embodied in this notice of Mrs. Reed, are mainly obtained from the Life and Correspondence of President Reed. *Vide* volume II., chapter XII.

The maiden name of Mrs. Reed was De Berdt. She was born in London on the twenty-second of October, 1746. There, about the year 1763, she became acquainted with Mr. Joseph Reed, of New Jersey, then a student at the Temple. She had fond parents and lived in affluence, but from these she at length turned, and, being married in May, 1770, "followed the lover of her youth to these wild Colonies." Philadelphia became the home of the happy couple. The wife of an American, she imbibed the sentiments and manifested the spirit of an American, and to the day of her death showed herself worthy to be the wife of an American soldier. "During five years of war, more than half the time her family was broken up, and for a long period the young wife, with her little children and an aged mother, was driven to seek a distant and precarious refuge." Her husband was an Adjutant-General, and was in the camp much of the time, till he was chosen President—or, as we now say, Governor—of Pennsylvania, in 1778. Her letters written to him, breathe a patriotic and submissive spirit, and a cheerful trust in that "presiding Power" from whom all solace is derived in seasons of danger, disappointment and affliction.

She was placed at the head of the voluntary association of Philadelphia ladies at its formation in May, and as early as the twentieth of the following month, it will be seen, by an extract from a letter written by Mr. Reed to General Washington, the business of the society was progressing admirably: "The ladies have caught the happy contagion, and in a few days Mrs. Reed will have the honor of writing to you on the subject. It is expected she will have a sum equal to £100,000, to be laid out according to your Excellency's direction, in such a way as may be thought most honorable and gratifying to the brave old soldiers who have borne so great a share of the burden of this war. I thought it best to mention it in this way to your Excellency for your consideration, as it may tend to forward the benevolent scheme of the donors with dispatch. I must observe that the ladies have excepted such articles of necessity, as clothing, which the states are bound to provide."

The following letter, written the next month, explains itself:

"ESTHER REED TO WASHINGTON.

"Philadelphia, July 4th, 1780.

"SIR,—The subscription set on foot by the ladies of this city for the use of the soldiery, is so far completed as to induce me to transmit to your Excellency an account of the money I have received, and which, although it has answered our expectations, does not equal our wishes, but I am persuaded will be received as a proof of our zeal for the great cause of America, and our esteem and gratitude for those who so bravely defend it.

"The amount of the subscription is 200,580 dollars, and £625 *6s.* 8*d.* in specie, which makes in the whole, in paper money, 300,634 dollars.

"The ladies are anxious for the soldiers to receive

the benefit of it, and wait your directions how it can best be disposed of. We expect some considerable addition from the country, and have also wrote to the other States in hopes the ladies there will adopt similar plans, to render it more general and beneficial.

"With the utmost pleasure I offer any further attention and care in my power to complete the execution of the design, and shall be happy to accomplish it agreeable to the intention of the donors and your wishes on the subject.

"The ladies of my family join me in their respectful compliments and sincerest prayer for your health, safety, and success.

"I have the honor to be,

"With the highest respect,

"Your obedient humble servant,

"E. Reed."

During the months of July and August, though in feeble health, Mrs. Reed held frequent correspondence with General Washington on the best mode of administering relief to the destitute soldiers. Her desire to make herself useful may be inferred from the tone of a letter addressed to her husband from the banks of the Schuylkill, on the twenty-second of August. Among other things, she says, "I received this morning a letter from the General, and he still continues his opinion that the money in my hands should be laid out in linen; he says, no supplies he has at present or has a prospect of are any way adequate to the wants of the army.

His letter is, I think, a little formal, as if he was hurt by our asking his opinion a second time, and our not following his directions, after desiring him to give them. The letter is very complaisant, and I shall now endeavor to get the shirts made as soon as possible. *This is another circumstance to urge my return to town, as I can do little towards it here.*"

The responsible and onerous duties of Mrs. Reed during the summer of 1780, were no doubt injurious to her already poor health, and hastened the approach of death. Early in September she was laid upon a bed of fatal illness, and before the month had closed, as before mentioned, she was in the "mysterious realm." The Council and Assembly adjourned to pay their last respect to her exalted virtues. Her remains were deposited in the Presbyterian burying-ground in Arch Street, and the following epitaph was inscribed on her tomb:

"In memory of ESTHER, the beloved wife of Joseph Reed,
President of this State, who departed this life
On the 18th of September, A. D. 1780, aged 34 years.
Reader! If the possession of those virtues of the heart
Which make life valuable, or those personal endowments which
Command esteem and love, may claim respectful and affectionate
Remembrance, venerate the ashes here entombed.
If to have the cup of temporal blessings dashed
In the period and station of life in which temporal blessings
May be best enjoyed, demands our sorrow, drop a tear, and
Think how slender is that thread on which the joys
And hopes of life depend."

COMPLETION OF BUNKER HILL MONUMENT.

> The tardy pile, slow rising there,
> With tongueless eloquence shall tell
> Of them who for their country fell.
>
> SPRAGUE.

> Ladies, you deserve
> To have a temple built *you.*
>
> SHAKSPEARE.

The Bunker Hill Monument Association was incorporated in June, 1823. Nothing further was done that year. At the second annual meeting, which was held on the seventeenth of June, efficient plans were devised to carry forward the enterprise; and at the end of another year, just half a century after the battle, the corner stone was laid. General Lafayette was then on a visit to the United States, and was appropriately chosen to take a leading part in this interesting ceremony. The monument did not get fairly under way till the spring of 1827. This apparent tardiness was owing to the circumstance that the material was to be brought from a granite quarry in Quincy, and a rail road — the first in the United States — had to be built from the quarry to the wharf in Quincy to convey the stone.

In 1828, the funds were exhausted, and the work was not resumed till 1834. Within a year the work was again suspended for the same cause. Nothing further was done, and but little said, till 1839, when it was announced that two gentlemen—Amos Lawrence, Esq., of Boston, and Judah Truro, Esq., of New Orleans — would give ten thousand each, provided a sum sufficient to complete the monument could be raised. This liberal offer caused some momentary stimulation; but no proposal immediately made was deemed expedient.

The affairs of the Association now wore, as they had done once or twice before, a gloomy aspect. In the annual report, made on the seventeenth of June, 1840, doubts were expressed whether the present generation would see the monument completed. The same discouraging remark was made soon after, in one of the sewing circles of Boston, when, instead of depressing the spirits, it raised the ambition and quickened the thoughts of the ladies, and several of them proposed to get up a Fair. It was a happy suggestion; was forthwith sanctioned by the board of directors; prompted the issuing of a circular by a sub-committee of the same; raised the stentorian voice of a free and patriotic press, and met with immediate favor all over the land.

The ladies had moved in the matter — *had taken the work into their own hands* — and all doubts in regard to its speedy completion seemed to vanish. The Fair was announced to be held in Quincy Hall, Boston, to commence on the fifth of September, 1840

Every female in the land was invited to contribute some article of her own hands' production, to the exhibition. The patriotic spirit of the *mothers* of the Revolution was now warm in the hearts of their *daughters*, and ten thousand hands, engaged in the work of preparation, were "plying the needle with exquisite art."

The ladies were to have the complete management of the Fair; and, all things in readiness, it commenced. The product of so much industry and ingenuity, dispensed at the hands of the ladies, presented a scene to the thousands who gathered around the numerous well-stored tables, that is described by a writer—doubtless an eye-witness—as "brilliant and inspiring."*

The Fair continued till the fifteenth of the month. Its success was chronicled from day to day in a journal called "The Monument," printed in the Hall. It was the grandest movement of the kind ever made in the country; was conducted throughout in the most admirable manner, and wound up in triumph. Its net proceeds were $30,035 50. To this sum and the $20,000 pledged by the two gentlemen before mentioned, was soon added enough, from other sources, to make the fund $55,153 27; and the work went on to its completion.† Thus,

---

* Frothingham's Siege of Boston.

† The last stone was raised on the morning of the twenty-third of July, 1842; the government of the Association and a multitude of other people were present on the occasion. Just before this act took place, a cannon was raised to the apex and discharged—a morning salute to call

at length, a "duty had been performed;" this imperishable offering to Freedom, "which had its commencement in manly patriotism," was "crowned by garlands of grace and beauty."

---

the people together to engage in the matins of Freedom. Edward Carnes, Jr., of Charlestown, accompanied the stone in its ascent, waving the American flag as he went up, and the Charlestown Artillery were meanwhile firing salutes to announce to the surrounding country the interesting event.

LYDIA DARRAH.

The brave man is not he who feels no fear,
For that were stupid and irrational;
But he whose noble soul its fear subdues,
And bravely dares the danger nature shrinks from.

JOANNA BAILLIE.

We find the following anecdote of the amiable and heroic Quakeress, Lydia Darrah, in the first number of the American Quarterly Review:

When the British army held possession of Phila delphia, General Howe's head quarters were in Second street, the fourth door below Spruce, in a house which was before occupied by General Cad-walader. Directly opposite, resided William and Lydia Darrah, members of the Society of Friends. A superior officer of the British army, believed to be the Adjutant General, fixed upon one of their chambers, a back room, for private conference; and two of them frequently met there, with fire and candles, in close consultation. About the second of December, the Adjutant General told Lydia that they would be in the room at seven o'clock, and remain late; and that they wished the family to retire early to bed; adding, that when they were going away, they would call her to let them out, and extinguish their fire and candles. She accordingly sent all the family to bed; but, as the officer had been so particular, her curiosity was excited. She took off her shoes, and put her ear to the key-hole of the conclave. She overheard an order read for all the British troops to march out, late in the evening of the fourth, and attack General Washington's army, then encamped at White Marsh. On hearing this, she returned to her chamber and laid herself down. Soon after, the officers knocked at her door, but she rose only at the third summons, having feigned to be asleep. Her mind was so much agitated that, from this moment, she could neither eat nor sleep; supposing it to be in her power to save the lives of thousands of her countrymen; but not knowing how she was to convey the necessary information to General Washington, nor daring to confide it even to her husband. The time left, was, however, short; she quickly determined to make her way, as soon as possible, to the American outposts. She informed her family, that, as they were in want of flour, she would go to Frankfort for some; her husband insisted that she should take with her the servant maid; but, to his surprise, she positively refused. She got access to General Howe, and solicited — what he readily granted, — a pass through the British troops on the lines. Leaving her bag at the mill, she hastened towards the American lines, and encountered on her way an American,

Lieutenant Colonel Craig, of the light horse, who, with some of his men, was on the look-out for information. He knew her, and inquired whither she was going. She answered, in quest of her son, an officer in the American army; and prayed the Colonel to alight and walk with her. He did so, ordering his troops to keep in sight. To him she disclosed her momentous secret, after having obtained from him the most solemn promise never to betray her individually, since her life might be at stake, with the British. He conducted her to a house near at hand, directed a female in it to give her something to eat, and he speeded for head quarters, where he brought General Washington acquainted with what he had heard. Washington made, of course, all preparation for baffling the meditated surprise. Lydia returned home with her flour; sat up alone to watch the movement of the British troops; heard their footsteps; but when they returned, in a few days after, did not dare to ask a question, though solicitous to learn the event. The next evening, the Adjutant General came in, and requested her to walk up to his room, as he wished to put some questions. She followed him in terror; and when he locked the door, and begged her, with an air of mystery to be seated, she was sure that she was either suspected, or had been betrayed. He inquired earnestly whether any of her family were up the last night he and the other officer met: — she told him that they all retired at eight o'clock. He observed — "I know *you* were asleep, for I knocked at your chamber door three times before you heard me;—I am entirely at a loss to imagine who gave General Washington information of our intended attack, unless the walls of the house could speak. When we arrived near White Marsh, we found all their cannon mounted, and the troops prepared to receive us; and we have marched back like a parcel of fools."

WIDOW STOREY.*

Stick to your aim; the mongrel's hold will slip,
But only crow-bars loose the bull-dog's lip;
Small as he looks, the jaw that never yields,
Drags down the bellowing monarch of the fields.

HOLMES.

The first man who commenced a settlement in the town of Salisbury, Vermont, on the Otter creek, was Amos Storey, who, in making an opening in the heart of the wilderness on the right of land to which the first settler was entitled, was killed by the fall of a tree. His widow, who had been left in Connecticut, immediately resolved to push into

---

* For this anecdote and that of Mrs. Hendee, we are indebted to the Hon. Daniel P. Thompson, of Montpelier, author of "The Green Mountain Boys," "Locke Amsden," &c. In a note to the author, in a letter which contained these anecdotes, he appropriately observes that "the women of the Green Mountains deserve as much credit for their various displays of courage, endurance and patriotism, in the early settlement of their State, as was ever awarded to their sex for similar exhibitions in any part of the world. In the controversy with New York and New Hampshire, which took the form of war in many instances; in the predatory Indian incursions, and in the war of the Revolution, they often displayed a capacity for labor and endurance, a spirit and firmness in the hour of danger, and a resolution and hardihood in defending their families, and their threatened land against all enemies, whether domestic or foreign, that would have done honor to the dames of Sparta."

the wilderness, with her ten small children, to take his place and preserve and clear up his farm. And this bold resolution she carried out to the letter, in spite of every difficulty, hardship and danger which for years constantly beset her in her solitary location in the woods. Acre after acre of the dense and dark forest melted away before her axe, which she handled with the dexterity of the most experienced chopper. The logs and bushes were piled and burnt by her own strong and untiring hand: crops were raised, by which, with the fruits of her fishing and unerring rifle, she supported herself and her hardy brood of children. As a place of refuge from the assaults of Indians or dangerous wild beasts, she dug out an underground room, into which, through a small entrance made to open under an overhanging thicket in the bank of the stream, she nightly retreated with her children. And here she continued to reside, thus living and thus laboring, unassisted, till, by her own hand and the help which her boys soon began to afford her, she cleared up a valuable farm and placed herself in independent circumstances in life.

MRS. HENDEE.

I am their mother, who shall bar me from them.
SHAKSPEARE.

On the burning of Royalton, Vermont, by the Indians, in 1776, Mrs. Hendee, of that place, exhibited a praiseworthy and heroic character. The attack was sudden, and her husband being absent in the Vermont regiment, and she being in the field, the Indians seized her children, carried them across White river, at that place perhaps an hundred yards wide and quite deep for fording, and placed them under the keepers having the other persons they had collected, thirty or forty in number, in charge. On discovering the fate of her children, Mrs. Hendee resolutely dashed into the river, waded through, and fearlessly entering the Indian camp, regardless of their tomahawks menacingly flourished round her head, boldly demanded the release of her little ones, and persevered in her alternate upbraidings and supplications, till her request was granted. She then carried her children back through the river and landed them in safety on the other bank. But not content with what she had done, like a patriot, as she was, she immedi ately returned, begged for the release of the children of others; again was rewarded with success, and brought two or three more away; again returned and again succeeded, till she had rescued the whole fifteen of her neighbors' children who had been thus snatched away from their distracted parents. On her last return to the camp of the enemy, the Indians were so struck with her conduct that one of them declared that so brave a squaw deserved to be carried across the river, and offered to take her on his back and carry her over. She, in the same spirit, accepted the offer, mounted the back of the gallant savage, was carried to the opposite bank, where she collected her rescued troop of children, and hastened away to restore them to their over-joyed parents.

PATRIOTIC WOMEN OF OLD MIDDLESEX.

In the radiant front superior shines
That first paternal virtue, public zeal,
Who throws o'er all an equal wide survey,
And, ever musing on the common weal,
Still labors glorious with some great design.

THOMSON.

"Old Middlesex" being our native county, with peculiar pleasure and some local pride, we record the following anecdote. Should the historical ploughshare be driven through the other towns in the county, and the towns generally of Massachusetts, it would turn up similar gems in abundance, "of purest ray serene." We quote from Butler's History of Groton:

"After the departure of Colonel Prescott's regiment of 'minute-men,' Mrs. David Wright, of Pepperell, Mrs. Job Shattuck, of Groton, and the neighboring women, collected at what is now Jewett's Bridge, over the Nashua, between Pepperell and Groton, clothed in their absent husbands' apparel, and armed with muskets, pitchforks, and such other weapons as they could find; and having elected Mrs. Wright their commander, resolutely determined that no foe to freedom, foreign or domestic, should pass that bridge. For rumors were rife, that the regulars were approaching and frightful stories of slaughter flew rapidly from place to place, and from house to house.

"Soon there appeared one* on horseback, supposed to be treasonably engaged in conveying intelligence to the enemy. By the implicit command of Sergeant Wright, he is immediately arrested, unhorsed, searched, and the treasonable correspondence found concealed in his boots. He was detained prisoner, and sent to Oliver Prescott, Esq., of Groton, and his dispatches were sent to the Committee of Safety."

* Captain Leonard Whiting, of Hollis, N. H., a noted tory, who was the bearer of dispatches from Canada to the British in Boston.

THE CACIQUE'S NOBLE DAUGHTER.

I think of thee, sweet lady, as of one
  Too pure to mix with others, like some star,
Shining in pensive beauty all alone,
  Kindred with those around, yet brighter far.

MRS. WELBY.

In his history of the Conquest of Florida, Mr Theodore Irving repeats, very interestingly, the story of Juan Ortiz who, with three other Spaniards, fell into the hands of the Indians by stratagem. The four captives were taken to the village of Hirrihigua, the cacique, who ordered them to be executed on a day of religious festival. Three were shot with arrows; and then "Juan Ortiz, a youth, scarce eighteen years of age, of a noble family of Seville, was the fourth victim. As they were leading him forth, his extreme youth touched with compassion the hearts of the wife and daughters of the cacique, who interceded in his favor.

"The cacique listened to their importunities, and granted for the present the life of Ortiz;—but a wretched life did he lead. From morning until evening he was employed in bringing wood and water, and was allowed but little sleep and scanty food. Not a day passed that he was not beaten. On festivals he was an object of barbarous amusement to the cacique, who would oblige him to run, from sunrise until sunset, in the public square of the village, where his companions had met their untimely end, Indians being stationed with bows and arrows, to shoot him, should he halt one moment. When the day was spent, the unfortunate youth lay stretched on the hard floor of the hut, more dead than alive. At such times the wife and daughters of the cacique would come to him privately with food and clothing, and by their kind treatment his life was preserved.

"At length the cacique, determining to put an end to his victim's existence, ordered that he should be bound down upon a wooden frame, in the form of a huge gridiron, placed in the public square, over a bed of live coals, and roasted alive.

"The cries and shrieks of the poor youth reached his female protectors, and their entreaties were once more successful with the cacique. They unbound Ortiz, dragged him from the fire, and took him to their dwelling, where they bathed him with the juice of herbs, and tended him with assiduous care. After many days he recovered from his wounds, though marked with many a scar.

"His employment was now to guard the cemetery of the village. This was in a lonely field in the bosom of a forest. The bodies of the dead were deposited in wooden boxes, covered with boards, without any fastening except a stone or a log of wood laid upon the top; so that the bodies were often carried away by wild beasts.

"In this cemetery was Ortiz stationed, with a bow and arrows, to watch day and night, and was told that should a single body be carried away, he would be burnt alive. He returned thanks to God for having freed him from the dreaded presence of the cacique. hoping to lead a better life with the dead than he had done with the living.

"While watching thus one long wearisome night, sleep overpowered him towards morning. He was awakened by the falling lid of one of the chests, and running to it, found it empty. It had contained the body of an infant recently deceased, the child of an Indian of great note.

"Ortiz doubted not some animal had dragged it away, and immediately set out in pursuit. After wandering for some time, he heard, at a short distance within the woods, a noise like that of a dog gnawing bones. Warily drawing near to the spot, he dimly perceived an animal among the bushes, and invoking succor from on high, let fly an arrow at it. The thick and tangled underwood prevented his seeing the effect of his shot, but as the animal did not stir, he flattered himself that it had been fatal: with this hope he waited until the day dawned, when he beheld his victim, a huge animal of the panther kind, lying dead, the arrow having passed through his entrails and cleft his heart.

"Gathering together the mangled remains of the infant, and replacing them in the coffin, Ortiz dragged his victim in triumph to the village, with the arrow still in his body. The exploit gained him credit with the old hunters, and for some time softened even the ferocity of the cacique. The resentment of the latter, however, from the wrongs he had suffered from white men, was too bitter to be appeased. Some time after, his eldest daughter came to Ortiz, and warned him that her father had determined to sacrifice him at the next festival, which was just at hand, and that the influence of her mother, her sisters, and herself would no longer avail him. She wished him, therefore, to take refuge with a neighboring cacique named Mucozo, who loved her and sought her in marriage, and who, for her sake, would befriend him. 'This very night at midnight.' said the kind-hearted maiden, 'at the northern extremity of the village you will find a trusty friend who will guide you to a bridge, about two leagues hence; on arriving there, you must send him back, that he may reach home before the morning dawn, to avoid suspicion—for well he knows that this bold act, in daring to assist you, may bring down destruction upon us both. Six leagues further on, you will come to the village of Mucozo—tell him I have sent you, and expect him to befriend you in your extremity—I know he will do it—go, and may your God protect you!' Ortiz threw himself at the feet of his generous protectress, and poured out his acknowledgments for the kindness she had always shown him. The Indian guide was at the place appointed, and they left the village without alarming the warlike savages. When they came to the bridge, Ortiz sent back the guide, in obedience to the injunction of his mistress, and, continuing his flight, found himself, by break of day, on the banks of a small stream near the village of Mucozo.

"Looking cautiously around, he espied two Indians fishing. As he was unacquainted with their language, and could not explain the cause of his coming, he was in dread lest they should take him for an enemy and kill him. He, therefore, ran to the place where they had deposited their weapons and seized upon them. The savages fled to the village without heeding his assurances of friendly intention. The inhabitants sallied out with bows and arrows, as though they would attack him. Ortiz fixed an arrow in his bow, but cried out at the same moment, that he came not as an enemy but as an ambassador from a female cacique to their chief. Fortunately one present understood him, and interpreted his words. On this the Indians unbent their bows, and returning with him to their village, presented him to Mucozo. The latter, a youthful chieftain, of a graceful form and handsome countenance, received Ortiz kindly for the sake of her who had sent him; but, on further acquaintance, became attached to him for his own merits, treating him with the affection of a brother."

HUMANE SPIRIT OF A FOREST MAID.

"Beneath the gloom
Of overshadowing forests, sweetly springs
The unexpected flower."

Some of the noblest attributes of humanity are sometimes exhibited by the wild children of the forest. These attributes, in such cases, seem, like trees in the remotest wilderness, to have gained, by their spontaneous growth, surprising height, symmetry and beauty.

A lovelier character than Pocahontas, daughter of Powhatan, king of the country where the first white settlement in Virginia was made, is rarely found among any people. She was lovely in the broadest as well as noblest sense of that word—lovely in features, lovely in disposition, lovely in the highest adornments of Christian grace. She was, in 1607, "a girl of ten or twelve years of age, who, not only for feature, countenance and expression, much exceeded any of the rest of her people, but for wit and spirit was the only nonpareil of the country." Such was Pocahontas, as described by the first white man, probably, who ever saw her, and in whose behalf, at the above date, she displayed the tenderness and true grandeur of her nature.

The colonists, writes Mr. Hildreth, in his new History of the United States, "were specially instructed to seek for a passage to the South Sea; and it was thought that possibly the Chickahoming might lead thither. Having ascended as high as he could in his barge, Captain Smith followed up the stream in a canoe, with two colonists and two Indians for companions; and when the canoe would float no longer, he left the two colonists to guard it, and struck inland with a single Indian as a guide. Set upon unexpectedly by a large party of natives, who had already surprised and killed the two men left to guard the canoe, Smith bound his Indian guide to his arm as a buckler, and made a vigorous defence, killing three of the assailants; but as he retreated backward, he presently sank into a miry swamp, and was taken prisoner His captors would have killed him, but he amused them with a pocket compass. Carried in a sort of triumph through several villages, he was taken before Powhatan, the same chief whom he had visited in company with Newport. An attempt was made to engage his services — at least so Smith understood it — in surprising the colonists at Jamestown. Having failed in this, after much consultation, it was resolved to put him to death. He was dragged to the ground and his head placed upon a stone;

Powhatan raised a club to dash out his brains"—and now view the highly dramatic scene which follows, as pictured by Mrs. Sigourney in a few lines of masterly coloring:

> The sentenced captive see — his brow how white!
> Stretched on the turf, his manly form lies low,
> The war club poises for its fatal blow,
> The death-mist swims before his darkened sight;
> Forth springs the child, in tearful pity bold,
> Her head on his reclines, her arms his neck enfold,
>
> "The child! what madness fires her? Hence! Depart!
> Fly, daughter, fly! before the death-stroke rings;
> Divide her, warriors! from that English heart."
> In vain, for with convulsive grasp she clings:
> She claims a pardon from her frowning sire;
> Her pleading tones subdue his gathered ire,
> And so, uplifting high his feathery dart,
> That doting father gave the child her will,
> And bade the victim live and be his servant still.

After Smith had been an inmate of Powhatan's wigwam awhile, he was permitted to leave the Indians. Sometime after this the savages, becoming alarmed by witnessing Smith's wonderful feats, "laid a plan to get him into their power under the pretence of wishing an interview with him in their territory. But Pocahontas, knowing the desire of the warriors, left the wigwam after her father had gone to sleep, and ran more than nine miles through the woods to inform her friend Captain Smith of the danger that awaited him, either by stratagem or attack."

Subsequently the colony at Jamestown was threatened with famine, when, accompanied by a few companions, she was accustomed to go to the fort every day or two with baskets of corn, and thus her

> —"generous hand vouchsafed its tireless aid
> To guard a nation's germ."

At the age of seventeen or eighteen, Pocahontas married a pious young English officer, named Thomas Rolfe, and went with him to England, where she was baptized and called Rebecca, and where she soon died. Well may it be said of her, in the language of the poet, slightly altered,

> It is not meet such names should moulder in the grave.

HANNAH DUSTIN.

Experience teaches us
That resolution 's a sole help at need;
And this, my lord, our honor teacheth us,
That we be bold in every enterprise.

SHAKSPEARE.

On the fifteenth of March, 1697, a band of Indian prowlers broke into the house of Mr. Dustin, of Haverhill, Massachusetts, and captured his wife, her nurse,* and a babe about one week old. The last was killed before leaving the town. The other two were marched through the wilderness for several days till they came to a halt on an island in the Merrimac river about six miles above Concord, New Hampshire. There they were placed in a wigwam occupied by two men, three women, seven children of theirs, and an English boy who had been captured about a year previous at Worcester, Massachusetts. The captives remained there till the thirtieth of that month before they planned escape. On that day the boy was requested by Mrs. Dustin to ask his master where to strike "to kill instantly;"

* Mrs. Mary Neff.

and the savage was simple enough to tell, and also instructed him in the art of scalping. "At night," to use the concise language of Mr. Bancroft, "while the household slumbers, the captives, each with a tomahawk, strike vigorously, and fleetly, and with division of labor, — and of the twelve sleepers, ten lie dead; of one squaw the wound was not mortal; one child was spared from design. The love of glory next asserted its power; and the gun and tomahawk of the murderer of her infant, and a bag heaped full of scalps were choicely kept as trophies of the heroine. — The streams are the guides which God has set for the stranger in the wilderness: in a bark canoe, the three descend the Merrimac to the English settlements, astonishing their friends by their escape, and filling the land with wonder at their successful daring."

Mrs. Dustin had the happiness of meeting her husband and seven children, who had escaped from the house before the savages entered, and the honor of a very handsome present from Colonel Nicholson, governor of Maryland, as a reward for her heroism.*

* Eleven years after the capture of Mrs. Dustin, a party of French and Indians from Canada made an attack upon the inhabitants of Haverhill, and killed and captured about forty persons. Several women exhibited on the occasion a remarkable degree of sagacity, courage and presence of mind. We condense from Mirick's History of Haverhill.

Ann Whittaker escaped the tomahawk by hiding in an apple chest under the stairs. — A negro servant, named Hagar, covered a couple of children with tubs in the cellar and then concealed herself behind some meat barrels. The Indians trod on a foot of one of the children and took meat from the barrel behind which Hagar had hidden, without discovering any of them.—The wife of Thomas Hartshorn, took all her children except the babe — which she was afraid would cry — through a trap-door into the cellar. The enemy entered and plundered the house, but did not find the way into the cellar. They took the infant from its bed in the garret and threw it out of the window. Strange to say, though stunned, it lived and grew to rugged manhood. — The wife of Captain Simon Wainwright, after the enemy had killed her husband, let them into the house and treated them kindly. They at length demanded money, when she went out, as she pretended, to get it. They soon ascertained — though too late to find her — that she had fled with all her children but one, who was taken captive.

THE HEROINES OF BRYANT'S STATION.

> The brave example cannot perish
> Of courage.
>
> HOSMER.

> Nor could the boldest of our youth have dared
> To pass our outworks.
>
> POPE'S HOMER.

At the siege of Bryant's station near Lexington, Kentucky, in August, 1782, the water in the fort was exhausted; and as the nearest place to obtain a supply was a spring several rods off, it would require no small risk and, consequently, no common intrepidity to undertake to bring it. A body of Indians in plain sight, were trying to entice the soldiers to attack them without the walls, while another party was concealed near the spring, waiting, it was supposed, to storm one of the gates, should the besieged venture out. It was thought probable that the Indians in ambush would remain so until they saw indications that the other party had succeeded in enticing the soldiers to open engagement.

The position of things was explained to the women, and they were invited to each take a bucket and march to the spring in a body. "Some, as was natural, had no relish for the undertaking, and asked why the men could not bring water as well as themselves, observing that they were not bullet-proof, and the Indians made no distinction between male and female scalps. To this it was answered, that the women were in the habit of bringing water every morning to the fort; and that if the Indians saw them engaged as usual, it would induce them to think that their ambuscade was undiscovered; and that they would not unmask themselves for the sake of firing at a few women, when they hoped, by remaining concealed a few moments longer, to obtain complete possession of the fort: that if men should go down to the spring, the Indians would immediately suspect something was wrong, would despair of succeeding by ambuscade, and would instantly rush upon them, follow them into the fort, or shoot them down at the spring.

"The decision was soon made. A few of the boldest declared their readiness to brave the danger, and the younger and more timid rallying in the rear of these veterans, they all marched down in a body to the spring, within point blank shot of more than five hundred Indian warriors! Some of the girls could not help betraying symptoms of terror; but the married women, in general, moved with a steadiness and composure that completely deceived the Indians. Not a shot was fired. The party were permitted to fill their buckets, one after another, without interruption; and although their steps became quicker and quicker, on their return. and when near the fort, degenerated into a rather unmilitary celerity, with some little crowding in passing the gate, yet not more than one-fifth of the water was spilled, and the eyes of the youngest had not dilated to more than double their ordinary size." *

* M'Clung's Sketches of Western Adventure.

MRS. DAVIESS.

'Tis late before
The brave despair.

THOMSON.

Samuel Daviess was an early settler at a place called Gilmer's Lick, in Lincoln county, Kentucky. In the month of August, 1782, while a few rods from his house, he was attacked early one morning by an Indian; and attempting to get within doors, he found that his house was already occupied by other Indians. Pursued by his foe, he ran into a cornfield and lay concealed till the savage gave up the chase and returned to the house. He then ran to his brother's station, five miles off, gave the alarm, and was soon returning with five stout, well armed men.

Meanwhile the Indians — four in number — who had entered the house while the fifth was in pursuit of Mr. Daviess, routed Mrs. Daviess and the children from their beds, and they soon understood that they must take up a line of march — they knew not whither. As soon as she was dressed, Mrs. Daviess "commenced showing the Indians one article of clothing and then another, which pleased them very much; and in that way delayed them at the house nearly two hours. In the mean time, the Indian who had been in pursuit of her husband returned, with his hands stained with poke berries, which he held up, and with some violent gestures and waving of his tomahawk, attempted to induce the belief, that the stain on his hands was the blood of her husband, and that he had killed him. She was enabled at once to discover the deception, and instead of producing any alarm on her part, she was satisfied that her husband had escaped uninjured.

"After the savages had plundered the house of every thing that they could conveniently carry off with them, they started, taking Mrs. Daviess and her children — seven in number — as prisoners, along with them. Some of the children were too young to travel as fast as the Indians wished, and discovering, as she believed, their intention to kill such of them as could not conveniently travel, she made the two oldest boys carry them on their backs. The Indians, in starting from the house, were very careful to leave no signs of the direction they had taken, not even permitting the children to break a twig or weed as they passed along. They had not gone far before an Indian drew his knife and cut off a few inches of Mrs. Daviess' dress, so that she would not be interrupted in traveling.

"Mrs. Daviess was a woman of cool, deliberate courage, and accustomed to handle the gun, so that she could shoot well, as many of the women were in the habit of doing in those days. She had con templated, as a last resort, that if not rescued in the course of the day, when night came on and the Indians had fallen asleep, she would deliver herself and children by killing as many of the Indians as she could — thinking that in a night attack as many of them as remained would most probably run off." *

Mr. Daviess and his comrades reaching the house and finding it empty, hastened on in pursuit of the Indians. They had gone but a few miles before they overtook the retreating party. Two Indian spies in the rear, first discovered the pursuers, and running on, overtook the three others, with the prisoners, and knocked down and scalped, though they did not kill, the oldest boy. At that moment the pursuers fired at the Indians, but missed. The latter were now alarmed and confused, and Mrs. Daviess, taking advantage of this circumstance, jumped into a sink hole with her infant in her arms; and the Indians fleeing, every child was saved.

"Kentucky, in its early days, like most new countries, was occasionally troubled by men of abandoned character, who lived by stealing the property of others, and, after committing their depredations, retired to their hiding places, thereby eluding the operation of the law. One of these marauders, a man of desperate character, who had committed extensive thefts from Mr. Daviess, as well as from his

---

* Collins's Historical Sketches of Kentucky

COFFIN DEL.
J.W. ORR. N.Y.

neighbors, was pursued by Daviess and a party whose property he had taken, in order to bring him to justice. While the party were in pursuit, the suspected individual, not knowing any one was pursuing him, came to the house of Daviess, armed with his gun and tomahawk—no person being at home but Mrs. Daviess and her children. After he had stepped into the house, Mrs. Daviess asked him if he would drink something—and having set a bottle of whiskey upon the table, requested him to help himself. The fellow, not suspecting any danger, set his gun up by the door, and while drinking, Mrs. Daviess picked up his gun, and placing herself in the door, had the gun cocked and leveled upon him by the time he turned around, and in a peremptory manner ordered him to take a seat, or she would shoot him. Struck with terror and alarm, he asked what he had done. She told him he had stolen her husband's property and that she intended to take care of him herself. In that condition she held him a prisoner, until the party of men returned and took him into their possession. *

* Collins.

A KENTUCKY AMAZON.

This is true courage.
WHITEHEAD'S ROMAN FATHER.

During the summer of 1787, writes Mr. McClung, in his Sketches of Western Adventure, "The house of Mr. John Merrill, of Nelson county, Kentucky, was attacked by the Indians, and defended with singular address and good fortune. Merrill was alarmed by the barking of a dog about midnight, and upon opening the door in order to ascertain the cause of the disturbance, he received the fire of six or seven Indians, by which one arm and one thigh were broken. He instantly sank upon the floor, and called upon his wife to close the door. This had scarcely been done when it was violently assailed by the tomahawks of the enemy, and a large breach soon effected. Mrs. Merrill, however, being a perfect amazon, both in strength and courage, guarded it with an axe, and successively killed or badly wounded four of the enemy as they attempted to force their way into the cabin.

"The Indians ascended the roof, and attempted to enter by way of the chimney; but here again they were met by the same determined enemy. Mrs. Merrill seized the only feather bed which the cabin afforded, and hastily ripping it open, poured its contents upon the fire. A furious blaze and stifling smoke instantly ascended the chimney, and brought down two of the enemy, who lay for a few moments at the mercy of the lady. Seizing the axe, she quickly dispatched them, and was instantly afterwards summoned to the door, where the only remaining savage now appeared, endeavoring to effect an entrance, while Mrs. Merrill was engaged at the chimney. He soon received a gash in the cheek, which compelled him, with a loud yell, to relinquish his purpose, and return hastily to Chillicothe, where, from the report of a prisoner, he gave an exaggerated account of the fierceness, strength, and courage of the 'long knife squaw!' "

HEROISM AT INNIS SETTLEMENT.

Courage alone can save us.

SOUTHEY.

The account of the Indians' attack on the Innis settlement, near Frankfort, Kentucky, in April, 1792, has been differently related by different writers. The most reliable account is doubtless that given by the Rev. Abraham Cook, a minister of the Baptist denomination and the brother of Jesse and Hosea Cook, whose wives were the heroines of the settlement. The attack was made on the twenty-eighth of the month, by about one hundred Indians, and at three points almost simultaneously. The first onset was upon the Cooks who lived in cabins close together, and where was displayed a degree of intrepidity rarely matched.

"The brothers were near their cabins, one engaged in shearing sheep, the other looking on. The sharp crack of rifles was the first intimation of the proximity of the Indians; and that fire was fatal to the brothers—the elder fell dead, and the younger was mortally wounded, but enabled to reach the cabin.

The two Mrs. Cook, with three children — two whites and one black — were instantly collected in the house, and the door, a very strong one, made secure. The Indians, unable to enter, discharged their rifles at the door, but without injury, as the balls did not penetrate through the thick boards of which it was constructed. They then attempted to cut it down with their tomahawks, but with no better success. While these things occurred without, there was deep sorrow, mingled with fearless determination and high resolve within. The younger Cook, mortally wounded, immediately the door was barred, sank down on the floor, and breathed his last; and the two Mrs. Cook were left the sole defenders of the cabin, with the three children. There was a rifle in the house, but no balls could be found. In this extremity, one of the women got hold of a musket ball, and placing it between her teeth, actually bit it into two pieces. With one she instantly loaded the rifle. The Indians, failing in their attempts to cut down the door, had retired a few paces in front, doubtless to consult upon their future operations. One seated himself upon a log, apparently apprehending no danger from within. Observing him, Mrs. Cook took aim from a narrow aperture and fired, when the Indian gave a loud yell, bounded high in the air, and fell dead. This infuriated the savages, who threatened — for they could speak English — to burn the house and all the inmates. Several speedily climbed to the top of the cabin, and kindled a fire on the boards of the roof. The devouring element began to take ef fect, and with less determined and resolute courage within, the certain destruction of the cabin and the death of the inmates, must have been the consequence. But the self possession and intrepidity of these Spartan females were equal to the occasion. One of them instantly ascended to the loft, and the other handed her water, with which she extinguished the fire. Again and again the roof was fired, and as often extinguished. The water failing, the undaunted women called for some eggs, which were broken and the contents thrown upon the fire, for a time holding the flames at bay. Their next resource was the bloody waistcoat of the husband and brother-in-law, who lay dead upon the floor. The blood with which this was profusely saturated, checked the progress of the flames—but, as they appeared speedily to be gathering strength, another, and the last expedient . . . . proved successful. The savage foe yielded, and the fruitful expedients of female courage triumphed. One Indian, in bitter disappointment, fired at his unseen enemy through the boards, but did not injure her, when the whole immediately descended from the roof.

"About the time the attack commenced, a young man named McAndre, escaped on horseback, in view of the Indians, who, it was supposed, would give the alarm to the older neighboring settlements. As soon as they descended from the house top, a few climbed some contiguous trees, and instituted a sharp look out. While in the trees, one of them fired a second ball into the loft of the cabin, which cut to pieces a bundle of yarn hanging near the head of Mrs. Cook, but without doing further injury. Soon after, they threw the body of the dead Indian into the adjacent creek, and precipitately fled."

BOLD EXPLOIT AT TAMPICO.

A thousand hearts are great within my bosom;
Advance our standards.

SHAKSPEARE.

Rocks have been shaken from their solid base;
But what shall move a dauntless soul?

JOANNA BAILLIE.

At the capture of Tampico, which took place on the fourteenth of November, 1846, a noteworthy act was performed by a lady, whose patriotism and daring should not be forgotten. She not only gave Commodore Connor full information in regard to the defence of the place, with a plan of the harbor, town and forts, but when the squadron was approaching, though opposed by the city council and even menaced, she hoisted the American flag and persisted in waving it beneath the very eye of the *ayuntamiento!* This intrepid woman was Mrs. Ann Chase, wife of the American Consul.

DICEY LANGSTON.

Thou soul of love and bravery!

MOORE.

Dicey Langston was the daughter of Solomon Langston, of Laurens district, South Carolina. She possessed an intrepid spirit, which is highly serviceable in times of emergency, and which, as she lived in the days of the Revolution, she had more than one opportunity to display. Situated in the midst of tories, and being patriotically inquisitive, she often learned by accident, or discovered by strategy, the plottings so common in those days, against the whigs. Such intelligence she was accustomed to communicate to the friends of freedom on the opposite side of the Ennoree river.

Learning one time that a band of loyalists—known in those parts as the "Bloody scout"—were about to fall upon the "Elder settlement," a place where a brother of hers and other friends were residing, she resolved to warn them of their danger. To do this she must hazard her own life. But off she started, alone, in the darkness of the night; traveled several miles through the woods, and over marshes and across creeks, through a country where foot-logs and bridges were then unknown; came to the Tyger, a rapid and deep stream, into which she plunged and waded till the water was up to her neck; she then became bewildered, and zigzagged the channel for some time; reached the opposite shore at length—for a helping Hand was beneath, a kind Providence guiding her:—hastened on; reached the settlement, and her brother and the whole community were safe!

She was returning one day from another settlement of whigs—in the Spartanburg district, when a company of tories met her and questioned her in regard to the neighborhood she had just left; but she refused to communicate the desired information. The leader of the band then held a pistol to her breast, and threatened to shoot her if she did not make the wished for disclosure. "Shoot me if you dare! I will not tell you!" was her dauntless reply, as she opened a long handkerchief that covered her neck and bosom, thus manifesting a willingness to receive the contents of the pistol, if the officer insisted on disclosures or life. The dastard, enraged at her defying movement, was in the act of firing, at which moment one of the soldiers threw up the hand holding the weapon, and the cowerless heart of the girl was permitted to beat on.

The brothers of Dicey were no less patriotic than she; and they having, by their active services on the side of freedom, greatly displeased the loyalists.

COFFIN DEL.
J.W. ORR N.Y.

these latter were determined to be revenged. A desperate band accordingly went to the house of their father, and finding the sons absent, they were about to wreak their vengeance on the old man, whom they hated for the sons' sake. With this intent one of the party drew a pistol; but just as it was aimed at the breast of her aged and infirm father, Dicey rushed between the two, and though the ruffian bade her get out of his way or receive in her own breast the contents of the pistol, she regarded not his threats, but flung her arms around her father's neck and declared she would receive the ball first, if the weapon must be discharged. Such fearlessness and willingness to offer her own life for the sake of her parent, softened the heart of the "bloody scout," and Mr. Langston lived to see his noble daughter perform other heroic deeds.

One time her brother James, in his absence, sent to the house for a gun which he had left in her care, with orders for her to deliver it to no one except by his direction. On reaching the house one of the company who where directed to call for it, made known their errand, whereupon she brought and was about to deliver the weapon. At this moment it occurred to her that she had not demanded the countersign agreed on between herself and brother. With the gun still in her hand, she looked the company sternly in the face, and remarking that they wore a suspicious look, called for the countersign. Hereupon one of them, in jest, told her she was too tardy in her requirements; that both the gun and its holder were in their possession. "Do you think so," she boldly asked, as she cocked the disputed weapon and aimed it at the speaker. "If the gun is in your possession," she added, "take charge of it!" Her appearance indicated that she was in earnest, and the countersign was given without further delay. A hearty laugh on the part of the "liberty men," ended the ceremony.

REBECCA MOTTE.

We can make our lives sublime.

LONGFELLOW

During the Revolutionary war, while Fort Motte, situated on Congaree river, in South Carolina, was in the hands of the British, in order to effect its surrender, it became necessary to burn a large mansion standing near the centre of the trench. The house was the property of Mrs. Motte. Lieut. Colonel Lee communicated to her the contemplated work of destruction with painful reluctance, but her smiles, half anticipating his proposal, showed, at once, that she was willing to sacrifice her property if she could thereby aid in the least degree towards the expulsion of the enemy and the salvation of the land. The reply she made to the proposal was that she was "gratified with the opportunity of contributing to the good of her country, and should view the approaching scene with delight!" *

*MRS. BREWTON, — since Foster — one of the most amiable and enlightened of the whig ladies, was an inmate of Mrs. Motte's family at the time of the destruction of her house. Meeting with her shortly after the signing of the preliminary articles of peace at Philadelphia,

The husband of this noble-hearted widow had so involved himself by securities for friends, that after the struggle for Independence was over, it was impossible for her to immediately meet all demands against the estate. She, however, resolved that they should some day be liquidated — that, life and health being continued long enough, all obligations of her husband's contracting should be good against herself. She purchased a large tract of rice land on credit, and by industry and economy was able, in a short time, to pay the old demands, and lived to accumulate a handsome property. She reminds us of Solomon's picture of the virtuous woman: "She considereth a field, and buyeth it: with the fruit of her hands she planteth a vineyard.' . . . "She looketh well to the ways of her household, and eateth not of the bread of idleness."

I inquired — "How it had happened, that she, a helpless, unprotected widow, without any charge of improper conduct, had so far incurred the enmity of the British commanders, as to have been arrested without ceremony, and hurried unprepared, into exile." She answered — "That she knew no act of hers which had merited such ungentlemanly and inhuman treatment." Entering, however, into conversation relative to the siege and surrender of Fort Motte, she gave at once a clue to the transaction. While the American forces were at a distance, Major M'Pherson, the commander of the post, suffered Mrs. Motte and her family to remain, and an apartment was allowed for their accommodation. But when the post at Thompson's, but a little removed from him, was attacked and carried, anticipating the fate which awaited him, immediate removal was not only advised, but insisted on. At the moment of departure, Mrs. Brewton seeing a quiver of arrows, which had been presented to Mr. Motte by a favorite African, said to her friend, "I will take these with me, to prevent their destruction by the soldiers." With the quiver in her hands, she was passing the gate, when Major M'Pherson, drawing forth a shaft, and applying the point to his finger, said, "what have you here, Mrs. Brewton?" "For God's sake be careful," she replied "these arrows are poisoned." The ladies immediately passed on to the out-house, which they were now to inhabit. In the siege which directly followed, when the destruction of the house was determined upon, and missiles eagerly sought for by Lieutenant Colonel Lee for conveying the fire to the shingles, these arrows being remembered, were presented by Mrs. Motte, with a wish for the happy accomplishment of the end proposed. It was afterwards known, that the first arrow missed its aim, and fell at the feet of the commander, who taking, it up, with strong expressions of anger, exclaimed, "I thank you, Mrs. Brewton." The second arrow took effect, and set fire to the roof, when the brisk discharge of a six pounder being maintained by Captain Finley, in the direction of the stair-case, every effort to extinguish it proved fruitless, until, from the apprehension of the roof falling in, the garrison were compelled to surrender at discretion. General Greene arriving soon after, paid to Major M'Pherson the tribute of applause due to his excellent defence, declaring, "that such gallantry could not fail to procure for him a high increase of reputation." This compliment, however, does not appear to have soothed the mortified soldier; for, walking immediately up to Mrs. Brewton, he said, "to *you* madam, I owe this disgrace; it would have been more charitable to have allowed me to perish by poison, than to be thus compelled to surrender my post to the enemy." This speech alone, accounts for the enmity against Mrs. Brewton. — [Knapp's American Anecdotes.

ANOTHER SACRIFICE FOR FREEDOM.

A patriot's birth-right thou may'st claim.

SHELLEY

The subject of the following anecdote was a sister of General Woodhull, and was born at Brookhaven, Long Island, in December, 1740. Her husband was a member of the Provincial Convention which met in May, 1775, and of the Convention which was called two years after, to frame the first state constitution.

While Judge William Smith was in the Provincial Congress, his lady was met, at a place called Middle Island, by Major Benjamin Tallmadge, who was then on his march across Long Island. He told her he was on his way to her house to capture the force then possessing Fort St. George, and that he might be obliged to burn or otherwise destroy her dwelling-house and other buildings in accomplishing this object. Ready to make any sacrifice for the good of her bleeding country, she promptly assured the Major that the buildings were at his disposal, to destroy or [illegible], as efforts to dislodge the enemy might require.

A PATRIOTIC DONATION.

> Large charity doth never soil,
> But only whitens soft white hands. — LOWELL.

When General Greene was retreating through the Carolinas, after the battle of the Cowpens, and while at Salisbury, North Carolina, he put up at a hotel, the landlady of which was Mrs. Elizabeth Steele. A detachment of Americans had just had a skirmish with the British under Cornwallis at the Catawba ford, and were defeated and dispersed; and when the wounded were brought to the hotel, the General no doubt felt somewhat discouraged, for the fate of the south and perhaps of the country seemed to hang on the result of this memorable retreat. Added to his other troubles was that of being penniless; and Mrs. Steele, learning this fact by accident, and ready to do any thing in her power to further the cause of freedom, took him aside and drew from under her apron two bags of specie. Presenting them to him she generously said, "Take these, for you will want them, and I can do without them."*

---

* Never did relief come at a more propitious moment; nor would it be straining conjecture to suppose that he resumed his journey with his spirits cheered and brightened by this touching proof of woman's devotion to the cause of her country. [Greene's Life of Nathaniel Greene.

"THE LITTLE BLACK-EYED REBEL."

Some there are
By their good deeds exalted

WORDSWORTH.

Mary Redmond, the daughter of a patriot of Philadelphia of some local distinction, had many relatives who were loyalists. These were accustomed to call her "the little black-eyed rebel," so ready was she to assist women whose husbands were fighting for freedom, in procuring intelligence. "The dispatches were usually sent from their friends by a boy who carried them stitched in the back of his coat. He came into the city bringing provisions to market. One morning when there was some reason to fear he was suspected, and his movements were watched by the enemy, Mary undertook to get the papers from him in safety. She went, as usual, to the market, and in a pretended game of romps, threw her shawl over the boy's head and secured the prize. She hastened with the papers to her anxious friends, who read them by stealth, after the windows had been carefully closed."

When the whig women in her neighborhood heard of Burgoyne's surrender, and were exulting in secret, the cunning little "rebel," prudently refraining from any open demonstration of joy, "put her head up the chimney and gave a shout for Gates!"

A BENEVOLENT QUAKERESS.*

How few, like thee, inquire the wretched out,
And court the offices of soft humanity!

ROWE.

Charity Rodman was born in Newport, Rhode Island, in the year 1765. Her father was a sea-captain, and died at Honduras while she was in infancy. She married Thomas Rotch, of Nantucket, Massachusetts, on the sixth of June, 1790. Soon afterwards the Rotch family removed to New Bedford, where they have since distinguished themselves by their energy and uprightness of character, and their success in the mercantile business, being extensively engaged in the whale-fishery. Of some of them, as traffickers, it may be said, as it was of the merchants of Tyre in the days of her glory: "they are among the honorable of the earth."

About the year 1801, Mrs. Rotch removed with her husband to Hartford, Connecticut, where she remained

* Some of the facts embodied in this article were gathered by the author while on a visit to Massillon, Ohio, in the summer of 1847, and were communicated to the public at that time through the columns of the Western Literary Messenger; others were lately and very obligingly furnished by Dr. William Bowen, of that place.

till 1811. She then, in a feeble state of health, and for its improvement, accompanied her husband on a journey through Ohio, and other parts of the West. The mildness of the winter was favorable to her constitution, and, restored to comfortable health, she returned to Hartford in the early part of the next summer. The following November she removed to Kendol, in Stark county, Ohio, near the site of the present village of Massillon.

There the mind of Mrs. Rotch, coöperating with the long-cherished wishes of her heart, originated and matured plans for the establishment of a "school for orphan and destitute children." Having traveled much, she had made extensive observations; and with an eye always open to the condition and wants of human kind, she early and often felt the force of a remark once made to her by an English friend: "That there were a great many children *wasted* in this country" — a painful truth, but no less applicable to Great Britain than to the United States.

Her husband died in 1823, and bequeathed to her, during life, his large and entire estate. His personal property was left in her hands to be disposed of as her philanthropic heart might dictate. This formed the basis of the school-fund which she left, and which, four or five years after her death, which occurred on the sixth of August, 1824, amounted to twenty thousand dollars. The interest of this sum has since purchased a farm of one hundred and eighty-five acres, one and a half miles from the village of Massillon, and erected, at a cost of five thousand dollars, a large brick edifice for educational and dwelling purposes, which has been open seven years and which sustains forty pupils. The real and personal estate of the institution, is now estimated at thirty-five thousand dollars.

A class of ten pupils enter annually and remain four years. The school is established on the manual labor plan; and the boys are thoroughly instructed in the art of husbandry, and the girls in culinary duties and the manufacture of their own wearing apparel. Children enter between the ages of ten and fourteen, hence the youngest leave as advanced in life as their fifteenth year, a period when their habits of industry and their moral principles usually become too well established to be easily changed.

This school, founded by the benevolence of a single individual — a devout, yet modest and quiet member of the Society of Friends — is destined to become a source of inestimable blessings. Every half century, five hundred otherwise neglected plants in the garden of humanity, will there be pruned and nurtured, and strengthened for the storms of life; and many of them will doubtless be fitted to bear fruit here to the glory of God, and be finally transplanted to bloom in eternal youth in the gardens above.

The offspring of Christian philanthropy, the school will stand as a lasting memorial of woman's worth. The highest ambition of its founder was to be a blessing to those who should come after her; and it may be said that while she did not live in vain, neither did she die in vain. Her death threw a legacy into the lap of orphanage, the benignant influence of which will long be felt.

The grave of Mrs. Rotch is overlooked by the monument of her munificence, but no marble nor enduring object marks the spot. Virtues like hers neither crave nor need *chiseled* words of praise; they are engraved on the hearts of the succored, to be remembered while those hearts continue to beat; and the feet of befriended children will keep a path open to the grave of their foster-mother, for ages.

A PIONEER IN SUNDAY SCHOOLS.*

—Doubtless unto thee is given
A life that bears immortal fruit
In such great offices as suit
The full-grown energies of heaven.

TENNYSON'S IN MEMORIAM.

The Ohio Company, which was organized in Boston in the year 1787, built a stockade fort during the next two years, at Marietta, and named it *Campus Martius*. The year it was completed, the Rev. Daniel Storey, a preacher at Worcester, Massachusetts, was sent out as a chaplain. He acted as an evangelist till 1797, when he became the pastor of a Congregational church which he had been instrumental in collecting in Marietta and the adjoining towns, and which was organized the preceding year. He held that relation till the spring of 1804. Probably he was the first Protestant minister whose voice was heard in the vast wilderness lying to the northwest of the Ohio river.

In the garrison at Marietta was witnessed the

* The facts contained in this article we find in a series of papers, by S. P. Hildreth, Esq., published in "The American Pioneer," in 1842.

formation and successful operation of one of the first Sunday schools in the United States. Its originator, superintendent and sole teacher, was Mrs. Andrew Lake, an estimable lady from New York. Every Sabbath, after "Parson Storey" had finished his public services, she collected as many of the children at her house as would attend, and heard them recite verses from the Scriptures, and taught them the Westminster catechism. Simple in her manner of teaching and affable and kind in her disposition, she was able to interest her pupils—usually about twenty in number—and to win their affections to herself, to the school, and, subsequently, in some instances, to the Saviour. A few, at least, of the little children that used to sit on rude benches, low stools and the tops of meal bags, and listen to her sacred instructions and earnest admonitions, have doubtless ere this became pupils, with her, in the "school of Christ" above.

THE WOMEN OF WYOMING.

The guardians of the land.

HOLMES.

Justice and gratitude, writes Miner,* "demand a tribute to the praiseworthy spirit of the wives and daughters of Wyoming. While their husbands and fathers were on public duty, they cheerfully assumed a large portion of the labor which females could do. They assisted to plant, made hay, husked and garnered the corn. As the settlement was mainly dependent on its own resources for powder, Mr. Hollenback caused to be brought up the river a pounder; and the women took up their floors, dug out the earth, put it in casks, and run water through it,—as ashes are bleached:—then took ashes, in another cask, and made ley—mixed the water from the earth with weak ley, boiled it, set it to cool, and the saltpetre rose to the top. Charcoal and sulphur were then used, and powder was produced for the public defence."

---

* History of Wyoming, page 212.

MARY GOULD.

> Far rung the groves and gleamed the midnight grass,
> With flambeau, javelin and naked arm;
> As warriors wheeled their culverins of brass,
> Sprung from the woods a bold athletic mass,
> Whom virtue fires and liberty combines.
>
> CAMPBELL.

> Such is the power of mighty love.
>
> DRYDEN.

Early in the evening of the third day of July, 1778—the date of the memorable Wyoming massacre—Mrs. Mary Gould, wife of James Gould, with the other females remaining in the village of Wyoming, sought safety in the fort. In the haste and confusion attending this act, she left a boy of hers about four years old, behind. Obeying the instincts of a mother, and turning a deaf ear to the admonitions of friends, she started off on a perilous search for the missing one. It was dark; she was alone, and the foe was lurking around; but the agonies of death could not exceed her agonies of suspense; so she hastened on. She traversed the fields which, but a few hours before,

> "Were trampled by the hurrying crowd;"

where

"— fiery hearts and armed hands
Encountered in the battle cloud,"

and where unarmed hands were now resting on cold and motionless hearts. After a search of between one and two hours, she found her child on the bank of the river, sporting with a little band of playmates. Clasping the jewel in her arms, she hurried back and reached the fort in safety.

THE MOTHER OF PRESIDENT POLK.

> Holy as heaven a mother's tender love!
> The love of many prayers, and many tears,
> Which changes not with dim, declining years.
>
> MRS. NORTON.

The late President Polk's mother, who died at Columbia, Tennessee, in the winter of 1851–2, was a member of the Presbyterian church, a highly exemplary Christian, and a faithful mother. The lessons which she taught her son in youth, were not forgotten when he had arrived at manhood, and risen to the highest office in the gift of a free and sovereign people. A single anecdote will show the abiding recollection and influence of her teachings.

A gentleman, who once visited Mr. Polk at the White House, remarked to him that his respect for the Sabbath was highly gratifying to the religious sentiment of the country; whereupon he made the following reply: "I was taught by a pious mother to fear God, and keep his commandments, and I trust that no cares of a government of my own, will ever tempt me to forget what I owe to the government of God."

TRIALS OF A PATRIOT

> Press on! if fortune play thee false
> To-day, to-morrow she'll be true.
>
> PARK BENJAMIN

During the latter part of the Revolution, Thomas McCalla lived in Chester district, South Carolina. He removed thither from Pennsylvania, with his young wife, in 1778. He was a whole-hearted whig; served in the American army before moving to the south, and again enlisted soon after reaching his new home. He was in all the engagements attending Sumter's operations against the enemy, till the seventeenth of August, 1780, when, by permission, he went to visit his family. A short time afterwards he again joined the fighting men, but was almost immediately taken prisoner, sent to Camden, thrown into jail and threatened daily with hanging. The persevering and heroic endeavors of his affectionate and patriotic wife, to obtain his release, are detailed in the following interesting manner by the author of the Women of the Revolution:

While this brave man was languishing in prison, expecting death from day to day, his wife remained in the most unhappy state of suspense. For about a month she was unable to obtain any tidings of him. The rumor of Sumter's surprise, and that of Steel, came to her ears; she visited the places where those disasters had occurred, and sought for some trace of him, but without success. She inquired, in an agony of anxiety, of the women who had been to Charlotte for the purpose of carrying clothes or provisions to their husbands, brothers, or fathers, not knowing but that he had gone thither with the soldiers; but none could give her the least information. Imagination may depict the harrowing scenes that must have passed, when females returning to their homes and children after carrying aid to the soldiers, were met by such inquiries from those who were uncertain as to the fate of their kindred. To these hapless sufferers no consolation availed, and too often was their suspense terminated by more afflicting certainty.

In the midst of Mrs. McCalla's distress, and before she had gained any information, she was called to another claim on her anxiety; her children took the small-pox. John was very ill for nine days with the disease, and his mother thought every day would be his last. During this terrible season of alarm, while her mind was distracted by cares, she had to depend altogether upon herself, for she saw but one among her neighbors. All the families in the vicinity were visited with the disease, and to many it proved fatal. As soon as her child was so far recovered as to be considered out of danger, Mrs. McCalla made preparations to go to Camden. She felt convinced that it was her duty to do so, for she clung to the hope that she might there learn something of her husband, or even find him among the prisoners.

With her to resolve was to act, and having set her house in order, she was in the saddle long before day, taking the old Charleston road leading down on the west side of the Catawba river. The mountain gap on Wateree creek was passed ere the sun rose, and by two o'clock she had crossed the river, passing the guard there stationed, and entered Camden. Pressing on with fearless determination, she passed the guard, and desiring to be conducted to the presence of Lord Rawdon, was escorted by Major Doyle to the head-quarters of that commander. His Lordship then occupied a large, ancient looking house on the east side of the main street. The old site of the town is now in part deserted, and that building left standing alone some four hundred yards from any other, as if the memories associated with it had rendered the neighborhood undesirable. It was here that haughty and luxurious nobleman fixed his temporary residence, "sitting as a monarch," while so many true-hearted unfortunates, whose fate hung on his will, were languishing out their lives in prison, or atoning for their patriotism on the scaffold.

Into the presence of this august personage Mrs. McCalla was conducted by the British major. Her impression at first sight was favorable; he was a fine looking young man, with a countenance not unprepossessing, which we may suppose was eagerly searched for the traces of human sympathy by one who felt that all her hopes depended on him. His aspect gave her some encouragement, and being desired to explain the object of her visit, she pleaded her cause with the eloquence of nature and feeling; making known the distressed situation of her family at home, the fearful anxiety of mind she had suffered on account of the prolonged absence of her husband and her ignorance of his fate, and her children's urgent need of his care and protection. From Major Doyle she had at length learned that he was held a prisoner by his lordship's orders. She had come, therefore, to entreat mercy for him; to pray that he might be released and permitted to go home with her. This appeal to compassion she made with all the address in her power, nor was the untaught language of distress wanting in power to excite pity in any feeling heart.

Lord Rawdon heard her to the end. His reply was characteristic. "I would rather hang such —— rebels than eat my breakfast." This insulting speech was addressed to his suppliant while her eyes were fixed on him in the agony of her entreaty, and the tears were streaming down her cheeks. His words dried up the fountain at once, and the spirit of the American matron was roused. "Would you?" was her answer, while she turned on him a look of the deepest scorn A moment after, with a struggle to control her feelings, for she well knew how much depended on that—she said, "I crave of your lordship permission to see my husband."

The haughty chief felt the look of scorn his cruel language had called up in her face, for his own conscience bore testimony against him, but pride forbade his yielding to the dictates of better feeling. "You should consider, madam," he answered, "in whose presence you now stand. Your husband is a rebel——"

Mrs. McCalla was about to reply — but her companion, the Major, gave her a look warning her to be silent, and in truth the words that sprang to her lips would have ill pleased the Briton. Doyle now interposed, and requested his lordship to step aside with him for a moment. They left the apartment, and shortly afterwards returned. Rawdon then said to his visitor, with a stately coldness that precluded all hope of softening his determination: "Major Doyle, madam, has my permission to let you go into the prison. You may continue in the prison *ten minutes only*. Major, you have my orders." So saying, he bowed politely both to her and the officer, as intimating that the business was ended, and they were dismissed. They accordingly quitted the room. . . . .

The sight of the prison-pen almost overcame the fortitude of the resolute wife. An enclosure like that constructed for animals, guarded by soldiers, was the habitation of the unfortunate prisoners, who sate within on the bare earth, many of them suffering with the prevalent distemper, and stretched helpless on the ground, with no shelter from the burning sun of September. "Is it possible," cried the matron, turning to Doyle, "that you shut up men in this manner, as you would a parcel of hogs!" She was then admitted into the jail, and welcome indeed was the sight of her familiar face to McCalla. The time allotted for the interview was too short to be wasted in condolement or complaint; she told him she must depart in a few minutes, informed him of the state of his family—inquired carefully what were his wants, and promised speedy relief. When the ten minutes had expired, she again shook hands with him, assuring him she would shortly return with clothes for his use, and what provisions she could bring, then turning walked away with a firm step, stopping to shake hands with young John Adair and the other captives with whom she was acquainted. The word of encouragement was not wanting, and as she bade the prisoners adieu, she said: "Have no fear; the women are doing their part of the service." "I admire your spirit, madam," Doyle observed to her, "but must request you to be a little more cautious."

Mrs. McCalla was furnished by the Major with a pass, which she showed to the officer on duty as she passed the guard on her return, and to the officer at the ferry. She rode with all speed, and was at home before midnight; having had less than twenty-four hours for the accomplishment of her whole enterprise; in that time riding one hundred miles, crossing the river twice, and passing the guard four times—visiting her husband, and having the interview with Lord Rawdon, in which probably for the first time in his ife he felt uneasiness from a woman's rebuke. It convinced him that even in the breast of woman a spirit of independence might dwell, which no oppression could subdue, and before which brute force must quail, as something of superior nature. How must the unexpected outbreaking of this spirit, from time to time, have dismayed those who imagined it was crushed forever throughout the conquered province!

It is proper to say that Mrs. McCalla met with kinder treatment from the other British officers to whom she had occasion to apply at this time, for they were favorably impressed by the courage and strength of affection evinced by her. Even the soldiers, as she passed them, paid her marks of respect. The tories alone showed no sympathy nor pity for her trials; it being constantly observed that there was deeper hostility towards the whigs on the part of their countrymen of different politics, than those of English birth.

Mrs. McCalla began her work immediately after her arrival at home; making new clothes, altering and mending others, and preparing provisions. Her preparations being completed, she again set out for Camden. This time she had the company of one of her neighbors, Mrs. Mary Nixon. Each of the women drove before her a pack-horse, laden with the articles provided for the use of their suffering friends. They were again admitted to the presence of Lord Rawdon to petition for leave to visit the prisoners, but nothing particular occurred at the interview. His lordship treated the matron who had offended him with much haughtiness, and she on her part felt for him a contempt not the less strong that it was not openly expressed. From this time she made her journeys about once a month to Camden, carrying clean clothes and provisions; being often accompanied by other women bound on similar errands, and conveying articles of food and clothing to their captive fathers, husbands, or brothers. They rode without escort, fearless of peril by the way, and regardless of fatigue, though the journey was usually performed in haste, and under the pressure of anxiety for those at home as well as those to whose relief they were going. On one occasion, when Mrs. McCalla was just about setting off alone upon her journey, news of a glorious event was brought to her; the news of the battle of King's Mountain, which took place on the seventh of October. She did not stop to rejoice in the victory of her countrymen, but went on with a lightened heart, longing, no doubt, to share the joy with him who might hope, from the changed aspect of affairs, some mitigation of his imprisonment.

. . . About the first of December, Mrs. McCalla went again to Camden. On the preceding trip she had met with Lord Cornwallis, by whom she was treated with kindness. Whatever hopes she had grounded on this, however, were doomed to disappointment; he was this time reserved and silent. She was afterwards informed by the Major that a considerable reverse had befallen his majesty's troops at Clermont, and the annoyance felt on this account—Doyle said—was the cause of his not showing as much courtesy as he usually did to ladies. "You must excuse him," observed the good-natured officer, who seems to have always acted the part of a peacemaker on these occasions; and he added that Cornwallis had never approved of the cruelties heretofore practised.

Towards the last of December the indefatigable wife again performed the weary journey to Camden. McCalla's health had been impaired for some months, and was now declining; it was therefore necessary to make a strenuous effort to move the compassion of his enemies, and procure his release. Rawdon was in command, and she once more applied to him to obtain permission for her husband to go home with her. As might have been anticipated, her petition was refused: his lordship informed her that he could do nothing in the premises; but that if she would go to Winnsboro' and present her request to Lord Cornwallis, he might possibly be induced to give her an order for the liberation of the prisoner.

To Winnsboro', accordingly, she made her way, determined to lose no time in presenting her application. It was on New Year's morning that she entered the village. The troops were under parade, and his lordship was engaged in reviewing them; there could be no admission, therefore, to his presence for some time, and she had nothing to do but remain a silent spectator of the imposing scene. A woman less energetic, and less desirous of improving every opportunity for the good of others, might have sought rest after the fatigues of her journey, during the hours her business had to wait; Sarah McCalla was one of heroic stamp, whose private troubles never caused her to forget what she might do for her country. She passed the time in noticing particularly every thing she saw, not knowing but that her report might do service. After the lapse of several hours, the interview she craved with Cornwallis was granted. He received her with courtesy and kindness, listened attentively to all she had to say, and appeared to feel pity for her distresses. But his polished expression of sympathy, to which her hopes clung with desperation, was accompanied with regret that he could not, consistently with the duties of his Majesty's service, comply unconditionally with her request. He expressed, nevertheless, entire willingness to enter into an exchange with General Sumter, releasing McCalla for any prisoner he had in his possession. Or he would accept the pledge of General Sumter that McCalla should not again serve until exchanged, and would liberate him on that security. "But, madam," he added, "it is Sumter himself who must stand pledged for the keeping of the parole. We have been too lenient heretofore, and have let men go who immediately made use of their liberty to take up arms against us."

With this the long-tried wife was forced to be content, and she now saw the way clear to the accomplishment of her enterprise. She lost no time in returning home, and immediately set out for Charlotte to seek aid from the American general. She found Sumter at this place, nearly recovered of the wounds he had received in the action at Blackstock's, in November. Her appeal to him was at once favorably received. He gave her a few lines, stating that he would stand pledged for McCalla's continuance at home peaceably until he should be regularly exchanged. This paper was more precious than gold to the matron whose perseverance had obtained it; but it was destined to do her little good. She now made the best of her way homeward. After crossing the Catawba, she encountered the army of General Morgan, was stopped, being suspected to be a tory, and taken into his presence for examination. The idea that she could be thus suspected afforded her no little amusement, and she permitted the mistake to continue for some time, before she produced the paper in Sumter's hand-writing which she well knew would remove every difficulty. She then informed the General of her visit to Winnsboro' on the first of January, and her sight of the review of the troops. Morgan thanked her for the information and dismissed her, and without further adventure she arrived at her own house.

A few days after her return, the British army, being on its march from Winnsboro', encamped on the plantation of John Service, in Chester district, and afterwards at Turkey creek. Mrs. McCalla went to one of those camps in the hope of seeing Lord Cornwallis. She succeeded in obtaining this privilege; his lordship recognised her as soon as she entered the camp, and greeted her courteously, questioning her as to her movements, and making many inquiries about Sumter and Morgan. On this last point she was on her guard, communicating no more information than she felt certain could give the enemy no manner of advantage, nor subject her friends to inconvenience At length she presented to the noble Briton the paper which she imagined would secure her husband's freedom. What was her disappointment when he referred her to Lord Rawdon, as the proper person to take cognizance of the affair! The very name was a death-blow to her hopes, for she well knew she could expect nothing from his clemency. Remonstrance and entreaty were alike in vain; Cornwallis was a courteous man, but he knew how, with a bland smile and well-turned phrase of compliment, to refuse compliance even with a request that appealed so strongly to every feeling of humanity, as that of an anxious wife pleading for the suffering and imprisoned father of her children. She must submit, however, to the will of those in power; there was no resource but another journey to Camden, in worse than doubt of the success she had fancied just within her reach.

It was a day or two after the battle of the Cowpens that she crossed the ferry on her way to Camden. She had not yet heard of that bloody action, but, observing that the guard was doubled at the ferry, concluded that something unusual had occurred. As she entered the village, she met her old friend Major Doyle, who stopped to speak to her. His first inquiry was if she had heard the news; and when she answered in the negative, he told her of the "melancholy affair" that had occurred at the Cowpens. The time, he observed, was most inauspicious for the business on which he knew she had come. "I fear, madam," he said, "that his lordship will not treat you well."

"I have no hope," was her answer, "that he will let Thomas go home; but, sir, it is my duty to make efforts to save my husband. I will thank you to go with me to Lord Rawdon's quarters."

Her reception was such as she had expected. As soon as Rawdon saw her, he cried angrily, "You here again, madam! Well—you want your husband—I dare say! Do you not know what the ——— rebels have been doing?"

"I do not, sir," replied the dejected matron, foı she saw that his mood was one of fury.

"If we had hung them," he continued, "we should have been saved this. Madam! I order you most positively never to come into my presence again!"

It was useless, Mrs. McCalla knew, to attempt to stem the tide; she did not therefore produce, nor even mention the paper given her by Sumter, nor apologise for the intrusion by saying that Lord Cornwallis had directed her to apply to him; but merely answered in a subdued and respectful tone by asking what she had done.

"Enough!" exclaimed the irritated noble. "You go from one army to another, and Heaven only knows what mischief you do! Begone."

She waited for no second dismissal, but could not refrain from saying, as she went out, in an audible voice, "My countrymen must right me." Lord Rawdon called her back and demanded what she was saying. She had learned by this time some lessons in policy, and answered, with a smile, "We are but simple country folk." His lordship probably saw through the deceit, for turning to his officer, he said, "Upon my life, Doyle, she is a wretch of a woman!" And thus she left him.

That great event — the battle of the Cowpens — revived the spirits of the patriots throughout the country. Every where, as the news spread, men who had before been discouraged flew to arms. The action took place on the seventeenth of January, 1781; on the twenty-second of the same month, six wagons were loaded with corn at Wade's island, sixty miles down the Catawba for the use of General Davison's division. The whole whig country of Chester, York and Lancaster may be said to have risen in mass, and was rallying to arms. Mecklenburg, North Carolina, was again the scene of warlike preparation; for the whigs hoped to give the enemy another defeat at Cowans or Batisford on the Catawba. On the twenty-fourth of January, General Sumter crossed tnis river at Landsford, and received a supply of corn from Wade's island, His object was to cross the districts to the west, in the rear of the advancing British army, to arouse the country and gather forces as he went, threaten the English posts at Ninety-Six and Granby, and go on to recover the State. While Cornwallis marched from his encampment on Service's plantation, the whigs of Chester, under the gallant Captains John Mills and James Johnston, were hovering near, watching the movements of the hostile army as keenly as the eagle watches his intended prey. Choosing a fit opportunity, as they followed in the rear, they pounced upon a couple of British officers, one of whom was Major McCarter, at a moment when they had not the least suspicion of danger, took them prisoners in sight of the enemy, and made good their retreat. By means of this bold exploit the liberation of McCalla was brought about, at a time when his wife was wholly disheartened by her repeated and grievous disappointments. When General Sumter passed through the country, a cartel of exchange was effected, giving the two British officers in exchange for the prisoners of Chester district in Camden and Charleston.

The person sent with the flag to accomplish this exchange in Camden, was Samuel Neely of Fishing creek. As he passed through the town to the quarters of Lord Rawdon, he was seen and recognized by the prisoners, and it may be supposed their hearts beat with joy at the prospect of speedy release. But in consequence of some mismanagement of the business, the unfortunate men were detained in jail several weeks longer. Neely was in haste to proceed to Charleston, being anxious, in the accomplishment of his mission in that city, to get his son Thomas out of the prison-ship, and in his hurry probably neglected some necessary formalities. His countrymen in Camden were kept in confinement after his return from Charleston with his son. Captain Mills was informed of this, and indignant at the supposed disrespect shown by Lord Rawdon to the cartel of General Sumter, wrote a letter of remonstrance to Rawdon, which he entrusted to Mrs. McCalla to be conveyed to him.

Our heroine was accompanied on this journey by Mrs. Mary Dixon, for she judged it impolitic that the letter should be delivered by one so obnoxious to his lordship as herself. Still she deemed it her duty to be on the spot to welcome her liberated husband, supply all his wants, and conduct him home. The distance was traversed this time with lighter heart than before, for now she had no reason to fear disappointment. When they arrived at Camden, they went to the jail. John Adair was standing at a window; they saw and greeted each other, the women standing in the yard below. Perhaps in consequence of his advice, or prudential considerations on their part, they determined not to avail themselves of the good offices of Major Doyle on this occasion. Adair directed them to send the jailor up to him, and wrote a note introducing his sister to the acquaintance of Lord Rawdon. The two women then proceeded to the quarters of that nobleman. When they arrived at the gate, Mrs. McCalla stopped, saying she would wait there, and her companion proceeded by herself. She was admitted into the presence of Lord Rawdon, who read the note of introduction she handed to him, and observed, referring to the writer—that the small-pox had almost finished him; still, he had come very near escaping from the jail; that he was "a grand 'scape-gallows." On reading the letter of Captain Mills his color changed, and when he had finished it, turning to Mrs. Nixon, he said in an altered tone: "I am sorry these men have not been dismissed, as of right they ought." He immediately wrote a discharge for eleven of the prisoners, and put it into her hands, saying: "You can get them out, madam. I am very sorry they have been confined so many weeks longer than they should have been." At the same time he gave Mrs. Nixon a guinea. "This," he said, "will bear your expenses."

His lordship accompanied her on her way out, and as she passed through the gate his eye fell on Mrs. McCalla, whom he instantly recognized. Walking to the spot where she stood near the gate, he said fiercely: "Did I not order you, madam, to keep out of my presence?" The matron's independent spirit flashed from her eyes, as she answered: "I had no wish, sir, to intrude myself on your presence; I stopped at the gate on purpose to avoid you." Unable to resist the temptation of speaking her mind for once, now that she had a last opportunity, she added: "I might turn the tables on you, sir, and ask, why did *you* come out to the gate to insult a woman? I have received from you nothing but abuse. My distresses you have made sport of, and I ceased long since to expect anything from you but ill-treatment. I am now not your supplicant; I came to *demand*, as a right, the release of my husband!" So saying, she bowed to him contemptuously, wheeled about, and deliberately walked off, without stopping to see how her bold language was received. Mrs. Nixon hastened after her, pale as death, and at first too much frightened to speak As soon as she found voice, she exclaimed: "Sally. you have ruined us, I am afraid! Why, he may put us both in jail!"

Mrs. McCalla laughed outright. "It is not the first time, Mary," she replied, "that I have given him to understand I thought him a villain!" The two made their way back to the prison, but even after they got there Mrs. Nixon had not recovered from her terror. She was informed that it would be some time before the prisoners could be released. The blacksmith was then sent for, and came with his tools. The sound of the hammering in the appartments of the jail, gave the first intimation to the women who waited to greet their friends, that the helpless captives were chained to the floor. This precaution had been adopted not long before, in consequence of some of the prisoners having attempted an escape. They were then put in hand-cuffs or chained by the ankle. These men left the place of their long imprisonment and suffering in company with the two women, and as they marched through the streets of Camden, passing the British guard, they sang at the top of their voices the songs of the "liberty-men."

INTREPIDITY OF MRS. ISRAEL.

> He is not worthy of the honey comb,
> That shuns the hive because the bees have stings.
>
> SHAKSPEARE.

During the Revolution, Israel Israel, a true whig and a worthy farmer, residing on the banks of the Delaware, near Wilmington, was, for a short time, a prisoner on board the frigate Roebuck, directly opposite his own house and land. While thus situated, it was reported by some loyalists by whose treachery he had been betrayed into the hands of the enemy, that he had said repeatedly that "he would sooner drive his cattle as a present to George Washington, than receive thousands of dollars in British gold for them." The commander hearing the report, to be revenged on the rebel, sent a small detachment of soldiers to drive his cattle, which were in plain sight of the frigate, down to the Delaware, and have them slaughtered before their owner's eyes. Mrs. Israel,* who was young and

* The maiden name of Mrs. Israel was Hannah Erwin. Her first meeting with her husband was romantic enough. Mr. Israel had

sprightly, and brave as a Spartan, seeing the movements of the soldiers as she stood in her doorway, and divining their purpose as they marched towards the meadow where the cattle were grazing, called a boy about eight years old, and started off in great haste, to defeat, if possible, their marauding project. They threatened and she defied, till at last they fired at her. The cattle, more terrified than she, scattered over the fields; and as the balls flew thicker she called on the little boy "Joe" the louder and more earnestly to help, determined that the assailants should not have one of the cattle. *They did not.* She drove them all into the barn-yard, when the soldiers, out of respect to her courage, or for some other cause, ceased their molestations and returned to the frigate.

---

sailed in a sloop, or packet, from Philadelphia, to visit New Castle where his mother and family resided. He observed on deck an extremely pretty girl, hardly seventeeen years of age, and very neatly and tastefully dressed, with the finest turned foot and ankle in the world. All who went on such voyages were then obliged to furnish themselves with provisions; and his attention was drawn by the young girl's kindly distribution of her little stock, handing it about from one to another, till but little was left for her own portion. In passing him, she modestly hesitated a moment, and then offered him a share. This led to conversation; he learned that she was the daughter of highly respectable parents, and resided in Wilmington. Love at first sight was as common in those days as now. After seeing his mother, he visited Wilmington; became better acquainted, offered himself and was accepted: and on his marriage, rented the farm above mentioned, and commenced life anew.—[Mrs. Ellet.

AN INCIDENT IN MISSIONARY LIFE.

Love's holy flame for ever burneth;
From heaven it came, to heaven returneth;
Too oft on earth a troubled guest,
. . . at times oppressed.
It here is tried and purified,
Then hath in heaven its perfect rest.
It soweth here with toil and care,
But the harvest time of love is there.

SOUTHEY.

No class of laborers in the broad harvest field of the world endure so many sacrifices of comfort and of home felicities as the missionaries to foreign countries. Of the trials peculiar to *mothers* who go forth on such an errand of humanity, the keenest must be their separation from their children. The pernicious habits and influences of a pagan community, often render it absolutely necessary that their offspring should be sent to a civilized land to be educated. This duty, however painful, is imperative, and they who accuse the mother of hardness because she does it, are either grossly ignorant, or haters of truth. Many instances of heroic firmness and almost superhuman calmness under such trials, are on record, but one may stand as a type of the whole.

Mrs. Comstock* of the Burmah Baptist mission felt called upon to part with her two children, whom God had given her while on the field of labor. The hour for separation came, and taking them by the hand, she led them down to the ship that was to bear them for ever from her sight. Having invoked the blessing of Heaven upon them, she gave each the parting kiss and, with streaming eyes, lifted her hands towards heaven and exclaimed: "My Saviour! I do this for thee."

Amid the jungles of the East,
  Where gloomiest forms of sin are rife,
Like flowerets in a desert drear,
  Her treasured ones had sprung to life.

And smiling round her, day by day,
  Though cares unnumbered weigh her heart,
Their prattle, full of music tones,
  Unceasing joy and hope impart.

Their little minds, like tender buds
  In vernal hours, she sees unfold,
And young affection in their eyes
  Is gleaming like a gem of gold.

But 'mid the toils that press her sore —
  The spirit-wants of 'wildered ones —
These buds must often miss the dew,
  And plead in vain for constant suns.

She sees their smiles, their music hears,
  And feels affection's holy thrall;
But duty's voice, from out the skies,
  In sweeter tones, is heard o'er all.

---

* Sarah Davis Comstock was the wife of the Rev. Grover S. Comstock, who was stationed at Kyouk Phyoo in the province of Arracan, Burmah. She was born at Brookline, Massachusetts, in 1812, and died at Ramree, April twenty-eighth, 1843.

To Western climes, illumed by truth,
  And blest with learning's sacred flowers,
These blossoms of her heart must go,
  To bloom henceforth in stranger bowers.

She leads them to the waiting ship;
  She kneels in anguish on the deck,
And while she breathes a silent prayer,
  Their arms like tendrils twine her neck.

She tears her from the loved away,
  Whom she on earth no more may see,
And looking up to heaven, exclaims,
  "My Saviour, I do this for thee!"

Then hastens to her task again,
  The pleasant task her Saviour's given,
That, finished all, she may ascend,
  And lure the distant ones to heaven

A KIND-HEARTED CHIPPEWA.

Both men and women belie their nature
When they are not kind.

BAILEY'S FESTUS.

In the early settlement of Ohio, Daniel Convers was captured by the savages; but he had the good fortune to be purchased by a noble-hearted Indian whose wife possessed a kindred spirit. His condition, we are informed in the Pioneer History of Ohio, "was not that of a slave, but rather an adoption into the family as a son. The Indian's wife, whom he was directed to call mother, was a model of all that is excellent in woman, being patient, kind-hearted, humane and considerate to the wants and comfort of all around her, and especially so to their newly adopted son. To sum up all her excellences in a brief sentence of the captive's own language, she was 'as good a woman as ever lived.'" *

* Mr. Convers escaped from his Chippewa friends, at Detroit. Touching the treatment he received from his adopted mother, a writer says: "How few among the more civilized race of whites would ever imitate the Christian charities of this untaught daughter of nature!"

HUMANITY OF A CHEROKEE

How poor an instrument
May do a noble deed.

SHAKSPEARE.

During the Revolution, a young Shawanese Indian was captured by the Cherokees and sentenced to die at the stake. He was tied, and the usual preparations were made for his execution, when a Cherokee woman went to the warrior to whom the prisoner belonged, and throwing a parcel of goods at his feet, said she was a widow and would adopt the captive as her son, and earnestly plead for his deliverance. Her prayer was granted, and the prisoner taken under her care. He rewarded her by his fidelity, for, in spite of the entreaties of his friends, whom he was allowed to visit, he never left her.

SELF-SACRIFICING SPIRIT OF THE MISSIONARY.

Thou know 'st not, Afric! sad of heart and blind,
Unskilled the precious Book of God to read;
Thou canst not know, what moved that soul refined,
Thy lot of wretchedness to heed,
And from her fireside, bright with hallowed glee,
To dare the boisterous surge and deadly clime for thee.
MRS. SIGOURNEY.

We know not how one may exhibit greater benevolence than to offer life for the spiritual good of the heathen; and he virtually does this who goes to some, at least, of the missionary stations. Those in Africa are the most unhealthy, and their history presents a frightful bill of mortality. In his journal of January, 1846, Dr. Savage, of the Protestant Episcopal mission in Africa, states that during the nine years previous to that date, the whole number of missionaries under the patronage of the different Boards, in Africa, had been sixty-one, and of that number forty were then dead. American Baptists alone lost eleven between 1826 and 1848. Five of them were buried in the single town of Monrovia. With such facts as these, touching African missions, staring the disciple of Christ in the face, it must require no com mon degree of moral courage for him to embark in the enterprise.

The following letter, by Miss Maria V. Chapin, of Vermont, was written prior to her leaving this country for West Africa, and breathes the sentiments of a self-sacrificing and heroic Christian. Multitudes of like examples, equally as noble, might be pointed out, but it seems to be needless: this letter may stand as a type of the spirit usually exhibited under similar circumstances. It was addressed to the Rev. Dr. Vaughan, then Secretary of the Foreign Committee of the Protestant Episcopal church:

"The question of my personally engaging in a mission to the heathen, has long been before my mind, and received, as it claimed, my most serious and prayerful consideration. This great work is now brought nearer to my mind than I could ever before regard it, and I trust it does not appear the less desirable. I have considered the subject in every light, so far as I am able from the information I have respecting it, and I can never take up the question again, to find reasons for going. My mind is now settled as to the duty, should no unforeseen providence prevent, of leaving home and country for a heathen land. A long adieu to my kindred and friends will rend the heart; I feel already that it will; but at the same time, the prospect of doing good to some poor heathen soul will fill it with joy, and the hope of advancing, in ever so small a degree, the cause of my Redeemer, will be a constant feast to the soul. The silent tear of parental affection and solicitude would indeed overpower me, had I not confidence that He who thus afflicts, will support, my beloved parents. Neither, in the present case, can I think it proper to follow, altogether, the opinion of friends. With the smiles of my heavenly Father, I must be happy, though friends forsake me. I feel an inexpressible pleasure in commending them to God, assured that they will be enabled to give up their child without regret, in the hope that she will do good to perishing souls. And I have, also, that blessed hope, that, should we never again meet in this world, we shall be a happy family circle at the right hand of God. Still, I feel my own insufficiency to decide a question of such importance as that of leaving all that the heart holds most dear on earth, to encounter the toils and hardships of a missionary life. Indeed, I would not decide for myself. I trust solely to Him who has promised grace and strength. Though, at times, great weakness has constrained me to shrink at the prospect before me, I have been consoled and supported in the assurance that God will perfect strength in my weakness. I feel a desire to act in accordance with the will of God; to do nothing which would be displeasing in His sight. I think I am willing to be, and to do, anything for the sake of the glory of God; and if I can only be sure that I am wholly under the guidance of His spirit, I shall be fully satisfied. It is difficult, I know, to analyze one's feelings, and ascertain the real character of the motives by which we are actuated; I feel my liability to be deceived, and my need of Divine assistance. The only question which concerns me, is, are my motives pure and holy? Never would I bear the missionary standard, without having in my heart the missionary spirit. I have calmly and deliberately weighed the subject, and feel that no attraction from its novelty, no impulse from its moral dignity, can bear up, and carry forward any one, amidst the long continued labors of almost uniform sameness which you represented to me; nothing but a thorough conviction of being in the path of duty, nothing but the approving smile of Heaven, can keep one from despondency, from sinking into hopeless inactivity; but I have calmly and deliberately weighed the subject, and feel a willingness to give up comforts, and submit to privations, to forsake ease and endure toil, to assemble no more 'with the great congregation,' but seek the Lord in the wilderness, or in the desert—in short, to make every sacrifice of personal ease and gratification, for the one great object of making known a crucified Saviour to those who are perishing in ignorance and sin. Indeed, what sacrifice can be too great, if what is done for Him who bought us with his own blood can be called a sacrifice, for those to make, who have themselves experienced the efficacy of a Saviour's blood? I have reflected, that should I go out, cheered by the smiles of friends, and encouraged by the approbation of the churches, yet soon, amidst a people of strange speech, I shall see these smiles only in remembrance, and hear the voice of encouragement only in dying whispers across the ocean. Yet, when I have considered the command of Christ, 'Go ye and teach all nations,'—and when in pouring out my soul on this subject to the Father of light, I have realized more of that sweet 'peace which passeth all understanding;' objections have all dwindled to a point; I have been enabled, by the eye of faith, to discover the finger of God, pointing me to the benighted African, and have heard his voice saying, with the affection of a Father and the authority of a Sovereign, 'Come, follow me' —'He that loveth father or mother more than me, is not worthy of me;' and adding, for my encouragement, 'I will never leave thee nor forsake thee.' I do feel that God calls me to become a missionary, and do, with this belief, resolve to consider myself as devoted to that service, hoping that God will qualify me, and make me a faithful servant for Christ's sake."*

*This letter was written in the fall of 1841. Miss Chapin, afterwards Mrs. Savage, embarked for Africa on the twenty-eighth of the following January, and reached Cape Palmas on the twenty-fifth of March. As might be anticipated, her labors soon closed. She died on the field, in December, 1843.

"That life is long which answers life's great end."

DARING EXPLOIT OF "TWO REBELS."

> Think'st thou there dwells no courage but in breasts
> That set their mail against the ringing spears,
> When helmets are struck down? Thou little knowest
> Of nature's marvels.
>
> MRS. HEMANS.

During the sieges of Augusta and Cambridge, two young men of the name of Martin, belonging to Ninety-Six district, South Carolina, were in the army. Meanwhile their wives, who remained at home with their mother-in-law, displayed as much courage, on a certain occasion, as was exhibited, perhaps, by any female during the struggle for Independence.

Receiving intelligence one evening that a courier, under guard of two British officers, would pass their house that night with important dispatches, Grace and Rachel Martin resolved to surprise the party and obtain the papers. Disguising themselves in their husbands' outer garments and providing themselves with arms, they waylaid the enemy. Soon after they took their station by the road-side, the courier and his escort made their appearance. At the proper moment, the disguised ladies sprang from their bushy covert, and presenting their pistols, ordered the party to surrender their papers. Surprised and alarmed, they obeyed without hesitation or the least resistance. The brave women having put them on parole, hastened home by the nearest route, which was a by-path through the woods, and dispatched the documents to General Greene by a single messenger, who probably had more courage than the trio that lately bore them.

Strange to say, a few minutes after the ladies reached home, and just as they had doffed their male attire, the officers, retracing their steps, rode up to the house and craved accommodations for the night. The mother of the heroines asked them the cause of their so speedy return after passing her house, when they exhibited their paroles and said that "two rebels" had taken them prisoners. Here the young ladies, in a rallying mood, asked them if they had no arms, to which query they replied, that, although they had, they were arrested so suddenly that they had no time to use them. We have only to add that they were hospitably entertained, and the next morning took their leave of the women as ignorant of the residence of their captors as when first arrested.

ELIZABETH MARTIN.

> The mothers of our Forest-land!
> Their bosoms pillowed *men.*
>
> W. D. GALLAGHER.

> —A fine family is a fine thing.
>
> BYRON.

The mother-in-law of the two patriotic women spoken of in the preceding article, was a native of Caroline county, Virginia. Her maiden name was Marshall. On marrying Mr. Abram Martin, she removed to South Carolina.

When the Revolutionary war broke out, she had seven sons old enough to enlist in their country's service; and as soon as the call to arms was heard, she said to them, "Go, boys, and fight for your country! fight till death, if you must, but never let your country be dishonored. Were I a man I would go with you."

Several British officers once called at her house, and while receiving some refreshments, one of them asked her how many sons she had. She told him, eight; and when asked where they were, she boldly replied, "Seven of them are engaged in the service of their country." The officer sneeringly observed that she had enough of them. "No, sir, I wish I had fifty!" was her prompt and proud reply.

Only one of those seven sons was killed during the war. He was a captain of artillery, served in the sieges of Savannah and Charleston, and was slain at the siege of Augusta. Soon after his death a British officer called on the mother, and in speaking of this son, inhumanly told her that he saw his brains blown out on the battle field. The reply she made to the monster's observation was: "He could not have died in a nobler cause."

When Charleston was besieged, she had three sons in the place. She heard the report of cannon on the occasion, though nearly a hundred miles west of the besieged city. The wives of the sons were with her, and manifested great uneasiness while listening to the reports; nor could the mother control her feelings any better. While they were indulging in silent and, as we may suppose, painful reflections, the mother suddenly broke the silence by exclaming, as she raised her hands: "Thank God! they are the children of the republic!"*

---

*Vide Women of the Revolution, vol. 1 p. 278.

THE MOTHER'S EFFECTUAL PETITION.

What rhetoric didst thou use
To gain this mighty boon?

ADDISON.

James M. Wilson was one of the unfortunate young men who engaged in the Cuban invasion, in 1851; and he was taken prisoner and sent to Spain. His mother petitioned for his release through President Fillmore, and so earnest, so full of the beauty of maternal love, and so touching was her appeal, that her request was granted, and the erring son was permitted to return to his mother's embrace. The following is a copy of the letter which she addressed to the President. It is said to have called forth flattering commendation from the heads of State and the highest encomiums from the Majesty of Spain.

NEW ORLEANS, Sept. 25, 1851.

DEAR FATHER OF OUR COUNTRY:—To you I look for help. My dear son is one of the unfortunate prisoners to Spain. He is all the child I have; is only nineteen years old, not twenty-two, as stated. He was innocent and unsuspecting, and the more easily duped. He saw no means of making a support for himself and me, we being poor: he could get no employment; my health was bad; he therefore hoped to do something by going to Cuba. But, alas! I am worse than poor! Death would have been more welcome. His father died, when he was very young, in Texas, which makes him more dear to me. Oh! cruel fate; why have I lived to see this? Perhaps to suit some wise design. God's will be done, not mine! I have prayed for his life from the time he left; it was spared. Dear President, will it be possible for you to do any thing? Can you comfort me? I am wearing away. Methinks I cannot bear up under the idea of ten years; perhaps executed, or detained for life, or the climate cause his death. I feel for all of them, and pray for all. It was not my will that he should go; he was seduced into it by others. Dear father of the land of my birth, can you do any thing? Will you ask for their release? Methinks you will, and it would be granted. Will you feel offended with me for appealing to you for comfort? If so, I beg pardon. My distress has stimulated me to venture to dare to address the President. To whom else could I look for comfort? If you could but see me, I know you would pity me. If any one knew I had approached you, they might think I presumed much. Perhaps I do. Yet methinks you will view it in charity.

With all due respect to your Excellency.

OPHELIA P. TALBOT.

NOTEWORTHY INTEGRITY.

Honesty, even by itself, though making many adversaries
Whom prudence might have set aside, or charity have softened,
Evermore will prosper at the last.

TUPPER.

We have often read an interesting story of a stock-broker who, just before his death, laid a wager on parole with a Parisian capitalist; and a few weeks after his death, the latter visited the widow and gave her to understand that her late husband had lost a bet of sixteen thousand francs. She went to her secretary, took out her pocket-book, and counted bank notes to the stated amount, when the capitalist thus addressed her: "Madame, as you give such convincing proof that you consider the wager binding, *I* have to pay you sixteen thousand francs. Here is the sum, for *I* am the loser, and not your husband."

An act that, in principle, matches the above, came to light not long since in Philadelphia. During the speculations of 1837–38, Mr. C., a young merchant of that city, possessed of a handsome fortune, caught the mania, entered largely into its operations, and for a time was considered immensely rich. But when the great revulsion occurred he was suddenly reduced to bankruptcy. His young wife immediately withdrew from the circles of wealth and fashion, and adapted her expenses, family and personal, to her altered circumstances.

At the time of Mr. C.'s failure, his wife was in debt to Messrs. Stewart and Company, merchants of Philadelphia, about two hundred dollars for articles which she had used personally. This debt, she had no means of liquidating. It became barred by the statute of limitation, before Mr. C. became solvent, though his circumstances gradually improved. After the lapse of twelve years, and when the creditors had looked upon the debt as lost, Mrs. C. was able to take the principle, add to it twelve years' interest, enclose the whole in a note and address it to Messrs. Stewart and Company.*

* Messrs. Stewart and Company, upon the receipt of the money, addressed a note in reply to Mrs. C., in which they requested her acceptance of the accompanying gift, as a slight testimonial of their high appreciation of an act so honorable and so rare as to call forth unqualified admiration. Accompanying the letter was sent a superb brocade silk dress, and some laces of exquisite texture and great value. —[Philadelphia Enquirer.

A FAITHFUL MOTHER.

—Her pure and holy spirit now
Doth intercede at the eternal throne.

MISS LANDON.

The following anecdote strikingly illustrates the strength of maternal love, the beauty of faith, and the efficacy of prayer. It was related by a blind preacher:

"When I was about eighteen years of age, there was a dancing party in Middleboro, Massachusetts, which I was solicited to attend, and act, as usual, in the capacity of musician. I was fond of such scenes of amusements then, and I readily assented to the request. I had a pious mother; and she earnestly remonstrated against my going. But, at length, when all her expostulations and entreaties failed in changing my purpose, she said: 'Well, my son, I shall not forbid your going, but remember, that all the time you spend in that gay company, I shall spend in praying for you at home.' I went to the ball, but I was like the stricken deer, carrying an arrow in his side. I began to play; but my convictions sank deeper and deeper, and I felt miserable indeed.

I thought I would have given the world to have been rid of that mother's prayers. At one time I felt so wretched and so overwhelmed with my feelings, that I ceased playing and dropped my musical instrument from my hand. There was another young person there who refused to dance; and, as I learned, her refusal was owing to feelings similar to my own, and perhaps they arose from a similar cause. My mother's prayers were not lost. That was the last ball I ever attended, except *one*, where I was invited to play again, but went and prayed and preached *instead*, till the place was converted into a Bochim, a place of weeping. The convictions of that wretched night never wholly left me, till they left me at the feet of Christ, and several of my young companions in sin ere long were led to believe and obey the gospel also."

ANECDOTE OF MRS. SPAULDING OF NEW HAMPSHIRE.*

Through the deep wilderness, where scarce the sun
Can cast his darts, along the winding path
The pioneer is treading.

STREET.

An energy
A spirit that will not be shaken.

WILLIS.

One of the first two settlers of Northumberland, New Hampshire, was Daniel Spaulding, who removed thither in the summer of 1767. On the way to his new home, with his wife and child, the last burnt himself so badly at Plymouth that the mother was obliged to remain and take care of him, while Mr. Spaulding proceeded to the end of the journey. She soon became uneasy, and, anxious to join her husband, started off with her child, twenty-one

*The substance of this anecdote we find in the second number of the first volume of a periodical called "Historical Collections," published nearly thirty years ago at Concord, New Hampshire, and edited by J. Farmer and J. B. Moore. The anecdote was communicated by Adino N. Brackett, Esq., of Lancaster, and appeared in the June number for 1822.

months old, to travel twenty-six miles through the wilderness. A friend who had agreed to accompany her the whole distance with a horse, returned after traveling about one third of the way. Undaunted and persevering, she pushed on, alone and on foot; waded through Baker's river with her child in her arms; was overtaken by a heavy "thunder gust" in the afternoon, and thoroughly drenched; seated herself beside a tree when darkness appeared, and held her child in her lap through a long and sleepless night; resumed her journey early the next morning; waded through a small pond, with the water waist-high; pushed on to another river, which, though swollen by the rain of the preceding day and looking rapid and terrifying, she forded in safety; and at eleven o'clock that day, the second of her journey, she met her husband, who was on his way back with a horse for her accommodation.*

*This pioneer matron of northern New Hampshire, was living at Lancaster, in 1822, then in her eighty-second year. She was a descendant, "in the third degree," of Mrs. Dustin, the heroine of Penacook.

THE WIFE OF COLONEL THOMAS.

Then since there is no other way but fight or die,
Be resolute, my lord, for victory.

SHAKSPEARE.

Jane Thomas, wife of John Thomas, Colonel of the Spartan regiment of South Carolina, was a native of Chester county, Pennsylvania. She was a woman of remarkable coolness and intrepidity, as a single act of hers, in the times that tried *women's* souls, plainly indicates.

Governor Rutledge having stored a quantity of arms and ammunition in the house of Colonel Thomas, under a guard of twenty-five men, the tories were determined to obtain these munitions. To this end they sent a large party under Colonel More of North Carolina. Apprised of their approach and not daring to engage with a force so superior, Colonel Thomas fled with his twenty-five soldiers, taking along as much ammunition as could be conveniently carried. Two young men and the women were now the sole occupants of the house. The tories marched up to the door, but instead of being invited by the ladies to enter, they were ordered off the premises. Not choosing to obey the commands of the mistress, they commenced firing into the logs of the house. The compliment was instantly returned from the upper story; and the women now loading the guns for the older of the two young men to discharge, a constant and perilous firing was kept up from the chamber, which soon made the assailants desperate. They forthwith attempted to demolish the "batten door," but it was too strongly barricaded. Finding that themselves were likely to share a worse fate then the door, they finally obeyed the original orders of the intrepid mistress; withdrew from the premises and fled. Mrs. Thomas soon afterwards descended, and opening the door, there met her returning husband. --The ammunition saved on that occasion by the courage of a woman, was the main supply, it is said, of Sumter's army in the skirmishes at Rocky Mount and Hanging Rock.

EXEMPLARY PIETY.

I've pored o'er many a yellow page
  Of ancient wisdom, and have won,
Perchance, a scholar's name — but sage
  Or bard have never taught thy son
Lessons so dear, so fraught with holy truth,
As those his mother's faith shed on his youth.

GEORGE W. BETHUNE.

A lady in the district of Beaufort, South Carolina, at the age of seventy-six, anxious once more to enjoy the society of all her children and grandchildren, invited them to spend a day with her. The interview was permitted and was very affecting. It "was conducted just as we should suppose piety and the relation sustained by the parties would dictate. She acknowledged God in this, as well as in every other way. Her eldest son, who is a minister of the Gospel in the Baptist denomination, commenced the exercises of the day, by reading the Scriptures and prayer. The whole family then joined in the song of praise to the Giver of every good and perfect gift. This service was concluded by a suitable exhortation from the same person. Eighty-five of her regular descendants were present. Forty-four children and grandchildren, arrived at maturity, sat at the same table at dinner. Of that number forty-three professed faith in Jesus Christ; of the four surviving sons of this excellent lady, two were preachers of the Gospel, and the other two deacons in the Baptist church.

"Two of her grandsons were also ministers of the same church. When the day was drawing to a close the matron called her numerous children around her, gave them each salutary advice and counsel, and bestowed upon all her parting blessing. The day was closed by her youngest son, with exercises similar to those with which it commenced.

"Mrs.—— lived eight years after this event, lea ving, at her death, one hundred and fifteen lineal descendants, in which large number not a swearer nor drunkard is to be found."*

---

*Jabez Burns, D. D.

BOLD ADVENTURE OF A PATRIOTIC GIRL.

Stand
Firm for your country: * *
* * it were a noble life,
To be found dead embracing her.
JOHNSON.

There is strength
Deep bedded in our hearts, of which we reck
But little.
MRS. HEMANS.

We find the following incident in the first volume of American Anecdotes, "original and select." The young heroine of the adventure afterwards married a rich planter named Threrwits, who lived on the Congaree. She has been dead more than half a century, but her name should be remembered while this republic is permitted to stand.

"At the time General Greene retreated before Lord Rawdon from Ninety-Six, when he had passed Broad river, he was very desirous to send an order to General Sumter, who was on the Wateree, to join him, that they might attack Rawdon, who had divided his force. But the General could find no man in that part of the state who was bold enough to undertake so dangerous a mission. The country to be passed through for many miles was full of blood thirsty tories, who, on every occasion that offered, imbrued their hands in the blood of the whigs. At length Emily Geiger presented herself to General Greene, and proposed to act as his messenger: and the General, both surprised and delighted, closed with her proposal. He accordingly wrote a letter and delivered it, and at the same time communicated the contents of it verbally, to be told to Sumter in case of accidents.

"Emily was young, but as to her person or adventures on the way, we have no further information, except that she was mounted on horseback, upon a side-saddle, and on the second day of her journey she was intercepted by Lord Rawdon's scouts. Coming from the direction of Greene's army, and not being able to tell an untruth without blushing, Emily was suspected and confined to a room; and as the officer in command had the modesty not to search her at the time, he sent for an old tory matron as more fitting for that purpose. Emily was not wanting in expedient, and as soon as the door was closed and the bustle a little subsided, she *ate up the letter*, piece by piece. After a while the matron arrived, and upon searching carefully, nothing was to be found of a suspicious nature about the prisoner, and she would disclose nothing. Suspicion being thus allayed, the officer commanding the scouts suffered Emily to depart whither she said she was bound; but she took a route somewhat circuitous to avoid further deten tion, and soon after struck into the road to Sumter's camp, where she arrived in safety. Emily told her adventure, and delivered Green's verbal message to Sumter, who, in consequence, soon after joined th main army at Orangeburgh."

RACHEL CALDWELL.

—The spell is thine that reaches
The heart.

HALLECK.

Prudence protects and guides us.

YOUNG.

Rachel Caldwell was the daughter of the Rev. Alexander Craighead and the wife of David Caldwell, D. D., whose history is somewhat identified with that of North Carolina. For several years he was at the head of a classical school at Guilford in that state, and in the vocation of teacher he had, at times, the efficient aid of his faithful and talented companion. She was a woman of exalted piety; and such a degree of success attended her "labor of love" in the school, that it became a common saying that "Dr. Caldwell makes the scholars, and Mrs. Caldwell makes the preachers."

More than once during the Revolution, the house of Dr. Caldwell, who was a stanch friend of his country, was assailed by tories:* and on one occa-

* The tories not only destroyed his property, but drove him into the woods, where he was often obliged to pass nights; and some of his

sion, while his wife was alone and the marauders were collecting plunder, they broke open a chest or drawer and took therefrom a table-cloth which was the gift of her mother. She seized it the moment the soldier had it fairly in his hand, and made an effort to wrest it from him. Finding she would be the loser in a trial of physical strength, she instinctively resorted to the power of rhetoric. With her grasp still firm on the precious article, she turned to the rest of the plunderers, who stood awaiting the issue of the contest, and in a beseeching tone and with words warm with eloquence, asked if some of their number had not wives for the love of whom they would assist her, and spare the one dear memorial of a mother's affection! Her plea, though short, was powerful, and actually moved one man to tears. With rills of sympathy running down his cheeks, he assured her he had a wife — a wife that he loved — and that for her sake the table-cloth should be given up. This was accordingly done, and no further rudeness was offered.

In the fall of 1780, a "way-worn and weary" stranger, bearing dispatches from Washington to Greene, stopped at her house and asked for supper and lodgings. Before he had eaten, the house began to be surrounded by tories, who were in pursuit of

---

escapes from captivity or death are said to have been almost miraculous.— He resumed his labors as teacher and pastor after the war; and continued to preach till his ninety-sixth year. He died in 1824, at the age of ninety-nine. His wife died the following year in the eighty-seventh of her age.

him. Mrs. Caldwell led him out at a back-door unseen in the darkness, and ordered him to climb a large locust tree, and there remain till the house was plundered and the pursuers had departed. He did so. Mrs. Caldwell lost her property, but her calmness and prudence saved the express, and that was what most concerned the patriotic woman.

THE MOTHER OF RANDOLPH

She led me first to God;
Her words and prayers were my young spirit's dew;
For when she used to leave
The fireside every eve,
I knew it was for prayer that she withdrew.

PIERPONT.

The biographers of John Randolph mention the interesting fact that his mother taught him to pray. This all-important maternal duty made an impression on his heart. He lived at a period when skepticism was popular, particularly in some political circles in which he had occasion to mingle; and he has left on record his testimony in regard to the influence of his mother's religious instruction. Speaking of the subject of infidelity to an intimate friend, he once made the following acknowledgment:

"I believe I should have been swept away by the flood of French infidelity if it had not been for one thing—the remembrance of the time when my sainted mother used to make me kneel by her side, taking my little hands folded in hers, and cause me to repeat the Lord's Prayer."

CORNELIA BEEKMAN.

The smallest worm will turn when trodden on,
And doves will peck, in safeguard of their brood.

SHAKSPEARE.

The vaunts
And menace of the vengeful enemy
Pass like the gust, that roared and died away
In the distant tree.

COLERIDGE.

Mrs. Cornelia Beekman was a daughter of Pierre Van Cortlandt, Lieutenant Governor of New York from 1777 to 1795; and she seems to have inherited her father's zeal for the rights of his country. She was born at the Cortlandt manor house, "an old fashioned stone mansion situated on the banks of the Croton river," in 1752; was married when about seventeen or eighteen, to Gerard G. Beekman; and died on the fourteenth of March, 1847. A few anecdotes will illustrate the noble characteristics of her nature.*

When the British were near her residence, which

---

* For a fuller account of her life, see the second volume of Mrs. Ellet's Women of the Revolution, to which work we are indebted for the substance of these anecdotes.

was a short distance from Peekskill, a soldier entered the house one day and went directly to the closet, saying, in reply to a question she put to him, that he wanted some brandy. She reproved him for his boldness and want of courtesy, when he threatened to stab her with a bayonet. Unalarmed by his oath-charged threats — although an old, infirm negro was the only aid at hand — she in turn threatened him, declaring that she would call her husband and have his conduct reported to his commander. Her sterness and intrepidity, coupled with her threats, subdued the insolent coward, and, obeying her orders, he marched out of the house.

A party of tories, under command of Colonels Bayard and Fleming, once entered her house, and, with a great deal of impudence and in the most insulting tone, asked if she was not "the daughter of that old rebel, Pierre Van Cortlandt?" "I am the daughter of Pierre Van Cortlandt, but it becomes not such as you to call my father a rebel," was her dauntless reply. The person who put the question now raised his musket, at which menacing act, she coolly reprimanded him and ordered him out of doors. His heart melted beneath the fire of her eye, and, abashed, he sneaked away.

In one instance, a man named John Webb, better known at that time as "Lieutenant Jack," left in her charge a valise which contained a new suit of uniform and some gold. He stated he would send for it when he wanted it, and gave her particular directions not to deliver it to any one without a written order from himself or his brother Samuel. About two weeks afterwards, a man named Smith rode up to the door in haste, and asked her husband, who was without, for Lieutenant Jack's valise. She knew Smith, and had little confidence in his *professed* whig principles; so she stepped to the door and reminded her husband that it would be necessary for the messenger to show his order before the valise could be given up.

"You know me very well, Mrs. Beekman; and when I assure you that Lieutenant Jack sent me for the valise, you will not refuse to deliver it to me, as he is greatly in want of his uniform."

"I do know you very well — *too well* to give you the valise without a written order from the owner or the Colonel."

Soon after this brief colloquy, Smith went away without the valise, and it was afterwards ascertained that he was a rank tory, and at that very hour in league with the British. Indeed Major Andre was concealed in his house that day, and had Smith got possession of Webb's uniform, as the latter and Andre were about the same size, it is likely the celebrated spy would have escaped and changed the reading of a brief chapter of American history. Who can tell how much this republic is indebted to the prudence, integrity, courage and patriotism of Cornelia Beekman?

THE MOTHER OF WEST.

O wondrous power! how little understood —
Entrusted to the mother's mind alone —
To fashion genius, form the soul for good,
Inspire a West, or train a Washington.

MRS. HALE.

When Benjamin West was seven years old, he was left, one summer day, with the charge of an infant niece. As it lay in the cradle and he was engaged in fanning away the flies, the motion of the fan pleased the child, and caused it to smile. Attracted by the charms thus created, young West felt his instinctive passion aroused; and seeing paper, pen and some red and black ink on a table, he eagerly seized them and made his first attempt at portrait painting. Just as he had finished his maiden task, his mother and sister entered. He tried to conceal what he had done, but his confusion arrested his mother's attention, and she asked him what he had been doing. With reluctance and timidity, he handed her the paper, begging, at the same time, that she would not be offended. Examining the drawing for a short time, she turned to her daughter and, with a smile, said, "I declare, he has made a likeness of Sally." She then gave him a fond kiss, which so encouraged him that he promised her some drawings of the flowers which she was then holding, if she wished to have them.

The next year a cousin sent him a box of colors and pencils, with large quantities of canvas prepared for the easel, and half a dozen engravings. Early in the morning after their reception, he took all his materials into the garret, and for several days forgot all about school. His mother suspected that the box was the cause of his neglect of his books, and going into the garret and finding him busy at a picture, she was about to reprimand him; but her eye fell on some of his compositions, and her anger cooled at once. She was so pleased with them that she loaded him with kisses and promised to secure his father's pardon for his neglect of school.

How much the world is indebted to Mrs. West for her early and constant encouragement of the immortal artist. He often used to say, after his reputation was established, "*My mother's kiss made me a painter!*"

HEROIC ENDURANCE.

'Tis not now who is stout and bold,
But who bears hunger best and cold.

BUTLER.

On the twenty-seventh of July, 1755, Mrs. Howe, of Hinsdale, New Hampshire, with seven children and two other women and their children, was taken captive by the Indians, and marched through the wilderness to Crown Point. There Mrs. Howe, with some of the other prisoners, remained several days. The rest were conducted to Montreal to be sold, but the French refusing to buy them, they were all brought back, except Mrs. Howe's youngest daughter, who was presented to Governor De Vaudreuil.

Ere long the whole party started for St. Johns by water. Night soon came on; a storm arose; the darkness became intense; the canoes separated, and just before day Mrs. Howe was landed on the beach, ignorant of the destiny of her children. Raising a pillow of earth with her hands, she laid herself down to rest with her infant on her bosom. A toilsome day's journey brought her and her captors to St. Johns, and pressing onward they soon reached St. Francis, the home of the latter. A council having been called and the customary ceremonies performed, Mrs. Howe, with her infant left to her care, was put in the charge of a squaw, whom she was ordered to call mother.

"At the approach of winter, the squaw, yielding to her earnest solicitations, set out with Mrs. Howe and her child, for Montreal, to sell them to the French. On the journey both she and her infant were in danger of perishing from hunger and cold; the lips of the child being at times so benumbed, as to be incapable of imbibing its proper nourishment. After her arrival in the city, she was offered to a French lady; who, seeing the child in her arms, exclaimed, 'I will not buy a woman, who has a child to look after.' I shall not attempt to describe the feelings with which this rebuff was received by a person who had no higher ambition than to become a slave. Few of our race have hearts made of such unyielding materials, as not to be broken by long-continued abuse; and Mrs. Howe was not one of this number. Chilled with cold, and pinched with hunger, she saw in the kitchen of this inhospitable house some small pieces of bread, floating in a pail amid other fragments, destined to feed swine; and eagerly skimmed them for herself. When her Indian mother found that she could not dispose of her, she returned by water to St. Francis, where she soon died of small pox, which she had caught at Montreal. Speedily after, the Indians commenced their winter hunting. Mrs. Howe was then ordered to return her child to the captors. The babe clung to her bosom; and she was obliged to force it away. They carried it to a place called 'Messiskow,' on the borders of the river Missiscoui, near the north end of lake Champlain upon the eastern shore. The mother soon followed, and found it neglected, lean, and almost perishing with hunger. As she pressed its face to her cheek, the eager, half-starved infant bit her with violence. For three nights she was permitted to cherish it in her bosom; but in the day-time she was confined to a neighboring wigwam, where she was compelled to hear its unceasing cries of distress, without a possibility of contributing to its relief.

"The third day the Indians carried her several miles up the lake. The following night she was alarmed by what is usually called the great earthquake, which shook the region around her with violent concussions. Here, also, she was deserted for two nights in an absolute wilderness; and, when her Indian connections returned, was told by them that two of her children were dead. Very soon after, she received certain information of the death of her infant. Amid the anguish awakened by these melancholy tidings, she saw a distant volume of smoke; and was strongly inclined to make her way to the wigwam from which it ascended. As she entered the door, she met one of the children, reported to be dead; and to her great consolation found that he was in comfortable circumstances. A good-natured Indian soon after informed her, that the other was alive on the opposite side of the lake, at the distance of a few miles only. Upon this information she obtained leave to be absent for a single day; and, with the necessary directions from her informant, set out for the place. On her way she found her child, lean and hungry, and proceeded with it to the wigwam. A small piece of bread, presented to her by the Indian family in which she lived, she had carefully preserved for this unfortunate boy; but, to avoid offending the family in which he lived, was obliged to distribute it in equal shares to all the children. The little creature had been transported at the sight of his mother; and, when she announced her departure, fell at her feet, as if he had been dead. Yet she was compelled to leave him; and satisfied herself, as far as she was able, by commending him to the protection of God. The family in which she lived, passed the following summer at St. Johns. It was composed of the daughter and son-in-law of her late mother. The son-in-law went out early in the season on an expedition against the English settlements. At their return, the party had a drinking frolic, their usual festival after excursions of this nature. Drunkenness regularly enhances the bodily strength of a savage, and stimulates his mind to madness. In this situation he will insult, abuse, and not unfrequently murder, his nearest friends. The wife of this man had often been a sufferer by his intemperance. She therefore proposed to Mrs. Howe that they should withdraw themselves from the wigwam until the effects of his present intoxication were over. They accordingly withdrew. Mrs. Howe returned first, and found him surly and ill-natured, because his wife was absent. In the violence of his resentment he took Mrs. Howe, hurried her to St. Johns, and sold her for a trifling sum to a French gentleman, named Saccapee.

"Upon a little reflection, however, the Indian perceived that he had made a foolish bargain. In a spirit of resentment he threatened to assassinate Mrs. Howe; and declared that if he could not accomplish his design, he would set fire to the fort. She was therefore carefully secreted, and the fort watchfully guarded, until the violence of his passion was over. When her alarm was ended, she found her situation as happy in the family, as a state of servitude would permit. Her new master and mistress were kind, liberal, and so indulgent as rarely to refuse anything that she requested. In this manner they enabled her frequently to befriend other English prisoners, who, from time to time, were brought to St. Johns.

"Yet even in this humane family she met with new trials. Monsieur Saccapee, and his son, an officer in the French army, became at the same time passionately attached to her. This singular fact is a forcible proof that her person, mind, and manners, were unusually agreeable. Nor was her situation less perplexing than singular. The good will of the whole family was indispensable to her comfort, if not to her safety; and her purity she was determined to preserve at the hazard of her life. In the house where both her lovers resided, conversed with her every day, and, together with herself, vere continually under the eye of her mistress, the lovers a father and a son, herself a slave, and one of them her master, it will be easily believed that she met with very serious embarrassments in accomplishing her determination. In this situation she made known her misfortunes to Colonel Peter Schuyler of Albany, then a prisoner at St. Johns. As soon as he had learned her situation he represented it to the Governor De Vaudreuil. The Governor immediately ordered young Saccapee into the army; and enjoined on his father a just and kind treatment of Mrs. Howe. His humanity did not stop here. Being informed that one of her daughters was in danger of being married to an Indian of St. Francis, he rescued her from this miserable destiny, and placed her in a nunnery with her sister. Here they were both educated as his adopted children.

"By the good offices of Colonel Schuyler, also, who advanced twenty-seven hundred livres for that purpose, and by the assistance of several other gentlemen, she was enabled to ransom herself, and her four sons. With these children she set out for New England in the autumn of 1758, under the protection of Colonel Schuyler, leaving her two daughters behind.* As she was crossing lake Cham-

* After the treaty of peace at Paris, Mrs. Howe went to Canada and brought home the younger daughter, who left the nunnery with a great deal of reluctance. The older went to France with Monsieur De Vaudreuil, and was there married to a man named Louis.

plain, young Saccapee came on board the boat, in which she was conveyed; gave her a handsome present; and bade her adieu. Colonel Schuyler being obliged to proceed to Albany with more expedition than was convenient for his fellow travelers, left them in the care of Major Putnam, afterwards Major-General Putnam. From this gentleman she received every kind office, which his well known humanity could furnish; and arrived without any considerable misfortune at the place of their destination." *

* Dwight's Travels.

MATERNAL HEROISM

Is there a man, into the lion's den
Who dares intrude to snatch his young away?
THOMSON.

During the campaign of 1777, a soldier of the Fifty-fifth regiment was sitting with his wife at breakfast, when a bomb entered the tent, and fell between the table and a bed where their infant was sleeping. The mother urged her husband to go round the bomb and seize the child, his dress being, from the position of things, more favorable than hers for the prosecution of the dangerous task: but he refused. and running out of the tent, begged his wife to follow, saying that the fusee was just ready to communicate with the deadly combustibles. The fond mother, instead of obeying, hastily tucked up her garments to prevent their coming in contact with the bomb; leaped past it; caught the child, and in a moment was out of danger.

In December, 1850, the house of Peter Knight, of Bath, Maine, caught fire, and a small child, asleep in the room where the flames burst out, would have perished but for the self-possession and daring of its mother. One or two unsuccessful attempts had been made by others to rescue it, when the mother, always the last to despair, made a desperate effort, and se cured the prize. When the two were taken from the window of the second story, the dress of Mrs Knight was in flames!

A MODERN DORCAS.

'Tis truth divine, exhibited on earth,
Gives charity her being.

COWPER.

Isabella, the wife of Dr. John Graham, was born in Scotland, on the twenty-ninth of July, 1742. At the age of seventeen she became a member of the church in Paisley of which the Rev. Dr. Witherspoon, afterwards President of Princeton college, was the pastor. Dr. Graham was a physician of the same town. Her marriage took place in 1765. The next year Dr. Graham was ordered to join his regiment then stationed in Canada. After spending a few months at Montreal, he removed to Fort Niagara, where he remained in the garrison four years.

Just before the Revolutionary war the sixteenth regiment of Royal Americans was ordered to the island of Antigua. Thither Dr. Graham removed with his family, and there he died in 1774. Mrs. Graham then returned to her native land.

In 1789 she came to this country, and permanently settled in the city of New York. She there opened a school for young ladies, and gained a high reputation in her profession. She united with the Presbyterian church of which John Mason, D. D., was pastor, and was noted, through all the latter years of her life, for the depth of her piety and her Christian benevolence. She made it a rule to give a tenth part of her earnings to religious and charitable purposes. In 1795 she received, at one time, an advance of a thousand pounds on the sale of a lease which she held on some building lots; and not being used to such large profits, she said, on receiving the money, "Quick, quick, let me appropriate the tenth before my heart grows hard."

Two years afterwards, a society was organized and chartered, for the relief of poor widows; and Mrs. Graham was appointed first directress. Each of the managers had a separate district, and she had the superintendence of the whole. A house was purchased by the society, where work was received for the employment of the widows; and a school was opened for the instruction of their children. "Besides establishing this school, Mrs. Graham selected some of the widows, best qualified for the task, and engaged them, for a small compensation, to open day schools for the instruction of the children of widows, in distant parts of the city: she also established two Sabbath schools, one of which she superintended herself, and the other she placed under the care of her daughter. Wherever she met with Christians sick and in poverty, she visited and comforted them; and in some instances opened small subscription lists to provide for their support.

She attended occasionally for some years at the Alms House for the instruction of the children there, in religious knowledge: in this work she was much assisted by a humble and pious female friend, who was seldom absent from it on the Lord's day.

"It was often her custom to leave home after breakfast, to take with her a few rolls of bread, and return in the evening about eight o'clock. Her only dinner on such days was her bread, and perhaps some soup at the Soup House, established by the Humane Society for the poor, over which one of her widows had been, at her recommendation, appointed." *

In the winter of 1804-5, before a Tract or Bible Society had been formed in New York, she visited between two and three hundred of the poorer families, and supplied them with a Bible where they were destitute. She also distributed tracts which were written, at her request, by a friend, "and lest it might be said it was cheap to give advice, she usually gave a small sum of money along with the tracts."

On the fifteenth of March, 1806, a society was organized in New York for providing an Asylum for Orphan Children; and Mrs. Graham occupied the chair on the occasion. Her sympathies were strongly enlisted in this organization, and she was one of the trustees at the time of her death.

"In the winter of 1807-8, when the suspension

---

* Mrs. Bethune's Life of Mrs. Graham, abridged.

of commerce by the embargo, rendered the situation of the poor more destitute than ever, Mrs. Graham adopted a plan best calculated in her view to detect the idle applicant for charity, and at the same time to furnish employment for the more worthy amongst the female poor. She purchased flax, and lent wheels where applicants had none. Such as were industrions took the work with thankfulness, and were paid for it; those who were beggars by profession, never kept their word to return for the flax or the wheel. The flax thus spun was afterwards woven, bleached, and made into table-cloths and towels for family use." *

When the Magdalen Society was established by some gentlemen, in 1811, a board of ladies was elected for the purpose of superintending the internal management of the house; and Mrs. Graham was chosen President. This office she continued to hold till her death. The next year the trustees of the Lancasterian School solicited the services of several women to instruct the pupils in the catechism. Mrs. Graham cheerfully assisted in this task, instruction being given one afternoon in each week.

"In the spring of 1814 she was requested to unite with some ladies, in forming a Society for the Promotion of Industry amongst the poor. The Corporation of the city having returned a favorable answer to their petition for assistance, and provided a house, a meeting of the Society was held, and Mrs. Graham once more was called to the chair. It was the last

---

* Mrs. Bethune.

time she was to preside at the formation of a new society. Her articulation, once strong and clear, was now observed to have become more feeble. The ladies present listened to her with affectionate attention; her voice broke upon the ear as a pleasant sound that was passing away. She consented to have her name inserted in the list of managers, to give what assistance her age would permit in forwarding so beneficent a work. Although it pleased God to make her cease from her labors, before the House of Industry was opened, yet the work was carried on by others, and prospered. Between four and five hundred women were employed and paid during the following winter. The Corporation declared in strong terms their approbation of the result, and enlarged their donation, with a view to promote the same undertaking for the succeeding winter."

Mrs. Graham died on the twenty-seventh of July, 1814. Of no woman of the age may it be said with more propriety, as it was of Dorcas: "This woman was full of good works and alms-deeds, which she did." Yet few women are more humble than was Mrs. Graham, or think less of their benevolent deeds. Her daughter, Mrs. Bethune, writing of her decease, says that she departed in peace, not trusting in her wisdom or virtue, like the philosophers of Greece and Rome; not even, like Addison, calling on the profligate to see a good man die; but, like Howard, afraid that her good works might have a wrong place in the estimate of her hope, her chief glory was that of a "sinner saved by grace."

SARAH HOFFMAN.

Still to a stricken brother turn.

WHITTIER.

In the act of incorporation of the Widow's Society, established in the city of New York, in 1797, with the name of Mrs. Graham, is associated that of Mrs. Sarah Hoffman. This lady was the daughter of David Ogden, one of the judges of the Supreme Court of New Jersey, before the elevation of the provinces into states. She was born at Newark, on the eighth of September, 1742; and married Nicholas Hoffman, in 1762. She early took delight in doing good, being thus prompted by deep religious principle. Cautious and discriminating, her charities were bestowed judiciously, and she was able to do much good without the largest means. In her benevolent operations, however, she usually acted in an associated capacity.

As already intimated, she was a member of the society formed "for the relief of poor widows with small children." That this institution prospered under the control of such women as Mrs. Hoffman and Mrs. Graham, may be inferred from their report made in April, 1803. "Ninety-eight widows and two hundred and twenty-three children," this document states, "were brought through the severity of the winter with a considerable degree of comfort."

Mrs. Hoffman, Mrs. Graham and their associates, often perambulated the districts of poverty and disease, from morning till night, entering the huts of want and desolation, and carrying comfort and consolation to many a despairing heart. They clambered to the highest and meanest garrets, and descended to the lowest, darkest and dankest cellars, to administer to the wants of the destitute, the sick, and the dying. They took with them medicine as well as food; and were accustomed to administer Christian counsel or consolation, as the case required, to the infirm in body and the wretched in heart. They even taught many poor creatures, who seemed to doubt the existence of an overruling Providence, to pray to Him whose laws they had broken and thereby rendered themselves miserable.*

In Mrs. Hoffman's character, to tenderness of feeling were added great firmness, strength of mind, and moral courage. She was often seen in the midst of contagion and suffering where the cheek of the warrior would blanch with fear. She exposed her own life, however, not like the warrior, to destroy, but to save; and hundreds *were* saved by her humane efforts, combined with those of her co-workers. Her

* Knapp's Female Biography.

life beautifully exemplified the truth of what Crabbe says of woman:

> ——In extremes of cold and heat,
> Where wandering man may trace his kind;
> Wherever grief and want retreat,
> In woman they compassion find.

And if, as the poet Grainger asserts,

> The height of virtue is to serve mankind,

Mrs. Hoffman reached a point towards which many aspire, but above which few ascend.

HEROISM OF SCHOHARIE WOMEN.

> Invaders! vain your battles' steel and fire.
> HALLECK.

During the struggle for Independence, there were three noted forts in the Schoharie settlement, called the Upper, Middle and Lower; and when, in the autumn of 1780, Sir John Johnson sallied forth from Niagara, with his five hundred or more British, tory and German troops, and made an attack on these forts, an opportunity was given for the display of patriotism and courage, as well by the women of the settlement as by the men.

When the Middle fort was invested, an heroic and noted ranger named Murphy, used his rifle balls so fast as to need an additional supply; and, anticipating his wants, Mrs. Angelica Vrooman caught his bullet mould, some lead and an iron spoon, ran to her father's tent, and there moulded a quantity of bullets amid

> "the shout
> Of battle, the barbarian yell, the bray
> Of dissonant instruments, the clang of arms,
> The shriek of agony, the groan of death."

While the firing was kept up at the Middle fort,

great anxiety prevailed at the Upper; and during this time Captain Hager, who commanded the latter, gave orders that the women and children should retire to a long cellar, which he specified, should the enemy attack him. A young lady named Mary Haggidorn, on hearing these orders, went to Captain Hager and addressed him as follows:—"Captain, I shall not go into that cellar. Should the enemy come, I will take a spear, which I can use as well as any *man*, and help defend the fort." The Captain, seeing her determination, made the following reply:—"Then take a spear, Mary, and be ready at the pickets to repel an attack." She cheerfully obeyed, and held the spear at the picket, till "huzzas for the American flag" burst on her ear, and told that all was safe.*

---

* *Vide* History of Schoharie county, p. 410—11.

A STERLING PATRIOT.

With nerve to wield the battle-brand,
And join the border-fray,
They shrank not from the foeman,
They quailed not in the fight,
But cheered their husbands through the day,
And soothed them through the night.

W. D. Gallagher.

The most noted heroine of the Mohawk valley, and one of the bravest and noblest mothers of the Revolution, was Nancy Van Alstine. Her maiden name was Quackinbush. She was born near Canajoharie, about the year 1733, and was married to Martin J. Van Alstine, at the age of eighteen. He settled in the valley of the Mohawk, and occupied the Van Alstine family mansion. Mrs. Van Alstine was the mother of fifteen children. She died at Wampsville, Madison county, in 1831.

In the month of August, 1780, an army of Indians and tories, led on by Brant, rushed into the Mohawk valley, devastated several settlements, and killed many of the inhabitants: and during the two following months, Sir John Johnson, made a descent and finished the work which Brant had begun. The two almost completely destroyed the settlements throughout the valley. It was during those trying times that Mrs. Van Alstine performed a portion of her heroic exploits which are so interestingly related by Mrs. Ellet.

"While the enemy, stationed at Johnstown, were laying waste the country, parties continually going about to murder the inhabitants and burn their dwellings, the neighborhood in which Mrs. Van Alstine lived remained in comparative quiet, though the settlers trembled as each sun arose, lest his setting beams should fall on their ruined homes. Most of the men were absent, and when, at length, intelligence came that the destroyers were approaching, the people were almost distracted with terror. Mrs. Van Alstine called her neighbors together, endeavored to calm their fears, and advised them to make immediate arrangements for removing to an island, belonging to her husband, near the opposite side of the river. She knew that the spoilers would be in too great haste to make any attempt to cross, and thought if some articles were removed, they might be induced to suppose the inhabitants gone to a greater distance. The seven families in the neighborhood were in a few hours upon the island, having taken with them many things necessary for their comfort during a short stay. Mrs. Van Alstine remained herself to the last, then crossed in the boat, helping to draw it far up on the beach. Scarcely had they secreted themselves before they heard the dreaded warwhoop, and descried the Indians in the distance. It was not long before one and another saw the homes they loved in flames. When the savages came to Van Alstine's house, they were about to fire that also, but the chief, interfering, informed them that Sir John would not be pleased if that house were burned—the owner having extended civilities to the baronet before the commencement of hostilities. 'Let the old wolf keep his den,' he said, and the house was left unmolested. The talking of the Indians could be distinctly heard from the island, and Mrs. Van Alstine rejoiced that she was thus enabled to give shelter to the houseless families who had fled with her. The fugitives, however, did not deem it prudent to leave their place of concealment for several days, the smoke seen in different directions too plainly indicating that the work of devastation was going on.

"The destitute families remained at Van Alstine's house till it was deemed prudent to rebuild their homes. Later in the following autumn an incident occurred which brought much trouble upon them. Three men from the neighborhood of Canajoharie, who had deserted the whig cause and joined the British, came back from Canada as spies, and were detected and apprehended. Their execution followed; two were shot, and one, a bold, adventurous fellow, named Harry Harr, was hung in Mr. Van Alstine's orchard. Their prolonged absence causing some uneasiness to their friends in Canada, some Indians were sent to reconnoitre and learn something of them. It happened that they arrived on the day of Harr's

15

execution, which they witnessed from a neighboring hill. They returned immediately with the information, and a party was dispatched — it is said by Brant — to revenge the death of the spies upon the inhabitants. Their continued shouts of 'Aha, Harry Harr!' while engaged in pillaging and destroying, showed that such was their purpose. In their progress of devastation, they came to the house of Van Alstine, where no preparations had been made for defence, the family not expecting an attack, or not being aware of the near approach of the enemy. Mrs. Van Alstine was personally acquainted with Brant, and it may have been owing to this circumstance that the members of the family were not killed or carried away as prisoners. The Indians came upon them by surprise, entered the house without ceremony, and plundered and destroyed everything in their way. Mrs. Van Alstine saw her most valued articles, brought from Holland, broken one after another, till the house was strewed with fragments. As they passed a large mirror without demolishing it, she hoped it might be saved; but presently two of the savages led in a colt from the stable, and the glass being laid in the hall, compelled the animal to walk over it. The beds which they could not carry away, they ripped open, shaking out the feathers and taking the ticks with them. They also took all the clothing. One young Indian, attracted by the brilliancy of a pair of inlaid buckles on the shoes of the aged grandmother seated in the corner, rudely snatched them from her feet, tore off the buckles, and flung the shoes in her face. Another took her shawl from her neck, threatening to kill her if resistance were offered. The eldest daughter, seeing a young savage carrying off a basket containing a hat and cap her father had brought her from Philadelphia, and which she highly prized, followed him, snatched her basket, and after a struggle succeeded in pushing him down. She then fled to a pile of hemp and hid herself, throwing the basket into it as far as she could. The other Indians gathered round, and as the young one rose clapped their hands, shouting 'Brave girl!' while he skulked away to escape their derision. During the struggle Mrs. Van Alstine had called to her daughter to give up the contest; but she insisted that her basket should not be taken. Having gone through the house, the intruders went up to the kitchen chamber, where a quantity of cream in large jars had been brought from the dairy, and threw the jars down stairs, covering the floor with their contents. They then broke the window glass throughout the house, and unsatisfied with the plunder they had collected, bribed a man servant by the promise of his clothes and a portion of the booty to show them where some articles had been hastily secreted. Mrs. Van Alstine had just finished cutting out winter clothing for her family—which consisted of her mother-in-law, her husband and twelve children, with two black servants—and had stowed it away in barrels. The servant treacherously disclosed the hiding place, and the clothing was soon added to the rest of the booty. Mrs. Van Alstine reproached the man for his perfidy, which she assured him would be punished, not rewarded by the savages, and her words were verified; for after they had forced him to assist in securing their plunder, they bound him and put him in one of their wagons, telling him his treachery to the palefaces deserved no better treatment. The provisions having been carried away, the family subsisted on corn, which they pounded and made into cakes. They felt much the want of clothing, and Mrs. Van Alstine gathered the silk of milk-weed, of which, mixed with flax, she spun and wove garments. The inclement season was now approaching, and they suffered severely from the want of window glass, as well as their bedding, woolen clothes, and the various articles, including cooking utensils, taken from them. Mrs. Van Alstine's most arduous labors could do little towards providing for so many destitute persons; their neighbors were in no condition to help them, the roads were almost impassable, besides being infested by Indians, and their finest horses had been taken. In this deplorable situation, she proposed to her husband to join with others who had been robbed in like manner, and make an attempt to recover their property from the Indian castle, eighteen or twenty miles distant, where it had been carried. But the idea of such an enterprise against an enemy superior in numbers and well prepared for defence, was soon abandoned. As the cold became more intolerable and the necessity for doing something more urgent,

Mrs. Van Alstine, unable to witness longer the sufferings of those dependent on her, resolved to venture herself on the expedition. Her husband and children endeavored to dissuade her, but firm for their sake, she left home, accompanied by her son, about sixteen years of age. The snow was deep and the roads in a wretched condition, yet she persevered through all difficulties, and by good fortune arrived at the castle at a time when the Indians were all absent on a hunting excursion, the women and children only being left at home. She went to the principal house, where she supposed the most valuable articles must have been deposited, and on entering, was met by the old squaw who had the superintendence, who demanded what she wanted. She asked for food; the squaw hesitated; but on her visitor saying she had never turned an Indian away hungry, sullenly commenced preparations for a meal. The matron saw her bright copper tea-kettle, with other cooking utensils, brought forth for use. While the squaw was gone for water, she began a search for her property, and finding several articles gave them to her son to put into the sleigh. When the squaw, returning, asked by whose order she was taking those things, Mrs. Van Alstine replied, that they belonged to her; and seeing that the woman was not disposed to give them up peaceably, took from her pocket-book a paper, and handed it to the squaw, who she knew could not read. The woman asked whose name was affixed to the supposed order, and being told it was that of 'Yankee Peter'—a man who had great influence among the savages, dared not refuse submission. By this stratagem Mrs. Van Alstine secured, without opposition, all the articles she could find belonging to her, and put them into the sleigh. She then asked where the horses were kept. The squaw refused to show her, but she went to the stable, and there found those belonging to her husband, in fine order—for the savages were careful of their best horses. The animals recognised their mistress, and greeted her by a simultaneous neighing. She bade her son cut the halters, and finding themselves at liberty they bounded off and went homeward at full speed. The mother and son now drove back as fast as possible, for she knew their fate would be sealed if the Indians should return. They reached home late in the evening, and passed a sleepless night, dreading instant pursuit and a night attack from the irritated savages. Soon after daylight the alarm was given that the Indians were within view, and coming towards the house, painted and in their war costume, and armed with tomahawks and rifles. Mr. Van Alstine saw no course to escape their vengeance but to give up whatever they wished to take back; but his intrepid wife was determined on an effort, at least, to retain her property. As they came near she begged her husband not to show himself—for she knew they would immediately fall upon him—but to leave the matter in her hands. The intruders took their course first to the stable, and bidding all the rest remain within doors, the matron went out alone, followed to the door by her family, weeping and entreating her not to expose herself. Going to the stable she enquired in the Indian language what the men wanted. The reply was 'our horses.' She said boldly — 'They are ours; you came and took them without right; they are ours, and we mean to keep them.' The chief now came forward threateningly, and approached the door. Mrs. Van Alstine placed herself against it, telling him she would not give up the animals they had raised and were attached to. He succeeded in pulling her from the door, and drew out the plug that fastened it, which she snatched from his hand, pushing him away. He then stepped back and presented his rifle, threatening to shoot her if she did not move; but she kept her position, opening her neckhandkerchief and bidding him shoot if he dared. It might be that the Indian feared punishment from his allies for any such act of violence, or that he was moved with admiration of her intrepidity; he hesitated, looked at her for a moment, and then slowly dropped his gun, uttering in his native language expressions implying his conviction that the evil one must help her, and saying to his companions that she was a brave woman and they would not molest her. Giving a shout, by way of expressing their approbation, they departed from the premises. On their way they called at the house of Col. Frey, and related their adventure, saying that the white woman's courage had saved her and her property, and were there fifty such brave women as the wife of 'Big Tree,' the Indians would never have troubled the inhabitants of the Mohawk valley. She experienced afterwards the good effects of the impression made at this time. . . . .

"It was not long after this occurrence that several Indians came upon some children left in the field while the men went to dinner, and took them prisoners, tomahawking a young man who rushed from an adjoining field to their assistance. Two of these — six and eight years of age — were Mrs. Van Alstine's children. The savages passed on towards the Susquehanna, plundering and destroying as they went. They were three weeks upon the journey, and the poor little captives suffered much from hunger and exposure to the night air, being in a deplorable condition by the time they returned to Canada. On their arrival, according to custom, each prisoner was required to run the gauntlet, two Indian boys being stationed on either side, armed with clubs and sticks to beat him as he ran. The eldest was cruelly bruised, and when the younger, pale and exhausted, was led forward, a squaw of the tribe, taking pity on the helpless child, said she would go in his place, or if that could not be permitted, would carry him. She accordingly took him in her arms, and wrapping her blanket around him, got through with some severe blows. The children were then washed and clothed by order of the chief, and supper was given them. Their uncle — then also a prisoner —

heard of the arrival of children from the Mohawk, and was permitted to visit them. The little creatures were sleeping soundly when aroused by a familiar voice, and joyfully exclaiming, 'Uncle Quackinbush!' were clasped in his arms. In the following spring the captives were ransomed, and returned home in fine spirits." *

Prior to the commencement of hostilities, Mr. Van Alstine had purchased a tract of land on the Susquehanna, eighteen miles below Cooperstown; and thither removed in 1785. There as at her former home, Mrs. Van Alstine had an opportunity to exhibit the heroic qualities of her nature. We subjoin two anecdotes illustrative of forest life in the midst of savages.

"On one occasion an Indian whom Mr. Van Alstine had offended, came to his house with the intention of revenging himself. He was not at home, and the men were out at work, but his wife and family were within, when the intruder entered. Mrs. Van Alstine saw his purpose in his countenance. When she inquired his business, he pointed to his rifle, saying, he meant 'to show Big Tree which was the best man.' She well knew that if her husband presented himself he would probably fall a victim unless she could reconcile the difficulty. With this view she commenced a conversation upon subjects in which she knew the savage would take an interest, and admiring his dress, asked permission

* Women of the Revolution.

to examine his rifle, which, after praising, she set down, and while managing to fix his attention on something else poured water into the barrel. She then gave him back the weapon, and assuming a more earnest manner, spoke to him of the Good Spirit, his kindness to men, and their duty to be kind to each other. By her admirable tact she so far succeeded in pacifying him, that when her husband returned he was ready to extend to him the hand of reconciliation and fellowship. He partook of some refreshment, and before leaving informed them that one of their neighbors had lent him the rifle for his deadly purpose. They had for some time suspected this neighbor, who had coveted a piece of land, of unkind feelings towards them because he could not obtain it, yet could scarcely believe him so depraved. The Indian, to confirm his story, offered to accompany Mrs. Van Alstine to the man's house, and although it was evening she went with him, made him repeat what he had said, and so convinced her neighbor of the wickedness of his conduct, that he was ever afterwards one of their best friends. Thus by her prudence and address she preserved, in all probability, the lives of her husband and family; for she learned afterwards that a number of savages had been con cealed near, to rush upon them in case of danger to their companion.

"At another time a young Indian came in and asked the loan of a drawing knife. As soon as he had it in his hand he walked up to the table, on which there was a loaf of bread, and unceremoniously cut several slices from it. One of Mrs. Van Alstine's sons had a deerskin in his hand, and indignantly struck the savage with it. He turned and darted out of the door, giving a loud whoop as he fled. The mother just then came in, and hearing what had passed expressed her sorrow and fears that there would be trouble, for she knew the Indian character too well to suppose they would allow the matter to rest. Her apprehensions were soon realized by the approach of a party of savages, headed by the brother of the youth who had been struck. He entered alone, and inquired for the boy who had given the blow. Mr. Van Alstine, starting up in surprise, asked impatiently, 'What the devilish Indian wanted?' The savage, understanding the expression applied to his appearance to be anything but complimentary, uttered a sharp cry, and raising his rifle, aimed at Van Alstine's breast. His wife sprang forward in time to throw up the weapon, the contents of which were discharged into the wall, and pushing out the Indian, who stood just at the entrance, she quickly closed the door. He was much enraged, but she at length succeeded in persuading him to listen to a calm account of the matter, and asked why the quarrel of two lads should break their friendship. She finally invited him to come in and settle the difficulty in an amicable way. To his objection that they had no rum, she answered—'But we have tea;' and at length the party was called in, and a speech made by the leader in favor of the 'white squaw,' after which the tea was passed round. The Indian then took the grounds, and emptying them into a hole made in the ashes, declared that the enmity was buried forever. After this, whenever the family was molested, the ready tact of Mrs. Van Alstine, and her acquaintance with Indian nature, enabled her to prevent any serious difficulty. They had few advantages for religious worship, but whenever the weather would permit, the neighbors assembled at Van Alstine's house to hear the word preached. His wife, by her influence over the Indians, persuaded many of them to attend, and would interpret to them what was said by the minister. Often their rude hearts were touched, and they would weep bitterly while she went over the affecting narrative of our Redeemer's life and death, and explained the truths of the Gospel. Much good did she in this way, and in after years many a savage converted to Christianity blessed her as his benefactress."

HEROIC CONDUCT AT MONMOUTH.

Proud were they by such to stand,
  In hammock, fort or glen;
To load the sure old rifle—
  To run the leaden ball—
To watch a battling husband's place,
  And fill it should he fall.

W. D. GALLAGHER.

During the battle of Monmouth, a gunner named Pitcher was killed; and when the call was made for some one to take the place of her fallen husband, his wife, who had followed him to the camp, and thence to the field of conflict, unhesitatingly stepped forward, and offered her services. The gun was so well managed as to draw the attention of General Washington to the circumstance, and to call forth an expression of his admiration of her bravery and her fidelity to her country. To show his appreciation of her virtues and her highly valuable services, he conferred on her a lieutenant's commission. She afterwards went by the name of *Captain Molly*.

The poet Glover tells us, in his Leonidas, that Xerxes boasted

"His ablest, bravest counselor and chief
In Artemisia, Caria's matchless queen;"

and Herodotus also very justly eulogizes the same

character. Yet Artemisia was scarcely more serviceable to Xerxes in the battle of Salamis, than "Captain Molly" to Washington in the battle of Monmouth. One served in a Grecian expedition, to gratify her great spirit, vigor of mind and love of glory; the other fought, partly, it may be, to revenge the death of her husband, but more, doubtless, for the love she bore for an injured country, "bleeding at every vein." One was rewarded with a complete suit of Grecian armor; the other with a lieutenant's commission, and both for their bravery. If the queen of Caria is deserving of praise for her martial valor, the name of the heroic wife of the gunner, should be woven with hers in a fadeless wreath of song.

COURAGE OF A COUNTRY GIRL.

> Honor and shame from no condition rise,
> Act well your part, there all the honor lies.
>
> Pope

In December, 1777, while Washington was at Valley Forge and the enemy was in Philadelphia, Major Tallmadge was stationed between the two places with a detachment of cavalry, to make observations and to limit the range of British foragers. On one occasion, while performing this duty, he was informed that a country girl had gone into Philadelphia — perhaps by Washington's instigation — ostensibly to sell eggs, but really and especially to obtain information respecting the enemy; and curiosity led him to move his detachment to Germantown. There the main body halted while he advanced with a small party towards the British lines. Dismounting at a tavern in plain sight of their outposts, he soon saw a young girl coming out of the city. He watched her till she came up to the tavern; made himself known to her, and was about to receive some valuable intelligence, when he was informed that the British light horse were advancing. Stepping to the door he saw them in full pursuit of his patroles. He hastily mounted, but before he had started his charger, the girl was at his side begging for protection. Quick as thought, he ordered her to mount behind him. She obeyed, and in that way rode to Germantown, a distance of three miles. During the whole ride, writes the Major in his Journal, where we find these details, "although there was considerable firing of pistols, and not a little wheeling and charging, she remained unmoved, and never once complained of fear."

THE LEDYARDS AT FORT GRISWOLD

Ah never shall the land forget
  How gushed the life-blood of the brave;
Gushed warm with hope and courage yet,
  Upon the soil they fought to save.

BRYANT

How few like thee enquire the wretched out,
And court the offices of soft humanity.

ROWE.

"It will be remembered that at the time of the burning of New London, Connecticut, a detachment of the army of the traitor Arnold, under whose personal direction that feat of vandalism was performed, was directed to attack and carry Fort Griswold at Groton, on the opposite side of the river. It was then under the command of Colonel Ledyard, a brave and meritorious officer, whose memory will live in the warm affections of his country, as that of one of the early martyrs to her liberty, whilst the granite pile which now lifts its summit above the spot where he was sacrificed, shall long remain to bear the record of his death. The fort was, in truth, little more than an embankment of earth, thrown up as a breast-work for the handful of troops it surrounded, and with a strong log-house in the center. The force which attacked it was altogether superior to that of its defenders, even when the difference in their position is taken into view. The case was so hopeless, that the slightest share of prudence would have suggested retreat. But the chafed and gallant spirits of Ledyard and his men would not permit them to retire before a marauding enemy, however powerful, without making at least one effort to beat him back. With a boldness and heroism scarcely ever surpassed, they stood their ground, until overwhelming numbers of the enemy were in the fort, and engaged hand to hand with its heroic defenders. Fierce and terrible, for a few moments, was the encounter, and it was not until the last ray of hope was gone, and nothing but a useless effusion of blood would have resulted from further resistance, that they at length yielded. In doing so, however, they were inclined to believe that the gallantry displayed by their little band, would at least shelter them from indignity. Ledyard had turned the handle of his sword to the commander of the assailants, and in answer to the question, 'who commands this fort,' replied, 'I did, sir, but you do now,' when he was pierced to the heart with his own weapon, and by the dastardly hand in which he had just placed it. An almost indiscriminate butchery now commenced; many falling instantly dead and some being desperately wounded. The fort was then entirely at the disposal of the enemy. The barbarity, however, did not end there. When it was found that several of the prisoners were still alive, the British soldiers piled their mangled bodies in an old cart and started it down the steep and rugged hill, towards the river, in order that they might be there drowned. But stumps and stones obstructed the passage of the cart; and when the enemy had retreated — for the aroused inhabitants of that region soon compelled them to the step — the friends of the wounded came to their aid and thus several lives were saved."*

One of the "ministering angels" who came the next morning to the aid of the thirty-five wounded men, who lay all night freezing in their own blood, was Miss Mary Ledyard, a near relative of the Colonel. "She brought warm chocolate, wine, and other refreshments, and while Dr. Downer of Preston was dressing their wounds, she went from one to another, administering her cordials, and breathing into their ears gentle words of sympathy and encouragement. In these labors of kindness she was assisted by another relative of the lamented Colonel Ledyard — Mrs. John Ledyard — who had also brought her household stores to refresh the sufferers, and lavished on them the most soothing personal attentions. The soldiers who recovered from their wounds, were accustomed, to the day of their death, to speak of these ladies in terms of fervent gratitude and praise."†

---

* Democratic Review, vol. 20, pp. 93-4.

† Mrs. Ellet.

SENECA HEROINES.

They fought like brave *men,* long and well.
HALLECK.

In the celebrated battle between the French and Indians, which occurred near Victor, in the western part of New York, in 1687, five Seneca women took an active part in the bloody conflict. Mr. Hosmer, the poet, alludes to the circumstance in one of his celebrated "Lectures on the Iroquois," from the manuscript of which we have been permitted to copy, as follows:

"The memory of illustrious women who have watched in defence of altar and hearth, the deeds of the sterner sex, has been enshrined in song, and honored by the Historic Muse. Joan of Arc, and the dark-eyed maid of Saragossa in all coming time will be chivalric watch-words of France and Spain, but not less worthy of record, and poetic embalmment, were the *five** devoted heroines who followed their red lords to the battle-field near ancient Ganagarro, and fought with unflinching re-

* *Vide* Doc. His, Vol. 1. p. 256.

solution by their sides. Children of such wives could not be otherwise than valiant. Bring back your shield, or be brought upon it, was the Spartan mother's stern injunction to her son: but roused to a higher pitch of courage, the wild daughters of the Genesee stood in the perilous pass, and in the defence of their forest homes, turned not back from the spear, "the thunder of the captains, and the shouting."

MARTHA BRATTON.

Not to the ensanguined field of death alone
Is valor limited.

SMOLLET.

Our country first, their glory and their pride.

J. T. FIELDS.

Martha Bratton was the wife of William Bratton a native of Pennsylvania. She was born in Rowan county, North Carolina. They settled near York ville, in South Carolina, where she died in 1816. Two or three anecdotes will suffice to illustrate her character.

In June, 1780, a party of British and tory marauders, were attacked by a company of whigs under Colonel Bratton, at Mobley Meeting House, in Fairfield district, South Carolina, and defeated. Advertised of this disaster, Colonel Turnbull, commander of a detachment of British troops at Rocky Mount, Chester county, ordered Captain Huck to proceed with his cavalry to the frontier of the province, collecting all the royal army on his march, and if possible to subdue the rebels. An engage ment soon took place between Captain Huck and Col onel Bratton; but before the battle, the Colonel's wife had an opportunity to display her character in a truly heroic manner. The evening preceding, Huck arrived at the Colonel's house, and entering in an uncivil manner, demanded of his wife where her husband was. She boldly replied "He is in Sumter's army!" Huck then tried to persuade her to induce her husband to join the British, and even went so far as to promise him a commission, in case he would do so. But neither persuasion nor argument availed any thing. With the firmness of a true patriot, she assured him that she would rather see him—faithful to his country—perish in Sumter's army, than clothed with any power or graced with any honor royalty could bestow! At this point, a soldier, exasperated at her bold and fearless manner, seized a reaping hook that hung in the piazza and threatened to kill her if she did not give particular and full information in regard to her husband. But with the weapon still at her throat, she promptly refused; and, but for the interference of the officer second in command, she would have lost her life.

Huck now ordered her to prepare supper for himself and the whole band. With this request she complied, and then retired to an upper apartment with her children. Supper over, Huck posted his sentinels along the road and went with his officers to another house, half a mile off, to pass the night.

Convinced that the royalists would seek revenge for their late defeat at Mobley's Meeting House, and naturally fearing that his own family might be among the victims, Colonel Bratton had that day marched from Mecklenburg county, North Carolina, with seventy-five men. Late in the evening he drew near his house, and learning that the enemy were there, and ascertaining their number, he made speedy preparations for an attack. The guard of the royalists was neglected, and he found no trouble in reconnoitering the encampment. All things ready, the attack was made before Huck had finished his morning nap. He awoke only to attempt to rally his men and then lie down again to sleep for ever! The tories seeing their leader fall, fled, or made the attempt. Some *did* escape, others were killed, others taken prisoners. The firing ceased about day light, when Mrs. Bratton made her appearance. She received the wounded on both sides, and showed them impartial attention, setting herself to work immediately, dressing their wounds and trying to relieve their pains. She who was so brave in the hour of danger, was no less humane in a time of suffering. *

Prior to the fall of Charleston at a period when

---

* The following toast was drunk at Brattonsville, York district, on the twelfth of July, 1839, at a celebration of Huck's Defeat.

"The memory of Mrs. Martha Bratton.—In the hands of an infuriated monster, with the instrument of death around her neck, she nobly refused to betray her husband; in the hour of victory she remembered mercy, and as a guardian angel, interposed in behalf of her inhuman enemies. Throughout the Revolution she encouraged the whigs to fight on to the last; to hope on to the end. Honor and gratitude to the woman and heroine, who proved herself so faithful a wife —so firm a friend to liberty!"

ammunition was very scarce, Governor Rutledge intrusted to her a small stock of powder. This fact some tory ascertained, and communicated to the British at a station not far off. A detachment was forthwith sent out to secure the treasure, of which movement Mrs. Bratton received early intimation. Resolving that the red coats should not have the prize, she laid a train of powder from the depot to the spot she chose to occupy; and when they came in sight, she blew it up. "Who has dared to do this atrocious act? Speak quickly, that they may meet the punishment they deserve," was the demand of the officer in command. "Know then, 'twas *I*," was the dauntless reply of Mrs. Bratton, "and let the consequences be what they will," she added, "I glory in having frustrated the mischief contemplated by the merciless enemies of my country."

A POOR WOMAN'S OFFERING.

The world is but a word;
Were it all yours, to give it in a breath,
How quickly were it gone!

SHAKSPEARE.

The following anecdote was related, a few years ago, by the Rev. W. S. Plumer, while addressing the Virginia Baptist Education Society. We regret that he did not give the name of the good woman who possessed such commendable zeal for the missionary cause.

"A poor woman had attended a missionary meeting a few years since. Her heart was moved with pity. She looked around on her house and furniture to see what she could spare for the mission. She could think of nothing that would be of any use. At length she thought of her five children, three daughters and two sons. She entered her closet, and consecrated them to the mission. Two of her daughters are now in heathen lands, and the other is preparing to go. Of her sons, one is on his way to India, and the other is preparing for the ministry, and inquiring on the subject of a missionary life."

THE MOTHER OF PRESIDENT JACKSON.

How often has the thought
Of my mourn'd mother brought
Peace to my troubled spirit, and new power
The tempter to repel.
Mother, thou knowest well
That thou has bless'd me since my natal hour.

PIERPONT.

The mother of General Jackson had three children. Their names were Hugh, Robert and Andrew. The last was the youngest and lost his father when an infant. Like the mother of Washington, she was a very pious woman, and strove to glorify God as much in the rearing of her children as in the performance of any other duty. She taught Andrew the leading doctrines of the Bible, in the form of question and answer, from the Westminister catechism; and those lessons he never forgot. In conversation with him some years since, says a writer, "General Jackson spoke of his mother in a manner that convinced me that she never ceased to exert a secret power over him, until his heart was brought into reconciliation with God." This change, however, he did not experience till very late in life—after he had retired from the Presidency. He united with the Presbyterian church near the close of the year 1839, then in his seventy-third year. Just before his death, which occurred in June, 1845, he said to a clergyman, "My lamp of life is nearly out, and the last glimmer is come. I am ready to depart when called. The Bible is true. . . . Upon that sacred volume I rest my hope of eternal salvation, through the merits and blood of our blessed Lord and Saviour, Jesus Christ."

If departed spirits, the saintly and ascended, are permitted to look from their high habitation, upon the scenes of earth, with what holy transport must the mother of Andrew Jackson have beheld the death-bed triumph of her son. The lad whom she early sent to an academy at the Waxhaw meeting-house, hoping to fit him for the ministry, had become a man, and led the hosts of the land through many a scene of conflict and on to a glorious and decisive victory; had filled the highest office in the world, and was now an old man, able, in his last earthly hour, *by the grace of God attending her early, pious instruction*, to challenge death for his sting and to shout "victory" over his opening grave.

THE YOUNG HEROINE OF FORT HENRY.

> Judge me not ungentle,
> Of manner's rude, and insolent of speech,
> If, when the public safety is in question,
> My zeal flows warm and eager from my tongue.
>
> ROWE'S JANE SHORE.

The siege of Fort Henry, at the mouth of Wheeling creek, in Ohio county, Virginia, occurred in September, 1777. Of the historical *fact* most people are aware; yet but few, comparatively, knew how much the little band in the garrison, who held out against thirty or forty times their number of savage assailants, were indebted, for their success, to the courage and self-devotion of a single female.

The Indians kept up a brisk firing from about sunrise till past noon, when they ceased and retired a short distance to the foot of a hill. During the forenoon the little company in the fort had not been idle. Among their number were a few sharp shooters, who had burnt most of the powder on hand to the best advantage. Almost every charge had taken effect; and probably the savages began to see that they were losing numbers at fearful odds, and had doubtless retired for consultation. But they had less occasion for anxiety, just at that time, than the men, women and children in the garrison. As already hinted, the stock of powder was nearly exhausted. There was a keg in a house ten or twelve rods from the gate of the fort, and as soon as the hostilities of the Indians were suspended, the question arose, who shall attempt to seize this prize? Strange to say, every soldier proffered his services, and there was an ardent contention among them for the honor. In the weak state of the garrison, Colonel Shepard, the commander, deemed it advisable that only one person should be spared; and in the midst of the confusion, before any one could be designated, a girl named Elizabeth Zane,* interrupted the debate, saying that her life was not so important, at that time, as any one of the soldier's, and claiming the privilege of performing the contested service. The Colonel would not, at first, listen to her proposal; but she was so resolute, so persevering in her plea, and her argument was so powerful, that he finally suffered the gate to be opened, and she passed out. The Indians saw her before she reached her brother's house, where the keg was deposited; but, for some unknown cause, they did not molest her, until she re-appeared with the article under her arm. Probably divining the nature of her burden, they discharged a volley as she was running towards the

* We learn, from Withers, that Miss Zane has since had two husbands.

The name of the second was Clarke, a resident of Ohio. She was living, not long since, near St. Clairsville.

gate; but the whizzing balls only gave agility to her feet, and herself and the prize were quickly safe within the gate. The result was that the soldiers inspired with enthusiasm by this heroic adventure, fought with renewed courage, and, before the keg of powder was exhausted, the enemy raised the siege

A BENEVOLENT WIDOW

Charity ever
Finds in the act reward.

BEAUMONT AND FLETCHER.

Several years ago, a poor widow had placed a smoked herring,—the last morsel of food she had in the house—on the table for herself and children, when a stranger entered and solicited food, saying that he had had nothing to eat for twenty-four hours. The widow unhesitatingly offered to share the herring with him, remarking, at the same time, "We shall not be forsaken, or suffer deeper for an act of charity."

As the stranger drew near the table and saw the scantiness of the fare, he asked, "And is this all your store? Do you offer a share to one you do not know? Then I never saw charity before. But, madam, do you not wrong your children by giving a part of your morsel to a stranger?" "Ah," said she, with tears in her eyes, "I have a boy, a darling son, somewhere on the face of the wide world, unless Heaven has taken him away; and I only act towards you as I would that others should act towards him. God, who sent manna from heaven, can provide for us as he did for Israel; and how should I this night offend him,

COFFIN DEL.
J.W.ORR N.Y.

if my son should be a wanderer, destitute as you, and he should have provided for him a home, even as poor as this, were I to turn you unrelieved away!"

The stranger whom she thus addressed, was the long absent son to whom she referred; and when she stopped speaking, he sprang from his feet, clasped her in his arms, and exclaimed, "God, indeed, has provided just such a home for your wandering son, *and has given him wealth to reward the goodness of his benefactress.* My mother! O, my mother!" *

---

* Abridged from Cyclopedia of Moral and Religious Anecdotes.

ANNE FITZHUGH.

Who shall find a valiant woman?
The price of her is as things brought from afar.

PROVERBS.

'T is the last
Duty that I can pay to my dear lord.

FLETCHER.

The wife of Colonel William Fitzhugh, of Maryland, while he was absent at one time during the Revolution, was surprised by the news that a party of British soldiers was approaching her house. She instantly collected her slaves; furnished them with such weapons of defence as were at hand; took a quantity of cartridges in her apron, and, herself forming the van, urged her sable subalterns on to meet the foe. Not looking for resistance, the advancing party, on beholding the amazon with her sooty invincibles, hastily turned on their heels and fled.

On a subsequent occasion, a detachment of soldiers marched at midnight to Colonel Fitzhugh's house, which was half a mile from the shore, and near the mouth of the Patuxent river, and knocked at the

COFFIN
J.W. ORR Sc. N.Y.

door. The Colonel demanding who was there, and receiving for reply that the visitants were "friends to King George," told the unwelcome intruders that he was blind and unable to wait upon them, but that his wife would admit them forthwith. Lighting a candle and merely putting on her slippers, she descended, awoke her sons, put pistols in their hands, and, pointing to the back door, told them to flee. She then let the soldiers in at the front door. They inquired for Colonel Fitzhugh, and said he must come down stairs at once and go as a prisoner to New York. She accordingly dressed her husband—forgetting meanwhile, to do as much for herself—and when he had descended, he assured the soldiers that his blindness, and the infirmities of age unfitted him to take care of himself, and that it could hardly be desirable for them to take in charge so decrepit and inoffensive a person. They thought otherwise; and his wife, seeing he must go, took his arm and said she would go too. The officer told her she would be exposed and must suffer, but she persisted in accompanying him, saying that he could not take care of himself, nor, if he could, would she permit a separation.

It was a cold and rainy night, and with the mere protection of a cloak, which the officer took down and threw over her shoulders before leaving the house, she sallied forth with the party. While on the way to their boat, the report of a gun was heard, which the soldiers supposed was the signal of a rebel gathering. They hastened to the boat, where a parole was written out with trembling hand, and placed in the old gentleman's possession. Without even a benediction, he was left on shore with his faithful and fearless companion, who thought but little of her wet feet as she stood and saw the cowardly detachment of British soldiers push off and row away with all their might for safety.

ESTHER GASTON.

> True fortitude is seen in great exploits
> That justice warrants and that wisdom guides.
>
> ADDISON.

> The good alone are great.
>
> BEATTIE.

On the morning of July thirtieth, 1770, Esther Gaston, afterwards the wife of Alexander Walker, hearing the firing at the battle of Rocky Mount, took with her a sister-in-law, and, well mounted, pushed on towards the scene of conflict. They soon met two or three cowardly men, hastening from the field of action. Esther hailed and rebuked then, and finding entreaties would not cause them to retrace their steps, she seized the gun from the hands of one of them, exclaiming, "Give *us* your guns, then, and we will stand in your places." The cowards, abashed, now wheeled, and, in company with the females, hurried on to face the cannon's mouth.

While the strife was still raging, Esther and her companion busied themselves in dressing the wounded and quenching the thirst of the dying. Even their helpless enemies shared in their humane services.

During the battle of Hanging Rock, which occurred the next week, Esther might be seen at Waxhaw church, which was converted for the time into a hospital, administering to the wants of the wounded. As kind as patriotic, with her hands filled with soothing cordials, she was seen, through all her life, knocking at the door of suffering humanity.

REMARKABLE PRESENCE OF MIND AND SELF-POSSESSION.

Were I the monarch of the earth,
And master of the swelling sea,
I would not estimate their worth,
Dear woman, half the price of thee.

GEO. P. MORRIS.

Mr. Ralph Izard, a true "liberty man," resided, during the struggle for Independence, near Dorchester, in South Carolina. He was for awhile aid-de-camp to the commander of the Light Troops, and was an especial object of British hatred. On one occasion, while at home, he came very near falling into the hands of the enemy. A number of British soldiers surrounded his house, and on discovering them he hid himself in the clothes-press. They were confident he was in the house, and having instituted a thorough but ineffectual search, threatened to burn the building, unless his wife would point out his place of concealment. She adroitly evaded answering directly all queries respecting his quarters. They next robbed his wardrobe; seized all the better articles they could find in the house, and even tried to force off her finger-rings. She still remained composed and courageous, yet courteous and urbane, knowing that much, every thing, in fact, depended on her self-control. Her calmness and apparent unconcern led the marauders to conclude that they had been misled in supposing Mr. Izard was in the house ; and at length they departed. He then sprang from his covert, and, rushing out by a back door, crossed the Ashley river and notified the Americans on the opposite side, of the state of things.

Meantime, the ruffians returned to the house, and, strange to say, went directly to the clothes-press. Again disappointed, they retired; but they were soon met by a body of cavalry, handsomely whipped, and all the fine articles belonging to Mr. Izard's wardrobe and house were restored.

THE WIFE OF GOVERNOR GRISWOLD.

Happy the man, and happy sure he was,
So wedded.

HURDIS.

The residence of the first Governor of Connecticut, was at Blackhall, near Long Island Sound. While British ships were lying at anchor in these waters on a certain occasion, a party of marines in pursuit of his Excellency, presented themselves at the door. It being impossible for him to escape by flight, his affectionate and thoughtful wife secreted him in a large new meat barrel or tierce—for although he was somewhat corpulent, he could not vie in physical rotundity with the early and honored Knickerbocker magistrates. He was cleverly packed away in the future home of doomed porkers, just as the soldiers entered and commenced their search. Not finding him readily, they asked his quick-witted wife one or two hard questions, but received no very enlightening answer. The Legislature had convened a day or two before at Hartford, and she intimated that he was or ought to be at the capital. Unsuccessful in their search, the soldiers took their boat and returned to the ship. Before they had reached the latter, his unpacked Honor was on a swift steed, galloping to Gubernatorial head-quarters.

BOLD EXPLOIT OF A YOUNG GIRL.

> Some god impels with courage not thy own.
>
> POPE'S HOMER.

Robert Gibbes was the owner of a splendid mansion on John's Island, a few miles from Charleston, South Carolina, known, during the Revolution, as the "Peaceful Retreat." On his plantation the British encamped on a certain occasion; and the American authorities sent two galleys up the Stono river, on which the mansion stood, to dislodge them. Strict injunctions had been given to the men not to fire on the house, but Mr. Gibbes not being aware of this fact, when the firing commenced, thought it advisable to take his family to some remote place for shelter. They accordingly started in a cold and drizzly rain and in a direction ranging with the fire of the American guns. Shot struck the trees and cut the bushes beside their path for some distance. When about a mile from the mansion, and out of danger, reaching the huts occupied by the negroes on the plantation, Mrs. Gibbes, being chilled and exhausted, was obliged to lie down. Here, when they supposed all were safe, and began to rejoice over their fortunate escape, to their great astonishment, they discovered that a boy named Fenwick, a member of the family, had been left behind.* It was still raining, was very dark, and imminent danger must attend an effort to rescue the lad. And who would risk life in attempting it? The servants refused. Mr. Gibbes was gouty and feeble, and prudence forbade him to again venture out. At length, the oldest daughter of the family, Mary Ann, only thirteen years old, offers to go alone. She hastens off; reaches the house, still in possession of the British; begs the sentinel to let her enter; and though repeatedly repulsed, she doubles the earnestness of her entreaties, and finally gains admittance. She finds the child in the third story; clasps him in her arms; hastens down stairs, and, passing the sentry, flees with the shot whizzing past her head; and herself and the child are soon with the rest of the family.

---

* In addition to her own family, Mrs. Gibbes had the care of the seven orphan children of Mrs. Fenwick, her sister-in-law, and two other children. It is not surprising, that, in the confusion of a sudden flight from the house, one of the number should be left behind.

SUSANNA WRIGHT.

> Work for some good, be it ever so slowly;
> Cherish some flower, be it ever so lowly;
> Labor—all labor is noble and holy.
>
> MRS. OSGOOD.

Susanna Wright removed to this country with her parents from Warrington, in Great Britain, in the year 1714. The family settled in Lancaster county, Pennsylvania. Susanna was then about seventeen. "She never married; but after the death of her father, became the head of her own family, who looked up to her for advice and direction as a parent, for her heart was replete with every kind affection."

She was a remarkable economist of time, for although she had the constant management of a large family, and, at times, of a profitable establishment, she mastered many of the sciences; was a good French, Latin and Italian scholar; assisted neighbors in the settlement of estates, and was frequently consulted as a physician.

"She took great delight in domestic manufacture, and had constantly much of it produced in her family. For many years she attended to the rearing of silk worms, and with the silk, which she reeled and prepared herself, made many articles both of beauty and utility, dying the silk of various colors with indigenous materials. She had at one time upwards of sixty yards of excellent mantua returned to her from Great Britain, where she had sent the raw silk to be manufactured."

This industrious and pious Quakeress, who seems to have possessed all the excellencies defined in Solomon's inventory of the virtuous woman, lived more than four score years, an ornament to her sex and a blessing to the race.

> "There was no need,
> In those good times, of trim callisthenics,—
> And there was less of gadding, and far more
> Of home-bred, heart-felt comfort, rooted strong
> In industry, and bearing such rare fruit
> As wealth may never purchase."

PATRIOTISM OF 1770.

In conduct, as in courage, you excel,
Still first to act what you advise so well.

POPE'S HOMER.

In the early part of February, 1770, the women of Boston publicly pledged themselves to abstain from the use of tea, "as a practical execution of the non-importation agreement of their fathers, husbands and brothers." We are credibly informed, writes the editor of the Boston Gazette of February ninth, "that upwards of one hundred ladies at the north part of the town, have, of their own free will and accord, come into and signed an agreement, not to drink any tea till the Revenue Acts are passed." At that date three hundred matrons had become members of the league.

Three days after the above date, the young women followed the example of their mothers, multitudes signing a document which read as follows: "We, the daughters of those patriots who have and do now appear for the public interest, and, in that, principally regard their posterity,—as such do with pleasure engage with them in denying ourselves the drinking of foreign tea, in hopes to frustrate a plan which tends to deprive the whole community of all that is valuable in life."

Multitudes of females in New York and Virginia, and, if we mistake not, some in other states, made similar movements; and it is easy to perceive, in the tone of those early pledges of self-denial for honor, liberty, country's sake, the infancy of that spirit which, quickly reaching its manhood, planned schemes of resistance to oppression on a more magnanimous scale, and flagged not till a work was done which filled half the world with admiration and the whole with astonishment.

MRS. SPALDING OF GEORGIA.

> Through trials hard as these, how oft are seen
> The tender sex, in fortitude serene.
>
> ANN SEWARD.

Mrs. Spalding was the niece of General Lachlan McIntosh, daughter of Colonel William McIntosh and mother of Major Spalding, of Georgia.

In 1778, after Colonel Campbell took possession of Savannah, Georgia, that section of the country was infested with reckless marauders, and many families fled to avoid their ruthlessness. Mr. Spalding retired with his wife and child to Florida; and twice during the Revolution, she traversed "the two hundred miles between Savannah and St. John's river, in an open boat, with only black servants on board, when the whole country was a desert, without a house to shelter her and her infant son."

The part she bore in the dangers of the Revolution and the anxieties to which she was necessarily subjected, so impaired her health that "many years afterwards it was deemed necessary that she should try the climate of Europe. In January, 1800, she, with her son and his wife, left Savannah in a British ship of twenty guns, with fifty men, built in all points to resemble a sloop of war, without the appearance of a cargo. When they had been out about fifteen days, the captain sent one morning at daylight, to request the presence of two of his gentlemen passengers on deck. A large ship, painted black and showing twelve guns on a side, was seen to windward, running across their course. She was obviously a French privateer. The captain announced that there was no hope of out-sailing her, should their course be altered; nor would there be hope in a conflict, as those ships usually carried one hundred and fifty men. Yet he judged that if no effort were made to shun the privateer, the appearance of his ship might deter from an attack. The gentlemen were of the same opinion. Mr. Spalding, heart-sick at thought of the perilous situation of his wife and mother, and unwilling to trust himself with an interview till the crisis was over, requested the captain to go below and make what preparation he could for their security. After a few minutes' absence the captain returned to describe a most touching scene. Mrs. Spalding had placed her daughter-in-law and the other inmates of the cabin for safety in the two staterooms, filling the berths with the cots and bedding from the outer cabin. She had then taken her station beside the scuttle, which led from the outer cabin to the magazine, with two buckets of water. Having noticed that the two cabin boys were heedless, she had determined herself to keep watch over the magazine. She did so till the danger was past. The captain took in his light sails, hoisted his boarding nettings, opened his ports, and stood on upon his course. The privateer waited till the ship was within a mile, then fired a gun to windward, and stood on her way. This ruse preserved the ship."*

---

* Mrs. Ellet.

COURAGEOUS ACT OF MRS. DILLARD.

Thy country, glorious, brave and fair,
Thine all of life — . . .
Her name alone thy heart's depths stirred,
And filled thy soul with war-like pride.
SARA J. CLARKE.

The day before the battle at the Green Spring, in the Spartanburg district, South Carolina, Colonel Clarke, of the Georgia volunteers, with about two hundred men, stopped at the house of Captain Dillard and were cordially welcomed to a good supply of refreshments. In the evening of the same day, Colonel Ferguson and another officer named Dunlap, with a party of tories, arrived at the same house and inquired of the mistress, if Colonel Clarke had been there, to which question she gave a direct and honest answer. He then inquired in regard to the time of Clarke's departure and the number of his men. She could not guess their number, but said they had been gone a long time. She was then ordered to get supper, which she did, though in a less hospitable spirit than she had prepared the previous meal. While at work, she overheard some of the conversation of the officers, by which she learned that they were bent on surprising Colonel Clarke, and would start for that purpose when supper was dispatched. As soon as the food was on the table, Mrs. Dillard hurried out at the back door, bridled a horse that stood in the stable, and mounting without saddle, rode till nearly daylight before reaching the Green Spring where Clarke had encamped, and where he was to be attacked by Ferguson, at the break of day or sooner, as she had learned before starting.

She had just aroused the whigs and notified them of their danger, when a detachment of two hundred picked, mounted men, commanded by Dunlap, rushed into the camp. They found their intended victims ready for the charge; were quickly driven out of the camp, and glad to escape by flight. Thus, fortunately for the friends of freedom, ended this battle, which, but for the daring of a single patriotic woman, would doubtless have resulted in the annihilation of the little band of Georgia volunteers.

PHOEBE PHILLIPS.

> The secret pleasure of a generous act
> Is the great mind's great bribe.
>
> DRYDEN.

Phoebe Foxcroft, afterwards the wife of Samuel Phillips, the joint founder, with his uncle, of the academy at Andover, Massachusetts, was a native of Cambridge, in the same state. Reared beneath the shades of "Old Harvard" and being the daughter of a man of wealth and high respectability, it is almost needless to say that she was well educated and highly refined. To mental attainments she added the finishing charm of female character, glowing piety. The last forty years or more of her life were passed at Andover, where, after the death of her husband, she assisted in founding the celebrated Theological seminary. She died in 1818.

It is said that she was accustomed, for years, to make the health of every pupil in the academy a subject of personal interest. Her attentions to their wants were impartial and incalculably beneficial. To those that came from remote towns, and were thus deprived of parental oversight, she acted the part of a faithful mother.

Affectionate, kind, generous, watchful, as a christian guardian; she was unbending, self-sacrificing and "zealous, yet modest," as a patriot. During the seven years' struggle for freedom, she frequently sat up till midnight or past, preparing bandages and scraping lint for the hospitals and making garments for the ragged soldiers.

An offender of justice was once passing her house on his way to the whipping-post, when a boy, who observed him from her window, could not withhold a tear. He tried to conceal his emotion, but Mrs. Phillips saw the pearl drop of pity, and while a kindred drop fell from her own eyes, she said to him, with much emphasis and as though laying down some golden maxim—"When you become a law maker, examine the subject of corporeal punishment, and see if it is not unnatural, vindictive and productive of much evil." She was very discriminating, and could detect talent as well as tears; and addressed the lad with a premonition that he was destined to become a legislator—which was indeed the case. Elected to the assembly of the state, with the sacred command of his early and revered mentor impressed on his memory, he early called the attention of that body to the subject of corporeal punishment; had the statute book revised and the odious law, save in capital offences, expunged, and the pleasure of announcing the fact to the original suggestor of the movement.

WORTHY EXAMPLE OF A POOR WIDOW.

> Howe'er it be, it seems to me
> 'Tis only noble to be good;
> Kind hearts are more than coronets,
> And simple faith than Norman blood.
>
> TENNYSON.

The following article was communicated to the Christian Watchman and Reflector, of Boston, for January thirtieth, 1851. The facts are given without coloring or embellishment. The subject of the article has gone to the grave, but the influence of her exemplary life has not ceased to be felt. Her

> "Speaking dust
> Has more of life than half its breathing moulds."

Some twenty years since, the writer became pastor of a church in the town of B. A few weeks after my settlement, I called at the humble dwelling of a poor widow, with whom I had already become somewhat acquainted. Having been apprised of the high estimation in which she was held by the church of which she was a member, for her cheerful and consistent piety, an interesting and profitable interview was anticipated. I had been seated but a few moments when she placed in my hand one dollar, and proceeded, by way of explanation, to make the following statements, which I give as nearly as possible in her own language:

"Before you came among us, our church and people where in a very depressed and disheartened condition. For two or three Sabbaths we had no religious services during the day. How sad to be as sheep without a shepherd, and to have the house of God closed on his holy day! If the Lord would only send us a pastor, I felt willing to do any thing in my power to aid in sustaining him. But then the thought occurred to me, What can *you* do, a poor widow, with four small children to support, and your house rent to pay? It is quite as much as you can do to meet necessary expenses. For a moment I was sad; but my mind still dwelt upon the subject, until finally this plan occurred to me: 'God has blessed you with excellent health, and you can sit up and work between the hours of nine and eleven or twelve o'clock at night; and what you thus earn you can give for that object.' I was at once relieved, and resolved before the Lord that, if he would send us a pastor, I would immediately commence my labors, and do what I could to aid in sustaining and encouraging him. I felt that now I could pray consistently, as I was willing to do my duty. With a faith and fervor to which I had before been a stranger, I besought the Lord speedily to favor us with an under-shepherd; and soon you came here to preach for us. I believed God sent you; and although at first you had no idea of remaining, I never doubted that you would become our pastor. As soon as you had accepted the call of the church, I began to work in accordance with my vow, and that dollar is the result of my earning, the last four weeks. And O, you would rejoice with me, could you know how much I have enjoyed these silent hours of night, when my children around me are wrapt in slumber, and all is as the stillness of the grave. The Lord has been with me continually, and I have had uninterrupted communion with him. When God had given us a pastor, I felt I must pray for a blessing to attend his labors among us; and, often have I been so impressed with the importance of a revival of religion, and the conversion of my children, and the people of this place, that I have been obliged to leave my work, and kneel down before my Maker, and earnestly plead with him that his Spirit may accomplish this work. Even after I had retired to rest, I have sometimes been obliged to arise and pray that he would save the souls of this people. And, blessed be his holy name, he has listened to prayer for this object also. When I heard of the numbers who attended the religious inquiry meeting, and the hopeful conversion of some to God, I felt I could say, 'This is the Lord, I have waited for him;' and I believe he will do greater things than these in our midst. Thus has God blessed one of the most unworthy of all his creatures; and I have often been led to sing, while I have been laboring here, lowly as is my condition,

'I would not change my blest estate,
With all that earth calls rich or great;
And, while my faith can keep her hold,
I envy not the sinner's gold.' "

My attention had been absorbed with this interesting and affecting narrative; nor had I any inclination to interrupt it with remarks of my own. I now thought I could read the secret of the apparent success which had attended my labors in so short a time. As soon as I could recover from my emotions, I said to her, I am grateful for your prayers and this proffered donation; but, as my parish affords me a competent support, I can on no account feel at liberty to appropriate to my own private use the money thus earned. No; you shall have the additional satisfaction, while you are toiling at these unseasonable hours of night, of knowing that what you place in my hands shall be sacredly devoted to the cause of Christian benevolence, which I am sure you ardently love. With this she expressed herself satisfied; and continued her toils and prayers.

It may be asked, What was the result? The answer is recorded with pleasure, and, I trust, with gratitude to God. Besides punctually attending all the meetings of the church, and laboring much in private for the eternal welfare of souls; besides supporting her family with more ease than formerly, as she stated to her pastor, at the close of the first year, and paying her assessments in several charitable societies to which she belonged, and also contributing something whenever a public collection was taken for benevolent objects; in addition to all this, she had placed in my hands ten dollars and a half, which was appropriated as stated above. Her donations for objects of religious charity must have amounted to at least *twelve dollars* during that year, which, it is presumed, exceeded the amount given for similar objects by any other member of the church, although quite a number possessed a comfortable share of wealth. It may be thought that she was engaged in some business which yielded a handsome profit to reward her toils. But no; her business was shoe-binding, not then by any means very profitable. And who, with her disposition and spirit, could not do something to aid the cause of God? But what she earned and gave was not all. Her prayers, it is believed, had secured for the church a pastor, and been the means, with others, of the commencement of a revival of religion, which continued to prevail to a greater or less extent, for three successive years, during which time a large number were hopefully converted and added to the church: and among them several of her older children, who were away from home

ELIZABETH ESTAUGH.

> A perfect woman, nobly planned,
> To warn, to comfort and command;
> And yet a spirit still, and bright
> With something of an angel light.
>
> WORDSWORTH.

Elizabeth Haddon was the oldest daughter of John Haddon, a well educated and wealthy, yet humble, Quaker, of London. She had two sisters, both of whom, with herself, received the highest finish of a practical education. Elizabeth possessed uncommon strength of mind, earnestness, energy and originality of character, and a heart overflowing with the kindest and warmest feelings. A single anecdote of her childhood, told by Mrs. Child, will illustrate the nobleness of nature which characterized her life:

"At one time, she asked to have a large cake baked, because she wanted to invite some little girls. All her small funds were expended for oranges and candy on this occasion. When the time arrived, her father and mother were much surprised to see her lead in six little ragged beggars. They were, however, too sincerely humble and religious to *express* any surprise. They treated the forlorn little ones very tenderly, and freely granted their daughter's request to give them some of her books and playthings at parting. When they had gone, the good mother quietly said, 'Elizabeth, why didst thou invite strangers, instead of thy schoolmates?' There was a heavenly expression in her eye, as she looked up earnestly, and answered, 'Mother, I wanted to invite *them*, they looked *so* poor.'"

When eleven years of age, she accompanied her parents to the Yearly Meeting of the Friends, where she heard, among other preachers, a very young man named John Estaugh, with whose manner of presenting divine truth she was particularly pleased. Many of his words were treasured in her memory. At the age of seventeen she made a profession of religion, uniting herself with the Quakers.

During her early youth, William Penn visited the house of her father, and greatly amused her by describing his adventures with the Indians. From that time she became interested in the emigrant Quakers, and early began to talk of coming to America. Her father at length purchased a tract of land in New Jersey, with the view of emigrating, but his affairs took a new turn, and he made up his mind to remain in his native land. This decision disappointed Elizabeth. She had cherished the conviction that it was her duty to come to this country; and when, at length, her father, who was unwilling that any of his property should lie unimproved, offered the tract of land in New Jersey to any relative who would settle upon it, she promptly agreed to accept of the proffered estate. Willing that their child should follow in the path of duty, at the end of three months, and after much prayer, the parents consented to let Elizabeth join "the Lord's people in the New World."

Accordingly, early in the spring of 1700, writes Mrs. Child, in whose sweet language, slightly condensed, the rest of the narrative is told, arrangements were made for her departure, and all things were provided that the abundance of wealth, or the ingenuity of affection, could devise.

A poor widow of good sense and discretion accompanied her, as friend and housekeeper, and two trusty men servants, members of the Society of Friends. Among the many singular manifestations of strong faith and religious zeal, connected with the settlement of this country, few are more remarkable than the voluntary separation of this girl of eighteen years old from a wealthy home and all the pleasant associations of childhood, to go to a distant and thinly inhabited country, to fulfill what she considered a religious duty. And the humble, self-sacrificing faith of the parents, in giving up their child, with such reverend tenderness for the promptings of her own conscience, has in it something sublimely beautiful, if we look at it in its own pure light. The parting took place with more love than words can express, and yet without a tear on either side. Even during the long and tedious voyage, Elizabeth never wept. She preserved a martyr-like cheerfulness and serenity to the end.

The house prepared for her reception stood in a clearing of the forest, three miles from any other dwelling. She arrived in June, when the landscape was smiling in youthful beauty; and it seemed to her as if the arch of heaven was never before so clear and bright, the carpet of the earth never so verdant. As she sat at her window and saw evening close in upon her in that broad forest home, and heard, for the first time, the mournful notes of the whippo-wil and the harsh scream of the jay in the distant woods, she was oppressed with a sense of vastness, of infinity, which she never before experienced, not even on the ocean. She remained long in prayer, and when she lay down to sleep beside her matron friend, no words were spoken between them. The elder, overcome with fatigue, soon sank into a peaceful slumber; but the young enthusiast lay long awake, listening to the lone voice of the whippo-wil complaining to the night. Yet, notwithstanding this prolonged wakefulness, she arose early and looked out upon the lovely landscape. The rising sun pointed to the tallest trees with his golden finger, and was welcomed with a gush of song from a thousand warblers. The poetry in Elizabeth's soul, repressed by the severe plainness of her education, gushed up like a fountain. She dropped on her knees, and, with an outburst of prayer, exclaimed fervently, "Oh, Father, very beautiful hast thou made this earth! How bountiful are thy gifts, O Lord!"

To a spirit less meek and brave, the darker shades of the picture would have obscured these cheerful gleams; for the situation was lonely and the inconveniences innumerable. But Elizabeth easily triumphed over all obstacles, by practical good sense and the quick promptings of her ingenuity. She was one of those clear strong natures, who always have a definite aim in view, and who see at once the means best suited to the end. Her first inquiry was what grain was best adapted to the soil of her farm; and being informed that rye would yield best, "Then I shall eat rye bread," was her answer. But when winter came, and the gleaming snow spread its unbroken silence over hill and plain, was it not dreary then? It would have been dreary indeed to one who entered upon this mode of life from mere love of novelty, or a vain desire to do something extraordinary. But the idea of extended usefulness, which had first lured this remarkable girl into a path so unusual, sustained her through all trials. She was too busy to be sad, and leaned too trustingly on her Father's hand to be doubtful of her way. The neighboring Indians soon loved her as a friend, for they found her always truthful, just, and kind. From their teachings, she added much to her knowledge of simple medicines. So efficient was her skill and so prompt her sympathy, that for many miles round, if man, woman, or child were alarmingly ill, they were sure to send for Elizabeth Haddon; and wherever she went, her observing mind gathered some hint for the improvement of farm or dairy. Her house and heart were both large; and as her residence was on the way to the Quaker meeting-house in Newtown, it became a place of universal resort to Friends from all parts of the country traveling that road, as well as an asylum for benighted wanderers.

The winter was drawing to a close, when late one evening, the sound of sleigh-bells was heard, and the crunching of snow beneath the hoofs of horses, as they passed into the barn-yard gate. The arrival of travelers was too common an occurrence to excite or disturb the well-ordered family.

Great logs were piled in the capacious chimney, and the flames blazed up with a crackling warmth, when two strangers entered. In the younger, Elizabeth instantly recognized John Estaugh, whose preaching had so deeply impressed her at eleven years of age. This was almost like a glimpse of home—her dear old English home! She stepped forward with more than usual cordiality, saying:

"Thou art welcome, Friend Estaugh; the more so for being entirely unexpected."

"And I am glad to see thee, Elizabeth," he replied with a friendly shake of the hand. "It was not until after I landed in America, that I heard the Lord had called thee hither before me; but I remember thy father told me how often thou hadst played the settler in the woods, when thou wast quite a little girl."

"I am but a child still," she replied, smiling.

"I trust thou art," he rejoined; "and as for these strong impressions in childhood, I have heard of many cases where they seemed to be prophecies sent of the Lord. When I saw thy father in London, I had even then an indistinct idea that I might sometime be sent to America on a religious visit."

"And hast thou forgotten, Friend John, the ear of Indian corn which my father begged of thee for me? I can show it to thee now. Since then I have seen this grain in perfect growth; and a goodly plant it is, I assure thee. See," she continued, pointing to many bunches of ripe corn, which hung in their braided husks against the walls of the ample kitchen: "all that, and more, came from a single ear, no bigger than the one thou didst give my father. May the seed sown by thy ministry be as fruitful!"

"Amen," replied both the guests.

The next morning, it was discovered that snow had fallen during the night in heavy drifts, and the roads were impassable. Elizabeth, according to her usual custom, sent out men, oxen and sledges, to open pathways for several poor families, and for households whose inmates were visited by illness. In this duty, John Estaugh and his friend joined heartily and none of the laborers worked harder than they. When he returned, glowing from this exercise, she could not but observe that the excellent youth had a goodly countenance. It was not physical beauty; for of that he had little. It was that cheerful, child-like, out-beaming honesty of expression, which we not unfrequently see in Germans, who, above all nations, look as if they carried a crystal heart within their manly bosoms.

Two days after, when Elizabeth went to visit her

patients, with a sled-load of medicines and provisions, John asked permission to accompany her. There, by the bedside of the aged and the suffering, she saw the clear sincerity of his countenance warmed with rays of love, while he spoke to them words of kindness and consolation; and there she heard his pleasant voice modulate itself into deeper tenderness of expression, when he took little children in his arms.

The next First day, which we call the Sabbath, the whole family attended Newtown meeting; and there John Estaugh was gifted with an out-pouring of the spirit in his ministry, which sank deep into the hearts of those who listened to him. Elizabeth found it so marvellously applicable to the trials and temptations of her own soul, that she almost deemed it was spoken on purpose for her. She said nothing of this, but she pondered upon it deeply. Thus did a few days of united duties make them more thoroughly acquainted with each other, than they could have been by years of fashionable intercourse.

The young preacher soon after bade farewell, to visit other meetings in Pennsylvania and New Jersey. Elizabeth saw him no more until the May following, when he stopped at her house to lodge, with numerous other Friends, on their way to the Quarterly Meeting at Salem. In the morning, quite a cavalcade started from her hospitable door, on horseback; for wagons were then unknown in Jersey. John Estaugh, always kindly in his impulses, busied himself with helping a lame and very ugly old woman, and left his hostess to mount her horse as she could. Most young women would have felt slighted; but in Elizabeth's noble soul the quiet deep tide of feeling rippled with an inward joy. "He is always kindest to the poor and the neglected," thought she; "verily he *is* a good youth." She was leaning over the side of her horse, to adjust the buckle of the girth, when he came up on horseback, and inquired if anything was out of order. She thanked him, with slight confusion of manner, and a voice less calm than her usual utterance. He assisted her to mount, and they trotted along leisurely behind the procession of guests, speaking of the soil and climate of this new country, and how wonderfully the Lord had here provided a home for his chosen people. Presently the girth began to slip, and the saddle turned so much on one side, that Elizabeth was obliged to dismount. It took some time to re-adjust it, and when they again started, the company were out of sight. There was brighter color than usual in the maiden's cheeks, and unwonted radiance in her mild deep eyes. After a short silence, she said, in a voice slightly tremulous, "Friend John, I have a subject of importance on my mind, and one which nearly interests thee. I am strongly impressed that the Lord has sent thee to me as a partner for life. I tell thee my impression frankly, but not without calm and deep reflection; for matrimony is a holy relation, and should be entered into with all sobriety. If thou hast no light on the subject, wilt thou gather into the stillness, and reverently listen to thy own inward revealings? Thou art to leave this part of the country to-morrow, and not knowing when I should see the again, I felt moved to tell thee what lay upon my mind."

The young man was taken by surprise. Though accustomed to that suppression of emotion which characterizes his religious sect, the color went and came rapidly in his face, for a moment; but he soon became calmer, and replied, "This thought is new to me, Elizabeth; and I have no light thereon. Thy company has been right pleasant to me, and thy countenance ever reminds me of William Penn's title page, 'Innocency with her open face.' I have seen thy kindness to the poor, and the wise management of thy household. I have observed, too, that thy warm-heartedness is tempered by a most excellent discretion, and that thy speech is ever sincere. Assuredly, such is the maiden I would ask of the Lord, as a most precious gift; but I never thought of this connexion with thee. I came to this country solely on a religious visit, and it might distract my mind to entertain this subject at present. When I have discharged the duties of my mission, we will speak further."

"It is best so," rejoined the maiden; "but there is one thing disturbs my conscience. Thou hast spoken of my true speech; and yet, Friend John, I have deceived thee a little, even now, while we conferred together on a subject so serious. I know not from what weakness the temptation came; but I will not hide it from thee. I allowed thee to suppose, just now, that I was fastening the girth of my horse securely; but, in plain truth, I was loosening the girth, John, that the saddle might slip, and give me an excuse to fall behind our friends; for I thought thou wouldst be kind enough to come and ask if I needed thy services."

They spoke no further concerning their union; but when he returned to England, in July, he pressed her hand affectionately, as he said, "Farewell, Elizabeth. If it be the Lord's will, I shall return to thee soon."

In October, he returned to America, and they were soon married, at Newtown meeting, according to the simple form of the Society of Friends. Neither of them made any change of dress for the occasion, and there was no wedding feast. Without the aid of priest or magistrate, they took each other by the hand, and, in the presence of witnesses, calmly and solemnly promised to be kind and faithful to each other. The wedded pair quietly returned to their happy home, with none to intrude upon those sacred hours of human life, when the heart most needs to be left alone with its own deep emotions.

During the long period of their union, she three times crossed the Atlantic, to visit her aged parents, and he occasionally left her for a season, when called abroad to preach. These temporary separations were felt as a cross, but the strong-hearted woman always cheerfully gave him up to follow his own convictions of duty. In 1742, he parted from her, to go on a religious visit 'to Tortola, in the West Indies. He died there, in the sixty-seventh year of his age. She published a religious tract of his, to which is prefixed a preface entitled "Elizabeth Estaugh's testimony concerning her beloved husband, John Estaugh." In this preface, she says, "Since it pleased Divine Providence so highly to favor me, with being the near companion of this dear worthy, I must give some small account of him. Few, if any, in a married state, ever lived in sweeter harmony than we did. He was a pattern of moderation in all things; not lifted up with any enjoyments, nor cast down at disappointments; a man endowed with many good gifts, which rendered him very agreeable to his friends, and much more to me, his wife, to whom his memory is most dear and precious."

Elizabeth survived her excellent husband twenty years, useful and honored to the last. The monthly Meeting of Haddonfield, in a published testimonial, speak of her thus: "She was endowed with great natural abilities, which, being sanctified by the spirit of Christ, were much improved; whereby she became qualified to act in the affairs of the church, and was a serviceable member, having been clerk to the women's meeting nearly fifty years, greatly to their satisfaction. She was a sincere sympathizer with the afflicted, of a benevolent disposition, and in distributing to the poor, was desirous to do it in a way most profitable and durable to them, and, if possible, not to let the right hand know what the left did. Though in a state of affluence as to this world's wealth, she was an example of plainness and moderation. Her heart and house were open to her friends, whom to entertain seemed one of her greatest pleasures. Prudently cheerful, and well knowing the value of friendship, she was careful not to wound it herself, nor to encourage others in whispering supposed failings or weaknesses. Her last illness brought great bodily pain, which she bore with much calmness of mind and sweetness of spirit. She departed this life as one falling asleep, full of days, like unto a shock of corn, fully ripe."

The town of Haddonfield, in New Jersey, took its name from her; and the tradition concerning her courtship is often repeated by some patriarch among the Quakers.

Her medical skill is so well remembered, that the old nurses of New Jersey still recommend Elizabeth Estaugh's salve as the "sovereignest thing on earth."

KATE MOORE.

From lowest place when virtuous things proceed,
The place is dignified by the doer's deed.
SHAKSPEARE.

Kate Moore is the daughter of Captain Moore, keeper of the Light House on Fairweather Island, sixty miles north of the city of New York, and about half way between the harbors of Black Rock and Bridgeport, Connecticut. The island is about half a mile from shore and contains five acres of land. On that little, secluded spot Captain Moore has resided nearly a quarter of a century, and has reared a family of five children, of whom Kate is the heroine.

Disasters frequently occur to vessels which are driven round Montauk Point, and sometimes in the Sound, when they are homeward bound; and at such times she is always on the alert. She has so thoroughly cultivated the sense of hearing, that she can distinguish amid the howling storm, the shrieks of the drowning mariners, and thus direct a boat, which she has learned to manage most dexterously, in the darkest night, to the spot where a fellow mortal is perishing

Though well educated and refined, she possesses none of the affected delicacy which characterizes too many town-bred misses; but, adapting herself to the peculiar exigences of her father's humble yet honorable calling, she is ever ready to lend a helping hand, and shrinks from no danger, if duty points that way. In the gloom and terror of the stormy night, amid perils at all hours of the day, and all seasons of the year, she has launched her barque on the threatening waves; and has assisted her aged and feeble father in saving the lives of twenty-one persons during the last fifteen years! Such conduct, like that of Grace Darling, to whom Kate Moore has been justly compared, needs no comment; it stamps its moral at once and indelibly upon the heart of every reader.

CAPTIVITY OF MRS. ROWLANDSON.

> Through sorrowing and suffering thou hast pass'd,
> To show us what a woman true may be.
>
> LOWELL.

Mrs. Mary Rowlandson, the wife of the Rev. Joseph Rowlandson, was taken prisoner by the Indians at Lancaster, Massachusetts, on the tenth of February, 1676, and remained in captivity till the third of the following May. The details of her sufferings, as related by herself, are too painful for many persons to read; but she bore them with such Christian fortitude, that nothing short of a brief account of her captivity would seem to be excusable in a work like this.

The day after the destruction of Lancaster, the Indians began their march; and Mrs. Rowlandson carried her infant till her strength failed and she fell. She was then furnished with a horse, without a saddle. Attempting to ride, she again fell. Towards night it began to snow; and gathering a few sticks, she made a fire. Sitting beside it on the snow, she held her child in her arms through the long and dismal night. For three or four days she had no sustenance but water; nor did her child share any better for nine days. During this time it was constantly in her arms or lap. At the end of that period, the frost of death crept into its eyes, and she was forced to relinquish it to be disposed of by the unfeeling sextons of the forest.

After its burial, Mrs. Rowlandson was sold by her Narraganset captor to a Sagamore named Quanopin, by which transfer she found in her new master's wife "a most uncomfortable mistress." Soon afterwards the Indians went on an expedition to Medfield, and on their return one of them gave her a Bible — her best friend and great support during her sufferings and trials. She retained it during her captivity.

The party of Indians with whom she continued, remained for some time near Petersham, in Worcester county. At length, hearing a report that the pale faces were in pursuit of them, they hastily decamped and continued their march till they crossed the Connecticut river, in the neighborhood of Gill or Bernardston. There Mrs. Rowlandson came in contact with the great chief, Philip, who treated her civilly and even politely. Ere long the Indians re-crossed the Connecticut, and returned into Worcester county. During this part of her pilgrimage, writes President Dwight, whose concise narrative we have followed, "Mrs. Rowlandson went through almost every suffering but death. She was beaten, kicked, turned out of doors, refused food, insulted in the grossest manner, and at times almost starved.

Nothing but experience can enable us to conceive what must be the hunger of a person, by whom the discovery of six acorns, and two chestnuts, was regarded as a rich prize. At times, in order to make her miserable, they announced to her the death of her husband and her children. One of the savages, of whom she enquired concerning her son, told her that his master had, at a time which he specified, killed and roasted him; that himself had eaten a piece of him, as big as his two fingers, and that it was delicious meat. On various occasions they threatened to kill her. Occasionally, but for short intervals only, she was permitted to see her children; and suffered her own anguish over again in their miseries. She was also obliged, while hardly able to walk, to carry a heavy burden over hills, and through rivers, swamps, and marshes; and that in the most inclement seasons. These evils were repeated daily; and, to crown them all, she was daily saluted with the most barbarous and insolent accounts of the burning and slaughter, the tortures and agonies, inflicted by them upon her countrymen. It is to be remembered that Mrs. Rowlandson was tenderly and delicately educated, and as ill fitted to encounter these distresses as persons who have received such an education, now are in this and other countries.

"There was, however, among the savages a marked difference of character. Some of them, both men and women, treated her with kindness. None of them exhibited so much insolence to her as her mistress. This woman felt all the haughtiness of rank, as much as if she had been a European or Asiatic princess; and spent almost as much time in powdering her hair, painting her face, and adorning herself with ear-rings, bracelets, and other ornaments, a part of their plunder from the English."

The captivity of Mrs. Rowlandson was terminated through the agency of Mr. Hoar, of Concord, Massachusetts. Under a commission from the Government he redeemed her for about eighty dollars, which sum was contributed by a Mr. Usher and some female friends in Boston.

MRS. BOZARTH.

To weakness strength succeeds, and power
From frailty springs.

PARK BENJAMIN.

There's no impossibility to him
Who stands prepared to conquer every hazard.

MRS. HALE.

In the spring of 1779, while two or three neighboring families, had, from fear, collected at the house of Mrs. Bozarth, in Green county, Pennsylvania, the little company was one day attacked by Indians. The children, who were playing without, first discovered the foe, and, giving the alarm, had not time to get within doors before they were overtaken, and began to fall beneath the tomahawk. The first man who stepped to the door when the alarm was heard, was shot, and fell back; and before the door could be closed, an Indian leaped over him into the house. The other man in the house caught the savage and threw him on the bed. He then called for a knife, but Mrs. Bozarth, being unable to find one, seized an axe and instantly dispatched the bold assailant. Another Indian now rushed in, and shot at and wounded the man before he was off the bed. Mrs Bozarth gave this second intruder several blows, when his cries brought a third to the door. Him she killed as he entered. The wounded savage was then dragged out; the door again closed and fastened; and, through the assistance of the wounded man, Mrs. Bozarth was able to keep out the rest of the murderous assailants until relieved by the arrival of friends.

THE HEROINE OF STEEL CREEK.

Here and there some stern, high patriot stood.
BYRON.

The subject of the following anecdote was the mother of eleven sons. Most of them were soldiers and some were officers in the war of the Revolution. Her residence was in Mechlenburg county, near Steel creek, North Carolina.

When Lord Cornwallis heard of the defeat of Ferguson at King's Mountain,* fearing an attack of his rear at Camden, he collected his forces and retreated towards Winnsboro. While on this march, his whole army halted for the night on the plantation of Robert Wilson. Cornwallis and his staff took possession of the house, and made an unstinted levy on the hospitality of the good lady. By asking such questions as a British lord would, under the circumstances, feel at liberty to propound, the General learned, in the course of the evening, that the husband of Mrs. Wilson, and some of her sons, were then his prisoners in Camden jail. Her kindness

* October seventh, 1780.

and urbanity led him to think that perhaps *she* was a friend to the Crown; and, after some preliminary remarks, intended to prepare her mind, for the leading consideration which he wished to enforce upon it, he at length addressed her as follows:

"Madam, your husband and your son are my prisoners; the fortune of war may soon place others of your sons—perhaps all your kinsmen, in my power. Your sons are young, aspiring and brave. In a good cause, fighting for a generous and powerful king, such as George III, they might hope for rank, honor and wealth. If you could but induce your husband and sons to leave the rebels, and take up arms for their lawful sovereign, I would almost pledge myself that they shall have rank and consideration in the British army. If you, madàm, will pledge yourself to induce them to do so, I will immediately order their discharge."

"I have seven sons," Mrs. Wilson replied, "who are now, or have been, bearing arms—indeed my seventh son, Zaccheus, who is only fifteen years old, I yesterday assisted to get ready to go and join his brothers in Sumter's army. Now, sooner than see one of my family turn back from the glorious enterprise, I would take these boys—pointing to three or four small sons—and with them would myself enlist, under Sumter's standard, and show my husband and sons how to fight, and, if necessary, to die for their country!"

Colonel Tarleton was one of the listeners to this colloquy, and when Mrs. Wilson had finished her reply, he said to Cornwallis: "Ah! General! I think you've got into a hornet's nest! Never mind, when we get to Camden, I'll take good care that old Robin Wilson never comes back again!" We may add that Tarleton's threat was never executed. Mr. Wilson and his worthy companion lived to old age, and died at Steel creek just before the war of 1812

BENEVOLENCE OF A COLORED WOMAN.

Great minds, like Heaven, are pleased in doing gooa.

ROWE.

The following anecdote is obtained from a reliable source. Did the spirit which pervaded the heart of its subject, thoroughly permeate the churches, the great work of carrying the Gospel to every nation, would soon be accomplished.

"In one of the eastern counties of New York lived a colored female, who was born a slave, but she was made free by the act gradually abolishing slavery in that state. She had no resources except such as she obtained by her own labor. On one occasion she carried to her pastor *forty dollars:* she told him that she wished him, with two dollars of this sum to procure for her a seat in his church; eighteen dollars she desired to be given to the American Board; and the remaining twenty dollars she requested him to divide among other benevolent societies according to his discretion."

REBECCA EDWARDS.

> Honor being then above life, dishonor must
> Be worse than death; for fate can strike but one.
> Reproach doth reach whole families.
>
> CARTWRIGHT'S SIEGE.

At the celebration of our national Independence, in 1797, the orator of the society of the Cincinnati of South Carolina, paid the following tribute to the magnanimity of Mrs. Rebecca Edwards:—"The Spartan mother, on delivering his shield to her son departing for the army, nobly bade him 'return with it or on it.' The sentiment was highly patriotic, but surely not superior to that which animated the bosom of the distinguished female of our own state, who, when the British officer presented the mandate which arrested her sons as objects of retaliation, less sensible of private affection than attached to her honor and the interest of her country, stifled the tender feelings of the mother, and heroically bade them despise the threats of their enemies, and steadfastly persist to support the glorious cause in which they had engaged—that if the threatened sacrifice should follow, they would carry a parent's blessing, and the good opinion of every virtuous citizen along with them to the grave: but if from the frailty of human nature—of the possibility of which she would not suffer an idea to enter her mind—they were disposed to temporize, and exchange their liberty for safety, they must forget her as a mother, nor subject her to the misery of ever beholding them again." *

* American Anecdotes, vol. 2, p. 11.

"THE BEAUTIFUL REBEL."

Trembling and fear
Are to her unknown.

SIR WALTER SCOTT.

The maiden name of Mrs. Lewis Morris was Ann Elliott. She was born at Maccabee, in 1762, and died in New York, in 1848. She was a firm and fearless patriot, and when the city of Charleston, South Carolina, was in possession of the red coats, she wore thirteen small plumes in her bonnet. She had so fair a face, so graceful a form and so patriotic a spirit, as to be called "the beautiful rebel." An English officer fell in love with her and offered to join the Americans, if she would favor his proposals. She ordered the friend who interceded for him to say to him, "that to her former want of esteem, was added scorn for a man capable of betraying his sovereign for selfish interest."

While she was engaged to Colonel Morris and he was on a visit one time at Maccabee, the house was suddenly surrounded by Black Dragoons. They were in pursuit of the Colonel, and it was impossi ble for him to escape by flight. What to do he knew not, but, quick as thought, she ran to the window, opened it, and, fearlessly putting her head out, in a composed yet firm manner, demanded what was wanted. The reply was, "We want the —— rebel." "Then go," said she, "and look for him in the American army," adding "How dare you disturb a family under the protection of both armies!" She was so cool, self-possessed, firm and resolute as to triumph over the dragoons, who left without entering the house

HARRIET B. STEWART.

Men sacrifice others — women themselves.
MRS. S. C. HALL.

Harriet Bradford Tiffany, afterwards the wife of the Rev. Charles S. Stewart, was born near Stamford, Connecticut, on the fourth of June, 1798. She lost her father when she was a small child, and till 1815, passed most of her time with an uncle, in Albany. At this date, an older sister married and settled in Cooperstown, and consequently Harriet took up her abode in that place. She became the subject of renewing grace in the summer of 1819; was married on the third of June, 1822, and sailed with her husband and nearly thirty other missionaries, all bound to the same field, on the nineteenth of November following. This little, heroic band, that, by the help of God, have since been mainly instrumental in making the Sandwich islands blossom like a rose, arrived at Honolulu, in Oahu, on the twenty seventh of April, 1823.

Mrs. Stewart left a beautiful town in a thriving part of the Empire State; tempting luxuries; a brilliant circle, and many endearing friends; but she had embarked in a glorious enterprise foı Christ's sake, and, hence, she settled down in a little log hut, in the town of Lahaiua, three days' sail from Oahu, contented and happy. On the first day of January 1824, she wrote as follows: "It is now fifteen months since I bade adieu to the dear valley which con tains much, very much, that is most dear to me; but since the day I parted from it, my spirits have been uniformly good. Sometimes, it is true, a cloud ot tender recollections passes over me, obscuring, for a moment, my mental vision, and threatening a day of darkness; but it is seldom. And as the returning sun, after a summer shower, spreads his beams over the retiring gloom of the heavens, and stretches abroad the shining arch of promise to cheer the face of nature, so, at such times, do the rays of the Sun of Righteousness speedily illumine the hopes of my soul, and fill my bosom with joy and peace."

A few months after the above date, writing to a friend, she says: "We are most contented and most happy, and rejoice that God has seen fit to honor and bless us by permitting us to be the bearers of his light and truth to this dark corner of the earth. Could you feel the same gladness that often fills our bosoms, in witnessing the happy influence of the Gospel on the minds and hearts of many of these interesting creatures, you would be satisfied, yes more than satisfied, that we should be *what we are, and where we are, poor missionaries in the distant islands of the sea.*"

In these brief extracts from her letters, shines, in its serenest lustre, the character of the Christian heroine: * and it would be an easy task to compile a volume of letters written on the field of moral conflict by American female missionaries, breathing a spirit equally as unselfish, cheerful and brave. All pioneer women in this enterprise are heroines, and if the conflicts and sublime victories of all claiming American citizenship, are not herein recorded, it is because, in a work of unambitious pretensions as it regards size, a few characters must stand as representatives of a class.

So pernicious was the influence of a tropical climate that, in the spring of 1825, the health of Mrs. Stewart began to fail; and at the end of a year, she was forced to leave the country. She sailed, with her husband, for London; and after tarrying three months in England, they embarked for home. They reached the valley of the Otsego in September, 1826. For three or four years, it was the prayer of Mrs. Stewart that she might be restored to health and permitted to return to the mission station; but in January, 1830, she was laid on a bed of declension and suffering, and in the following autumn, fully ripe, was gathered into the heavenly garner.

* For a full account of the life of Mrs. Stewart, we refer the reader to an interesting Memoir, by her husband.

A KIND AND BENEVOLENT WOMAN.

> Ah! woman — in this world of ours,
> What gift can be compared to thee.
>
> GEORGE P. MORRIS.

Mrs. Margaret Morris, of Burlington, New Jersey, kept a journal during the Revolution, for the amusement, it is said, of a sister, the wife of Dr. Charles Moore, of Philadelphia. A few copies were printed several years ago, for private circulation, supplying friends with a mirror which reflects the image of expanded benevolence and exalted piety. Belonging to the Society of Friends, she was not partial to

> "The shot, the shout, the groan of war;"

yet her principles were patriotic, and she no doubt rejoiced over all the victories and in the final and complete success of the "rebel" army. She became a widow at an early age, and died at Burlington, in 1816, aged seventy-nine years.

A single extract from her journal will illustrate the most prominent feature of her character:

"June 14th, 1777. By a person from Bordentown, we hear twelve expresses came in there to-day from camp. Some of the gondola-men and their wives being sick, and no doctor in town to apply to, they were told Mrs. Morris was a skillful woman, and kept medicines to give to the poor; and notwithstanding their late attempts to shoot my poor boy, they ventured to come to me, and in a very humble manner begged me to come and do something for them. At first I thought they designed to put a trick on me, get me aboard their gondola, and then pillage my house, as they had done some others; but on asking where the sick folks were, I was told they were lodged in the Governor's house. So I went to see them; there were several, both men and women, very ill with fever; some said, the camp or putrid fever. They were broken out in blotches; and on close examination, it appeared to be the itch fever. I treated them according to art, and they all got well. I thought I had received all my pay when they thankfully acknowledged my kindness; but lo! in a short time afterwards a very rough, ill-looking man came to the door and asked for me. When I went to him he drew me aside, and asked if I had any friends in Philadelphia. The question alarmed me, supposing there was some mischief meditated against that poor city; however, I calmly said—'I have an ancient father, some sisters, and other near friends there.'

"'Well,' said the man, 'do you wish to hear from them, or send any thing by way of refreshment to them? If you do, I will take charge of it, and bring you back any thing you may send for.'

"I was very much surprised, and thought, to be sure, he only wanted to get provisions to take to the gondolas; but when he told me his wife was one of those I had given medicine to, and this was the only thing he could do to pay me for my kindness, my heart leaped with joy, and I set about preparing something for my dear, absent friends. A quarter of beef, some veal, fowls and flour, were soon put up; and about midnight the man called and took them aboard his boat. He left them at Robert Hopkins' —at the point—whence my beloved friends took them to town.

"Two nights afterwards, a loud knocking at our front door greatly alarmed us, and opening the chamber window, we heard a man's voice, saying, 'Come down softly and open the door, but bring no light.'

"There was something mysterious in such a call; but we concluded to go down and set the candle in the kitchen.

"When we got to the front door, we asked, 'Who are you?'

"The man replied, 'A friend; open quickly.' So the dooı was opened; and who should it be but our honest gondola-man, with a letter, a bushel of salt, a jug of molasses, a bag of rice, some tea, coffee, and sugar, and some cloth for a coat for my poor boys; all sent by my kind sisters!

"How did our hearts and eyes overflow with love to them, and thanks to our Heavenly Father for such seasonable supplies! May we never forget it! Beii.g now so rich, we thought it our duty to hand out a little to the poor around us, who were mourning for want of salt; so we divided the bushel, and gave a pint to every poor person who came for it—having bundance left for our own use. Indeed, it seemed to us as if our little store was increased by distribution, like the bread broken by our Saviour to the multitude."

NOBLE EXAMPLE OF PIONEERS.

> In every rank, or great or small,
> 'T is industry supports us all.
>
> GAY.

> Count life by virtues — these will last
> When life's lame-footed race is o'er.
>
> MRS. HALE.

In the year 1843, the Hon. Samuel Wilkeson, of Buffalo — since deceased — communicated to the American Pioneer, a series of papers entitled "Early Recollections of the West." They present a graphic, yet painful picture of the perils, hardships and sufferings attendant on back-woods life in the midst of the aboriginal foresters. His father's family was one of twenty that removed from Carlisle and the adjacent towns, to the western part of Pennsylvania, in the spring of 1784. He pays the following tribute to the industry, perseverance and pious efforts of the mothers of the band:

The labor of all the settlers was greatly interrupted by the Indian war. Although the older settlers had some sheep, yet their increase was slow, as the country abounded in wolves. It was therefore the work of time to secure a supply of wool. Deerskin was a substitute for cloth for men and boys, but not for women and girls, although they were sometimes compelled to resort to it. The women spun, and generally wove all the cloth for their families, and when the wife was feeble, and had a large family, her utmost efforts could not enable her to provide them with anything like comfortable clothing. The wonder is, and I shall never cease to wonder, that they did not sink under their burthens. Their patient endurance of these accumulated hardships did not arise from a slavish servility, or insensibility to their rights and comforts. They justly appreciated their situation, and nobly encountered the difficulties which could not be avoided.

Possessing all the affections of the wife, the tenderness of the mother, and the sympathies of the woman, their tears flowed freely for others' griefs, while they bore their own with a fortitude which none but a woman could exercise. The entire education of her children devolved on the mother, and notwithstanding the difficulties to be encountered, she did not allow them to grow up wholly without instruction; but amidst all her numerous cares taught them to read, and instructed them in the principles of Christianity. To accomplish this, under the circumstances, was no easy task. The exciting influences which surrounded them, made the boys restless under restraint. Familiarized as they were to hardships from the cradle, and daily listening to stories of Indian massacres and depredations, and to the heroic exploits of some neighboring pioneer, who had taken an Indian scalp, or by some daring effort saved his own, ignorant of the sports and toys with which children in other circumstances are wont to be amused, no wonder they desired to emulate the soldier, or engage in the scarcely less exciting adventures of the hunter. Yet even many of these boys were subdued by the faithfulness of the mother, who labored to bring them up in the fear of God.

ANECDOTE OF MRS. SLOCUMB.

Our country yet remains:
By that dread name, we wave the sword on high,
And swear for her to live — with her to die!

CAMPBELL.

One of the spiciest specimens of colloquial sparring, *vis-a-vis*, in our Revolutionary annals, was between Colonel Tarleton and the wife of Lieutenant Slocumb, of Wayne county, North Carolina.* The Attic wit and Spartan boldness of the latter, exhibit original powers of mind, strength of will, and a degree of self-possession truly grand and ennobling. But the character of the heroine of "Pleasant Green," is most luminous in her conduct at the battle of Moore's Creek, which occurred on the twenty-seventh of February, 1776. She tells the story of her adventures on that bloody occasion, as follows:

"The men all left on Sunday morning. More than eighty went from this house with my husband; I looked at them well, and I could see that every man had mischief in him. I know a coward as

* *Vide* Women of the Revolution, vol. 1. pp. 306-7, etc.

soon as I set my eyes upon him. The tories more than once tried to frighten me, but they always showed coward at the bare insinuation that our troops were about.

"Well, they got off in high spirits, every man stepping high and light. And I slept soundly and quietly that night, and worked hard all the next day; but I kept thinking where they had got to—how far; where and how many of the regulars and tories they would meet; and I could not keep myself from the study. I went to bed at the usual time, but still continued to study. As I lay—whether waking or sleeping I know not—I had a dream; yet it was not all a dream. (She used the words, unconsciously, of the poet who was not then in being.) I saw distinctly a body wrapped in my husband's guard-cloak—bloody—dead; and others dead and wounded on the ground about him. I saw them plainly and distinctly. I uttered a cry, and sprang to my feet on the floor; and so strong was the impression on my mind, that I rushed in the direction the vision appeared, and came up against the side of the house. The fire in the room gave little light, and I gazed in every direction to catch another glimpse of the scene. I raised the light; every thing was still and quiet. My child was sleeping, but my woman was awakened by my crying out or jumping on the floor. If ever I felt fear it was at that moment. Seated on the bed, I reflected a few moments—and said aloud: 'I must go to him.' I told the woman I could not sleep, and would ride down the road. She appeared in great alarm; but I merely told her to lock the door after me, and look after the child. I went to the stable, saddled my mare — as fleet and easy a nag as ever traveled; and in one minute we were tearing down the road at full speed. The cool night seemed after a mile or two's gallop to bring reflection with it; and I asked myself where I was going, and for what purpose. Again and again, I was tempted to turn back; but I was soon ten miles from home, and my mind became stronger every mile I rode. I should find my husband dead or dying — was as firmly my presentiment and conviction as any fact of my life. When day broke I was some thirty miles from home. I knew the general route our little army expected to take, and had followed them without hesitation. About sunrise I came upon a group of women and children, standing and sitting by the road-side, each one of them showing the same anxiety of mind I felt. Stopping a few minutes I inquired if the battle had been fought. They knew nothing, but were assembled on the rode side to catch intelligence. They thought Caswell had taken the right of the Wilmington road, and gone towards the north-west (cape Fear). Again was I skimming over the ground through a country thinly settled, and very poor and swampy; but neither my own spirits nor my beautiful nag's failed in the least. We followed the well-marked trail of the troops.

"The sun must have been well up, say eight or nine o'clock, when I heard a sound like thunder, which I knew must be cannon. It was the first time I ever heard a cannon. I stopped still; when presently the cannon thundered again. The battle was then fighting. What a fool! my husband could not be dead last night, and the battle only fighting now! Still, as I am so near, I will go on and see how they come out. So away we went again, faster than ever; and I soon found, by the noise of the guns, that I was near the fight. Again I stopped. I could hear muskets, I could hear rifles, and I could hear shouting. I spoke to my mare and dashed on in the direction of the firing and the shouts, now louder than ever. The blind path I had been following brought me into the Wilmington road leading to Moore's creek bridge, a few hundred yards below the bridge. A few yards from the road, under a cluster of trees were lying perhaps twenty men. They were the wounded. I knew the spot; the very trees; and the position of the men I knew as if I had seen it a thousand times. I had seen it all night! I saw all at once; but in an instant my whole soul was centered in one spot; for there, wrapped in his bloody guard-cloak, was my husband's body! How I passed the few yards from my saddle to the place I never knew. I remember uncovering his head and seeing a face clothed with gore from a dreadful wound across the temple. I put my hand on the bloody face; 'twas warm; and an *unknown voice* begged for water. A small camp-kettle was lying near, and a stream of water was close by. I brought it; poured some in his mouth; washed his face; and behold — it was Frank Cogdell. He soon revived and could speak. I was washing the wound in his head. Said he 'It is not that; it is that hole in my leg that is killing me.' A puddle of blood was standing on the ground about his feet. I took his knife, cut away his trowsers and stockings, and found the blood came from a shot hole through and through the fleshy part of the leg. I looked about and could see nothing that looked as if it would do for dressing wounds but some heart-leaves. I gathered a handful and bound them tight to the holes; and the bleeding stopped. I then went to the others; and — Doctor! I dressed the wounds of many a brave fellow who did good fighting long after that day! I had not inquired for my husband; but while I was busy Caswell came up. He appeared very much surprised to see me; and was with his hat in hand about to pay some compliment: but I interrupted him by asking — 'Where is my husband?'

"'Where he ought to be, madam; in pursuit of the enemy. But pray,' said he, 'how came you here?'

"'Oh, I thought,' replied I, 'you would need nurses as well as soldiers. See! I have already dressed many of these good fellows; and here is one'— going to Frank and lifting him up with my arm under his head so that he could drink some more water—'would have died before any of you men could have helped him.'

"'I believe you,' said Frank. Just then I looked up, and my husband, as bloody as a butcher, and as muddy as a ditcher,* stood before me.

"'Why, Mary!' he exclaimed, 'What are you doing there? Hugging Frank Cogdell, the greatest reprobate in the army?'

"'I dont care,' I cried. 'Frank is a brave fellow, a good soldier, and a true friend to Congress.'

"'True, true! every word of it!' said Caswell. 'You are right, madam,' with the lowest possible bow.

"I would not tell my husband what brought me there. I was so happy; and so were all! It was a glorious victory; I came just at the height of the enjoyment. I knew my husband was surprised, but I could see he was not displeased with me. It was night again before our excitement had at all subsided. Many prisoners were brought in, and among them some very obnoxious; but the worst of the tories were not taken prisoners. They were, for the most part, left in the woods and swamps wherever they were overtaken. I begged for some of the poor prisoners, and Caswell readily told me none should be hurt but such as had been guilty of murder and house-burning. In the middle of the night I again mounted my mare and started for home. Caswell and my husband wanted me to stay till next morning, and they would send a party with me; but no! I

* It was his company that forded the creek, and, penetrating the swamp, made the furious charge on the British left and rear which decided the fate of the day.—[Mrs. Ellet.

wanted to see my child, and I told them they could send no party who could keep up with me. What a happy ride I had back! and with what joy did I embrace my child as he ran to meet me!"*

---

* Mrs. Slocumb was a dignified and generous matron, a kind and liberal neighbor, and a Christian of indomitable fortitude and inexhaustible patience. After four or five years' extreme bodily suffering, resulting from a complication of diseases, she died, on the sixth of March, 1836, aged seventy-six years.

CAPTAIN RICHARDSON SAVED BY HIS WIFE.

Love, lend me wings to make this purpose swift,
As thou hast lent me wit to plot this drift.
SHAKSPEARE.

During the struggle for Independence, Captain Richardson, of Sumter district, South Carolina, was obliged to conceal himself for a while in the thickets of the Santee swamp. One day he ventured to visit his family—a perilous movement, for the British had offered rewards for his apprehension, and patrolling parties were almost constantly in search of him.—Before his visit was ended, a small band of soldiers presented themselves in front of the house. Just as they were entering, with a great deal of composure and presence of mind, Mrs. Richardson appeared at the door, and found so much to do there at the moment, as to find it inconvenient to make room for the uninvited guests to enter. She was so calm, and appeared so unconcerned, that they did not mistrust the cause of her wonderful diligence, till her husband had rushed out of the back door and safely reached the neighboring swamp.

ɩ ΓRIKING INSTANCE OF PATIENCE.

Patience and resignation are the pillars
Of human peace on earth.

YOUNG.

The panegyric of Decker on patience is beautiful:

Patience, my lord! why 'tis the soul of peace:
Of all the virtues 'tis the nearest kin to heaven;
It makes men look like gods.

Not every Christian sufferer wears this garment in its celestial whiteness, as did the God-man, whom the same writer calls

"the best of men
That e'er wore earth about him."

One of the most patient beings in modern times was Miss Sarah Parbeck, of Salem, Massachusetts. A lady who visited her in 1845, gives the following account of the interview:

The door was opened by a very old lady, wrinkled and bowed down with age, who invited us to enter. The room was so dark, that, before my eyes were accommodated to the change, I could only see a figure dressed in white, sitting upon the bed and rocking to and fro. This motion was attended by a sound like the click of wooden machinery, which arose, as I afterwards discovered, from the bones, as they worked in their loosened sockets. As we approached, she extended her hand to my companion, and said, in a painful but affectionate voice, "Eliza, I am very glad to see thee;" and then asked my name and place of residence. She had just given me her hand, when a spasm seized her, and it was twitched suddenly from my grasp. It flew some four or five times with the greatest violence against her face, and then, with a sound, which I can only compare to that made by a child who has been sobbing a long time, in catching its breath, she threw up both her arms, and with a deep guttural groan was flung back upon her pillow, with a force inconceivable to one who has not witnessed it. The instant she touched the bed, she uttered that piercing shriek again, and sprung back to her former position, rocking to and fro, with those quick, heart-rending groans which I had heard while standing at the door. It was several minutes before she could speak, and then there was none to answer her. Both my companion and myself were choked with tears. Her poor mother went to the other side of the bed, and smoothed the coverlid, and re-arranged the pillows, looking sadly upon her poor child, writhing in torture which she could not alleviate. I became faint, and trembled with sudden weakness: a cold perspiration stood upon my face. The objects in the room began to swim about me, and I was obliged to take hold of the bedside for support. I have been in our largest hospitals, and have spent hours in going from room to room with the attending physician. I have witnessed there almost every form of human suffering, but I had never beheld any thing to be compared to that now before me. She afterwards told me, as if in apology for her screams, that when she was hurled back upon her pillow, both shoulders were dislocated, and as they sprung back into their sockets, the pain was far beyond endurance, and extorted from her these shrieks.

Her sentences were broken, uttered with much difficulty, and frequently interrupted by the terrible spasm I have described above. Yet this was her "quiet" state; this the time when she suffered *least.* Day after day, night after night, *fourteen weary years* have dragged themselves along, whilst her poor body has been thus racked. No relief; no hope of relief, except that which death shall give. When I asked her if her affliction did not at times seem greater than she could bear, "O! never," she replied. "I cannot thank God enough for having laid his heavy hand upon me. I was a thoughtless sinner, and had he not, in his mercy, afflicted me, I should probably have lost my immortal soul. I see only his kindness and love. The sweet communion I have with my Saviour more than compensates me for all I suffer. I am permitted to feel, in a measure, in my poor body, what he suffered to save me, and my soul can never grow weary in his praise." This last sentence, I must say, gave me an argument which put doubts of the verity and power of religion to flight.

more effectually than all the evidences which the wisdom of man has arrayed against the skeptic; and I could not but exclaim, "If this be delusion let me be deluded!"

She spoke in the most tender terms of her Saviour's love. Her conversation was in heaven, from whence also she looked for her Saviour, knowing that he should change her body of humiliation, and fashion it like unto his glorious body. I shall never forget the tones and language in which she entreated my sobbing companion to give that Saviour her heart. As she recovered from a spasm, I said to her, "do you not often desire to depart, and be with the Saviour you love so fervently?" She had hardly recovered her exhausted breath, but replied with great decision, "By the grace of God, *I have never had that wish.* Though death will be a welcome gift when my Father sees fit to bestow it upon me, yet, thanks to his supporting grace, I can wait his time without impatience. He sees that there is much dross to refine away, and why should I wish against his will?"

I remained by her side for more than an hour; such, however, were the attractions of her discourse, that I was unconscious of the time. I know not when I have been so drawn towards a fellow Christian, and never had I been led to such delightful contemplations of our Saviour's character—his faithfulness and love. I remarked to her, as I turned to go away, "God has made you a powerful preacher, here upon your bed of pain." "O," she replied, "if he will make me the instrument of saving but a single soul, I am willing to live and suffer here until my hair is gray with age." I noticed some bottles standing upon a small table, and asked her if she found any relief from opiates. "Through God's kindness," she answered, "I probably owe the preservation of my life thus far to an extract made from blackdrop." "Does it enable you to sleep?" "O no," she replied, "I have not known sleep for a very long time." "What!" I cried, "do you never rest?" A severe spasm here seized her, and it was some time before she could answer me; she had been attacked in this way some twelve or fifteen times whilst conversing with us, and frequently in the midst of a reply. When she recovered, she said the physicians thought she obtained rest in her "long spasm," which lasted for more than an hour. "During that time," she continued, "I am dead to every thing but a sense of the most extreme anguish. I see and hear nothing; I only feel as though I was being crushed in pieces by some immense weight." This was her rest! the rack! Yet, through all this suffering, the smiles of God penetrated to her heart. She sees him just, and acknowledges his love.

SUSANNAH ELLIOTT.

—— The painted folds thus fly,
And lift their emblems, printed high
On morning mist and sunset sky.

HOLMES.

She showed that her soft sex contains strong mind.

SIR W. DAVENANT.

Susannah Smith, afterwards the wife of Colonel Barnard Elliott, was a native of South Carolina. Ramsay, in his history of that state, and other authors, give a glowing account of her presentation of a pair of colors to the second South Carolina regiment of infantry, commanded by Col. Moultrie. The ceremony took place on the twenty-eighth of June, '76, two or three days after the attack on Fort Moultrie, Sullivan's island. The colors, which were embroidered by her own hand, were presented in these words: "Your gallant behavior in defenee of liberty and your country, entitles you to the highest honors: accept these two standards as a reward justly due to your regiment; and I make not the least doubt, under Heaven's protection, you will stand by them as long as they can wave in the air of liberty.'

Mrs. Elliott had a plantation called "The Hut," and while there she once had three American gentlemen as guests. These she was obliged to hurry into a closet one day, on the sudden approach of the enemy; and, opening a secret door, she showed them a narrow apartment back of the chimney, which she had contrived expressly for a hiding place. Two of the guests entered, and were saved, while the third, attempting to flee on horse-back, was overtaken and slain.

After the British had thoroughly, though ineffectually, searched the house, and failed, by many threats, to persuade the mistress to disclose the hiding place of the others, they demanded her silver. Pointing to some mounds of earth near by, as they made the demand, they asked if the plate was not buried there.* She told them, in reply, that those mounds were the graves of British soldiers who had died under her roof. The officers did not believe her, and made two of the soldiers dig till they came to one of the coffins, which was opened and which verified her assertion. The enemy then departed, when the two guests came forth, filled with gratitude to their kind and ingenious hostess for the free use of this singular apartment.

* The silver was buried in a trunk, and remained in a marshy bed till the close of the war. When disinterred, it had turned black.

ANECDOTES OF ANNA ELLIOTT.

"The spark of noble courage now awake,
And strive your excellent self to excel."

The wife of Charles Elliott, of Charleston, South Carolina, was one of those dames of Seventy-six who "appeared to concentrate every thought and every hour of existence to the interests of America." She cheered the prisoner, befriended the unjustly persecuted, comforted the sick, fed the hungry, and was humane alike to enemies and friends. Major Garden has paid her the following compliment: "I do not know an officer who did not owe to her some essential increase of comfort."

A British officer, whose cruel and persecuting disposition was well known to Mrs. Elliott, was walking with her in a flower garden one day, when, pointing to the chamomile he asked, "What is this, madam?" She at once replied, "The rebel flower." "And why," asked he, "is it called the rebel flower?" "Because," answered she, "it always flourishes most when trampled upon."

At another time, while an officer of the royal army was in her house at Charleston, a French officer, belonging to Pulaski's legion, passed; and pointing to him, he vociferated, "There, Mrs. Elliott, is one of your illustrious allies. What a pity the hero is minus his *sword*." The spirit of the woman was roused, and she replied, "Had two thousand such men been here to aid in the defence of our city, I should not at this moment, sir, have been subjected to the insolence of your observation."

When her father, the brave and zealous patriot, Thomas Ferguson, was put on board a transport ship at Charleston, preparatory to exile, she hastened from the country, where she chanced to be, and begged permission to receive his parting blessing. Her request being granted, she went on board the ship. Just as she entered the cabin, she was overcome with grief, and fainted. When recovered, she addressed her father as follows: "Let not oppression shake your fortitude, nor the hope of gentler treatment cause you for a moment to swerve from strict duty. Better times are in store for us: the bravery of the Americans, and the friendly aid of France, will achieve the deliverance of our country from oppression. We shall meet again, my father, and meet with joy."*

* A similar spirit was exhibited by the wife of Isaac Holmes, one of the number who were sent into exile at St. Augustine. Just as the guard were separating him from his family, she said to him, "Waver not in your principles, but be true to your country. Have no fears for your family; God is good, and will provide for them."

PATRIOTIC STRATAGEM.

What bosom beats not in its country's cause?
POPE.

While the Legislature of Virginia was in session at Charlottesville, Colonel Tarleton, with his famous band of cavalry, made a secret march to that place, in order to capture the Governor and some public stores there collected. Several of the Assembly-men were at the house of Colonel John Walker, a dozen miles distant, and directly on Tarleton's route. Colonel Walker was absent on duty in the lower part of the state. Tarleton came suddenly up to the door, and succeeded in making one or two prisoners, the other members fleeing to town. He then ordered breakfast for himself and his whole corps, which the shrewd lady of the house prepared in the slowest manner possible. This she did in order that the members who had fled to the capital, might attend to the removal or concealment of the stores, in the preservation of which she was deeply interested. Her stratagem succeeded; and, after tarrying a day or two at Charlottesville, Tarleton went empty away.

INFLUENCE OF A FAITHFUL TEACHER.

Spread out earth's holiest records here.
SPRAGUE.

"About the first of September, 1833, a deep and solemn interest upon the subject of religion, began to be visible in the Presbyterian church and congregation of Washingtonville, New York, and particularly in the Sabbath school. One teacher, feeling deeply the responsibility resting upon her, and the worth of immortal souls, before the school was dismissed on the Lord's day, affectionately requested her class, consisting of little girls about twelve or thirteen years of age, to remain after the rest of the school had retired. She then began, with an aching heart and with flowing tears, to reason and plead with them upon the subject of personal religion. They were deeply affected, and 'wept bitterly' in view of their lost condition. They then all knelt together before the Lord, and the teacher prayed for their salvation; and immediately the scholar next to her commenced praying for herself, and then the next, and so on, until the whole class, with ardent supplications, begged for the forgiveness of their sir and the salvation of their souls. It would take long to tell the history of this class, and relate particular instances of conversions, and the happy changes which took place in the families to which they belonged, and show the family altars which were established. These scholars, with their teacher and their fathers and mothers, brothers and sisters, were ere long seen commemorating a Saviour's dying love together. The revival extended itself to other towns, and the great day can alone unfold the astonishing results."

THE WIFE OF THOMAS HEYWARD.

What I will, I will, and there's an end.
SHAKSPEARE.

Immediately after the victory of the British at Guilford, order was given for the illumination of Charleston, South Carolina. This order, Major Garden informs us, * the wife of Thomas Heyward of that city refused to obey; and when an officer asked her the reason of her disobedience, she replied, "Is it possible for me, sir, to feel a spark of joy? Can I celebrate the victory of your army while my husband remains a prisoner at St. Augustine?" Enraged at her obstinacy, he told her she *should* illuminate. "Not a single light shall be placed, with my consent, on any occasion, in any window in the house," was her fearless reply. He then threatened to destroy her house before midnight. "You have power to destroy, sir," she said, "and seem well disposed to use it, but over my opinions you possess no control. I disregard your menaces, and resolutely declare, *I will not illuminate!*" As good as her word, she *did* not, nor was her house destroyed.

Revolutionary Anecdotes, First Series

Orders were given, at another time, for an illumination on the anniversary of the battle and surrender of Charleston,* and Mrs. Heyward again refused to obey. The mob was so indignant as to pelt her house with brickbats; and while engaged in the mean act, a feeble and emaciated sister of Mrs. Heyward — Mrs. George A. Hall — expired! When the town major heard of this painful circumstance, he tried to apologize to Mrs. Heyward, expressing regret for the indignities and damages, and offering to repair the building. She received his personal courtesies, but refused his proffered aid in making repairs, hinting, at the same time, that it was hardly possible for the authorities, in that way, to remedy insults the offering of which their baseness had probably prompted and and which they could and *should* have prevented.

---

* May twelfth, 1781.

NOBLE DECISION.

We are born to do benefits.
SHAKSPEARE.

When the news was received in Illinois, a few years ago, that, owing to a deficiency of funds, the Ceylon missionaries had been obliged to dismiss thousands of pupils from their schools, and that twenty-five dollars would revive any one of them, a minister of that state laid the subject before his small and poor church, and between pastor and people twenty-five dollars were promptly raised. Going home and communicating the intelligence to his wife, the minister learned that she had been weighing the subject, and was anxious, in some way, to raise enough herself alone to resuscitate a school. Her husband told her she could do it by dispensing with a tomb stone which had been ordered from New York for a child lately deceased, and which would cost twenty-five dollars. She promptly consented to have the order countermanded, saying that "living children demanded her money more than the one that was dead." By suffering the love of Christ to triumph over maternal feeling, she re-opened a mission school, and the day of judgment will reveal the great amount of good thereby accomplished.

A TENNESSEE HEROINE.

It is held
That valor is the chiefest virtue;
Most dignifies the haver: if it be,
The man I speak of cannot in the world.
Be singly counterpoised.

SHAKSPEARE.

Milton A. Haynes, Esq., of Tennessee, furnished for Mrs. Ellet's Women of the Revolution a lengthy and very interesting sketch of Sarah Buchanan, of East Tennessee. The following anecdotes, extracted therefrom, exhibit the heroism of her character:

On one occasion, Sarah and a kinswoman named Susan Everett were returning home from a visit a mile or two distant, careless of danger, or not thinking of its presence. It was late in the evening, and they were riding along a path through the open woods, Miss Everett in advance. Suddenly she stopped her horse, exclaiming, "Look, Sally, yonder are the red skins!" Not more than a hundred yards ahead was a party of Indians armed with rifles, directly in their path. There was no time for counsel, and retreat was impossible, as the Indians might easily intercept them before they could gain a fort in their rear. To reach their own block-house, four or five hundred yards distant, was their only hope of safety. Quick as thought, Sarah whispered to her companion to follow and do as she did, and then instantly assuming the position of a man on horseback, in which she was imitated by her relative, she urged her horse into a headlong gallop. Waving their bonnets in the air, and yelling like madmen, they came furiously down upon the savages, who had not seen them, crying out as they came — "Clear the track, you —— red skins!" The part was so well acted, that the Indians took them for the head of a body of troopers, who were making a deadly charge upon them, and dodging out of the path, fled for very life — and so did Sally and Susan! Before the savages had recovered from their fright, the two girls were safe within the gates of the fort, trembling like frightened fawns at the narrow escape which they had made.

On another occasion, when her husband and all the men of the fort were absent, two celebrated horse-thieves, who had taken refuge with the Indians, came and demanded of Mrs. Buchanan two of the Major's fine horses. Knowing their lawless character, she pretended acquiescence, and went with them to the stable, but on arriving at the door she suddenly drew a large hunting knife from under her apron, and assuming an attitude of defiance, declared that if either of them dared to enter the stable, she would instantly cut him down. Struck by her intrepid bearing, they fell back, and although they tried to overcome her resolution by threats and bravado, she maintained her ground, and the marauders were compelled to retire without the horses.

On Sunday night,* about the hour of midnight, while the moon was shining brilliantly, the Indian army under Watts and the Shawnee, advancing in silence, surrounded Buchanan's station. In order to effect an entrance into the fort by a *coup de main*, they sent runners to frighten and drive in the horses and cattle. This was done, and the animals came dashing furiously towards the fort; but the garrison, wrapped in slumber, heeded them not. The watchman, John McCrory, at this instant discovering the savages advancing within fifty yards of the gates, fired upon them. In an instant the mingled yells of the savage columns, the crack of their rifles, and the clatter of their hatchets, as they attempted to cut down the gate, told the little squad of nineteen men and seven women that the fearful war-cloud, which had been rising so long, was about to burst upon their devoted heads!

Aroused suddenly from deep slumber by the terrible war-whoop, every man and woman felt the horror of their situation. The first impulse with some was to surrender, and it is related of one woman that she instantly gathered her five children and attempted to go with them to the gate to yield

* In the autumn of 1792, while the war with the Creeks and Cherokees was raging in the Cumberland valley.

themselves to the Indians. Mrs. Buchanan seized her by the shoulder, and asked her where she was going.

"To surrender myself and children to the Indians—if I don't they'll kill us, any how," exclaimed the terrified woman. "Come back," said Mrs. Buchanan, "and let us all fight and die together." An old man, who waked up as it were in a dream, seemed paralyzed, and exclaimed, in a plaintive voice—"Oh, we shall all be murdered!"

"Get up then and go to fighting!" exclaimed Mrs. Buchanan; "I'd be ashamed to sit crouched up there when any one else is fighting. Better die nobly than live shamefully!"

In the mean time Major Buchanan had arranged his men in the block-houses so as to rake the Indians by a flank fire, and was pouring a galling fire into the head of the assaulting column. Yet, nothing dismayed, the daring foe crowded against the gates, their blows falling faster and heavier, while now and then they attempted to scale the pickets. At length, unable to do this or to force open the well-barred and ponderous gate, the bold warriors advanced to the block-houses, and standing before them, pointed their guns in at the port holes; both sides sometimes at the same instant firing through the same opening. It was the policy of Major Buchanan to impress upon them the idea that the fort contained a large garrison. To do this it was necessary for his men to fire their guns often, and occasionally in volleys. At this crisis the whisper went round—"All is lost. Our bullets are out!" But there were guardian angels whom these brave men knew not of. Scarcely had the words been spoken, when Mrs. Buchanan passed around with an apronful of bullets, which she and Nancy Mulherrin, the Major's sister, had moulded, during the fight, out of her plates and spoons. At the same time she gave to each of the tired soldiers some brandy which she carried in a pewter basin. During the contest they had thus moulded three hundred bullets. Not without their fun were these hardy men in this hour of peril. In order to keep up a show of good spirits, they frequently cried out to the Indians, "Shoot bullets, you squaws! Why don't you put powder in your guns?" This was understood, for Watts and many others spoke very good English, and they replied by daring them to come out and fight like men. In the midst of these banterings, Mrs. Buchanan discovered a large blunderbuss which had been standing in a corner during the fight and had not been discharged, and gave it to an Irishman named O'Connor to fire off. In telling the story afterwards the Irish man said: An' she gave me the wide-mouthed fusee and bade me to shoot that at the blasted creeters, and Jimmy O'Connor he took the fusee, and he pulled the trigger when the rest fired, for three or four times, and loaded her again every time, and so ye see, yer honor, when I pulled the trigger again, the fusee went off, it did, and Jimmy O'Connor went under the bed. This unequal contest lasted for four long hours, and when the first blush of morning began to appear in the east, most of the chiefs were killed or wounded. The boastful Shawnee was transfixed in death, leaning against the gate which he had so valorously assaulted; the White Owl's son and Unacate, or the White-man-killer, were mortally wounded, and John Watts was borne off on a litter, shot through both legs.

During this protracted fight Mrs. Buchanan aided the defenders by words and deeds, as if life or death depended upon the efforts which she was then making. She knew, and all knew, that if the assault could be repelled for four hours, relief would come from the neighboring posts. Foiled, discouraged, their leaders disabled, this formidable army of savage warriors precipitately retreated towards their country, bearing off most of their wounded, yet leaving many dead upon the field. This was the first formidable invasion of Cumberland valley, and its tide was rolled back as much by the presence of mind and heroic firmness of Sarah Buchanan and Nancy Mulherrin, as by the rifles of their husbands and friends. The fame of this gallant defence went abroad, and the young wife of Major Buchanan was celebrated as the greatest heroine of the West. From 1780 to 1796, there was not a year in which her family had not been exposed to peril, in which, of course, she was a partaker.*

* This heroic woman died at Buchanan's Station, on the twenty-third of November, 1831. She sleeps on the site of the old fort that witnessed her bravery; and Carcas, queen of Carcassone, who defended that city with such courage and resolution, when it was beseiged by Charlemagne, that the Emperor permitted her to retain the sovereignty of the place, has scarcely higher claims to historical commemoration.

AUTHOR.

MAGNANIMITY OF MRS. M'KAY.

> Greatness of mind, and nobleness, their seat
> In her build loveliest.
>
> MILTON.

"In the beginning of June, 1781, the British garrison at Augusta, Georgia, capitulated to the American forces, under command of General Pickens and Colonel Lee, of the partizan legion. Colonel Grierson, who was obnoxious to the Americans on account of his barbarities, was shot down by an unknown hand, after he was a prisoner. A reward of one hundred guineas was offered to any person who would point out the offender, but in vain. Colonel Brown, the British commander, expecting the same fate, conscious that he deserved it, from his unrelenting and vindictive disposition towards the Americans, was furnished with a guard, although he had hanged thirteen American prisoners, and had given others into the hands of the Indians to be tortured. On his way to Savannah, he passed through the settlements where he had burned a number of houses, and hung some of the relatives of the inhabitants. At Silverbluff, Mrs. M'Kay obtained leave of the

American officer, who commanded his safeguard, to speak to him; when she thus addressed him:—'Colonel Brown, in the late day of your prosperity, I visited your camp, and on my knees supplicated for the life of my only son, but you were deaf tc my entreaties; you hanged him, though a beardless youth, before my face. These eyes have seen him scalped by the savages under your immediate command, and for no better reason than that his name was M'Kay. As you are now a prisoner to the leaders of my country, for the present I lay aside all thoughts of revenge, but when you resume your sword, I will go five hundred miles to demand satisfaction at the point of it, for the murder of my son!'"

HEROIC CONDUCT OF A DAUGHTER.

> Fair was her face, and spotless was her mind,
> Where filial love with virgin sweetness joined.
>
> POPE.

Xantippe, a Roman lady, who nursed her father, the aged Cimonus, while he was a prisoner, and thereby saved his life, rendered herself immortal by this manifestation of filial affection. But the "Roman Charity" is not comparable to the following extraordinary deed of filial sacrifice.

The winter of 1783 was unusually severe, and the sufferings of the poor in the city of New York were very great. One family, consisting of the husband, wife and one daughter, were, on one occasion, reduced to the last stick of wood, and were wholly destitute of provisions. The daughter, who had thus far supported her aged and infirm parents by her industry, was out of work, and knew not what to do. At this juncture of affairs, she recollected that a dentist had advertised for sound fore-teeth, and offered three guineas a piece for all he was himself permitted to extract. In the midst of her grief, the generous girl suddenly brightened up,

COFFIN DEL.

and hastened to the dentist's office. She made known the condition of her parents, and offered to dispose of all her fore-teeth on his terms. The dentist, instead of extracting a tooth, with tears in his eyes, placed in her hands ten guineas, and sent her, rejoicing, to the relief of her parents.

HEROIC DECISION.

> No thought of flight,
> None of retreat, no unbecoming deed
> That argued fear.
>
> MILTON.

We have elsewhere in this work spoken of the perils necessary to be encountered by Christian missionaries, and particularly those who connect themselves with stations in Africa. The history of the Methodist Episcopal mission in that quarter of the globe, presents a noble, if not a long, list of soldiers who early fell there while contending with Error. They sank upon the battle field, with their armor on and covered with glory. They fell not before the hosts of paganism; they were conquered by the climate. Most of those who have not died on the field, have been obliged to shortly flee to their native land for the restoration of health. Here and there one has withstood the adverse nature of the climate, toiled for years, and done a noble work, which has caused rejoicing in Heaven and honored the name of Christ on earth.

Few persons, whose names are connected with the history of modern missions, have displayed a more devoted, self-sacrificing spirit, or greater moral courage, than Miss Sophronia Farrington. Prior to the autumn of 1834, of six missionaries who had entered the field in Africa under the patronage of American Methodists, three * were in their graves, and two † had returned to the United States for health. Miss Farrington stood alone, and the question arose, what she should do. The officers of the Missionary Society were willing she should return home, and her friends were urging it upon her. With her co-laborers all dead or fled, she seemed herself to be left to the alternative either to flee or fall. Should she choose the former course, the mission would be wholly, and, for ought she knew, for ever, abandoned. What then should she do? Like a hero, to use her own words, she had "offered her soul upon the altar of her God, for the salvation of that long benighted continent," and with courage that shames the facer of the cannon's mouth, she resolved to remain and toil alone, beside the graves of her fallen companions till more help should come or the Divine Husbandman close the labors of the lone vine-dresser. More help arrived in a few months, and, according to the annual report of 1836, the mission, of whose history she formed at one time the connecting link, "continued to loom up in bright perspective, and promise a rich reward for all the labors and sufferings of the faithful missionaries."

* Rev. M. B. Cox and Rev. O. S. Wright and wife.

† Rev. Mr. Spaulding and lady.

THE DAUGHTER OF AARON BURR.

'T is thine on every heart to 'grave thy praise,
A monument which Worth alone can raise.

BROOME.

Theodosia, the only daughter of Aaron Burr, was a woman of superior mental accomplishments, and very strong affections. She was married to Joseph Alston, Esq., afterwards Governor of South Carolina, in 1801. She was then in her eighteenth year. That she was an excellent wife may be gathered, not merely from the story of her life, but from the testimony of her husband. Writing to her father in 1813 —soon after her death—he says, "The man who has been deemed worthy of the heart of Theodosia Burr, and has felt what it was to be blest with such a woman's, will never forget his elevation." *

In regard to her attachment to her father, a writer, quoted in the appendix to Safford's Life of Blennerhassett, remarks as follows: "Her love for her father partook of the purity of a better world; holy, deep, unchanging; it reminds us of the affection which a celestial spirit might be supposed to entertain for a

* Memoirs of Aaron Burr, by Matthew L. Davis, vol. 2, p. 432.

parent cast down from heaven, for sharing in the sin of the 'Son of the Morning.' No sooner did she hear of the arrest of her father, than she fled to his side.* There is nothing in human history more touching than the hurried letters, blotted with tears, in which she announced her daily progress to Richmond; for she was too weak to travel with the rapidity of the mail."

Had her health permitted, and occasion presented itself, she would have matched in heroism any act in the life of Margaret Roper or Elizabeth Cazotte.†

The trial of her father for treason, and his virtual banishment, not only depressed her spirits, but fearfully racked her already feeble constitution, yet his disgrace abated not a tittle the ardor of her affection; and when he returned from Europe, though in feeble health, she resolved to visit him in the city of New York. She was then in South Carolina. Embarking in the privateer Patriot, on the thirteenth of January,

---

* He was imprisoned in Richmond, Virginia.—AUTHOR.

† Mrs. Roper accompanied her father, Sir Thomas More, to prison, and after he was executed and his head had lain fourteen days on London Bridge, she purchased it, and thus saved it from being thrown into the Thames. For this intrepidity, by the king's orders she was cast into prison—though she was soon permitted to escape.

Mademoiselle Cazotte was the daughter of an aged Frenchman, who, on one occasion, during the Revolution in his country, would have lost his life but for her courage. He was a "counter-revolutionist," and after an imprisonment, during which his daughter chose to be immured with him, on the second day of September, he was about to be slain. An axe was raised over his head, when Elizabeth threw herself upon him, and exclaimed, "Strike, barbarians; you cannot reach my father but through my heart." She did other heroic deeds.

1813, she was never heard of afterwards. The schooner may have fallen into the hands of pirates; but, as a heavy gale was experienced for several days soon after leaving Georgetown, the probability is that the craft foundered. Thus closed a life to which the panegyrical exclamation of Milton happily applies:

> O glorious trial of exceeding love
> Illustrious evidence, example high.

FEMALE INTREPIDITY.

> Be not dismayed — fear nurses up a danger,
> And resolution kills it in the birth.
>
> PHILLIPS.

During the war between the Indians and Ken tuckians, while the owner of a plantation in a thinly settled part of the state, was at work with his slaves in the field, a sable sentinel, who was posted near the house, saw a party of savages approaching. One of them was more fleet than he, and reaching the house at the same moment, they rushed within doors together. The planter's wife instantly closed the door and the negro and Indian grappled. The former was the stronger of the two, though the latter was the more expert. After a hard struggle, the negro threw the Indian, and held him fast until the woman beheaded him with a broad-axe. The negro then seized the guns, and began to fire at the other Indians through the loop-holes. The guns were loaded by the woman as fast as discharged. Their frequent report soon brought the laborers from the field, and the surviving Indians were driven away.

THE WIFE OF RICHARD SHUBRICK.

Be fire with fire;
Threaten the threatener, and out face the brow
Of bragging horror: so shall inferior eyes,
That borrow their behavior from the great,
Grow great by your example.

SHAKSPEARE.

The following anecdotes of Mrs. Richard Shubrick may be found in the First Series of Major Garden's Revolutionary Anecdotes. "There was," he writes, "an appearance of personal debility about her that rendered her peculiarly interesting: it seemed to solicit the interest of every heart, and the man would have felt himself degraded who would not have put his life at hazard to serve her. Yet, when firmness of character was requisite, when fortitude was called for to repel the encroachments of aggression, there was not a more intrepid being in existence.

"An American soldier, flying from a party of the enemy, sought her protection, and was promised it. The British, pressing close upon him, insisted that he should be delivered up, threatening immediate and universal destruction in case of refusal. The ladies, her friends and companions, who were in the house with her, shrunk from the contest, and were silent; but, undaunted by their threats, this intrepid lady placed herself before the chamber into which the unfortunate fugitive had been conducted, and resolutely said, 'To men of honor the chamber of a lady should be as sacred as the sanctuary! I will defend the passage to it though I perish. You may succeed, and enter it, but it shall be over my corpse.' 'By God,' said the officer, 'if muskets were only placed in the hands of a few such women, our only safety would be found in retreat. Your intrepidity, madam, gives you security; from me you shall meet no further annoyance.'

"At Brabant, the seat of the respectable and patriotic Bishop Smith, a sergeant of Tarleton's dragoons, eager for the aquisition of plunder, followed the overseer, a man advanced in years, into the apartment where the ladies of the family were assembled, and on his refusing to discover the spot in which the plate was concealed, struck him with violence, inflicting a severe sabre wound across the shoulders. Aroused by the infamy of the act, Mrs. Shubrick, starting from her seat, and placing herself betwixt the ruffian and his victim, resolutely said, 'Place yourself behind me, Murdoch; the interposition of my body shall give you protection, or I will die:' then, addressing herself to the sergeant, exclaimed, 'O what a degradation of manhood—what departure from that gallantry which was once the characteristic of British soldiers. Human nature is degraded by your barbarity;—but should you persist, then strike at *me*, for till I die, no further injury shall be done to *him*.' The sergeant, unable to resist such commanding eloquence, retired."*

---

* "The hope, however, of attaining the object in view, very speedily subjected the unfortunate Murdoch to new persecution. He was tied up under the very tree where the plate was buried, and threatened with immediate execution unless he would make the discovery required. But although well acquainted with the unrelenting severity of his enemy, and earnestly solicited by his wife, to save his life by a speedy confession of the place of deposit, he persisted resolutely, that a sacred trust was not to be betrayed, and actually succeeded in preserving it."

KEEN RETORT OF MRS. ASHE.

I have a thousand spirits in one breast,
To answer twenty thousand such as you.
SHAKSPEARE.

While General Leslie was staying with the British troops at Halifax, North Carolina, Colonel Tarleton and other officers held their quarters at the house of Colonel Ashe, whose wife was a firm friend of liberty. Her beau ideal of the hero was Colonel William Washington; and, knowing this fact, the sarcastic Tarleton took great delight in speaking diminutively of this officer in her presence. In his jesting way, he remarked to her one time, that he should like to have an opportunity of seeing her friend, Colonel Washington, whom he had understood to be a very small man. Mrs. Ashe promptly replied, "If you had looked behind you, Colonel Tarleton, at the battle of the Cowpens, you would have had that pleasure."*

* It is said that this taunt was so keenly felt that Tarleton laid his hand on the hilt of his sword. General Leslie entered the room at the moment, and seeing the agitation of Mrs. Ashe, and learning its cause, said to her, "Say what you please, Mrs. Ashe; Colonel Tarleton knows better than to insult a lady in my presence."

PHILANTHROPIC WIFE OF A DRUNKARD.

There's in you all that we believe of heaven.
OTWAY.

"The amazing influence of one Christian, who shows in her life the spirit of Christ, is illustrated in a striking manner, in the life of a lady who died not long since, in one of the principal cities of the United States. I am not permitted to give her name, nor all the particulars of her life. But what I relate may be relied upon, not only as facts, but as far below the whole truth. She had been for a long time afflicted with a drunken husband. At length the sheriff came, and swept off all her property, not excepting her household furniture, to discharge his grog bills. At this distressing crisis, she retired to an upper room, laid her babe upon the bare floor, kneeled down over it, and offered up the following petition: "O Lord, if thou wilt *in any way* remove from me this affliction, I will serve thee *upon bread and water*, all the days of my life." The Lord took her at her word. Her besotted husband immediately disappeared, and was never heard of again till after her death The church would now have maintained her, but she would not consent to become a charge to others. Although in feeble health, and afflicted with the sick headache, she opened a small school, from which she obtained a bare subsistence; though it was often no more than what was contained in the condition of her prayer—literally bread and water. She was a lady of pleasing address, and of a mild and gentle disposition. "In her lips was the law of kindness." Yet she possessed an energy of character and a spirit of perseverance, which the power of faith alone can impart. When she undertook any Christian enterprise, she was discouraged by no obstacles, and appalled by no difficulties. She resided in the most wicked and abandoned part of the city, which afforded a great field of labor. Her benevolent heart was pained at seeing the grog shops open upon the holy Sabbath. She undertook the difficult and almost hopeless task of closing these sinks of moral pollution upon the Lord's day, and succeeded. This was accomplished by the mild influence of persuasion, flowing from the lips of kindness, and clothed with that power which always accompanies the true spirit of the gospel. But she was not satisfied with seeing the front doors and windows of these houses closed. She would, therefore, upon the morning of the Sabbath, pass round, and enter these shops through the dwellings occupied by the families of the keepers, where she often found them engaged secretly in this wickedness. She would then remonstrate with them, until she persuaded them to abandon it, and attend public worship. In this manner, she abolisned, almost entirely, the sale of liquors upon the Sabbath, in the worst part of the city.

"She also looked after the poor, that the Gospel might be preached to them. She carried with her the number of those pews in the church which were unoccupied. And upon Sabbath mornings, she made it her business to go out in the streets and lanes of the city, and persuade the poor to come in and fill up these vacant seats. By her perseverance and energy, she would remove every objection, until she had brought them to the house of God. She was incessant and untiring in every effort for doing good. She would establish a Sabbath school, and superintend it until she saw it flourishing, and then deliver it into the hands of some suitable person, and go and establish another. She collected together a Bible class of apprentices, which she taught herself. Her pastor one day visited it, and found half of them in tears, under deep conviction. She was faithful to the church and to impenitent sinners. It was her habitual practice to reprove sin, and to warn sinners wherever she found them. At the time of her death, she had under her care a number of pious young men preparing for the ministry. These she had looked after, and brought out of obscurity. As soon as their piety nad been sufficiently proved, she would bring them to the notice of her Christian friends. She persuaded pious teachers to give them gratuitous instruction, and pious booksellers to supply them with books. In the same way, she procured their board in the families of wealthy Christians; and she formed little societies of ladies, to supply them with clothing. There was probably no person in the city whose death would have occasioned the shedding of more tears, or called forth more sincere and heartfelt grief." *

* Practical Directory for Young Christian Females.

THE MOTHER OF DR. DWIGHT.

Though renown
Plant laurels on the warrior's grave, and wreathe
With bays the slumbering bard — the mother's urn
Shall claim more dear memorials: gratitude
Shall there abide; affection, reverence, there
Shall oft revolve the precepts which now speak
With emphasis divine.

MRS. WEST.

The mother of Timothy Dwight was a daughter of Jonathan Edwards, and seems to have inherited a large share of her father's talents and spiritual graces. Her powers of mind were unusually strong; her knowledge was extensive and varied, and her piety highly fervid. She married at an early age; became a mother when eighteen; had a large family; and, though never negligent of domestic duties, she daily and assiduously devoted herself to the education of her children. She began to instruct Timothy, it is said, "as soon as he was able to speak; and such was his eagerness, as well as his capacity for improvement, that he learned the alphabet at a single lesson; and before he was four years old, was able to read the Bible with ease and correctness. . . . She taught him from the very dawn of his reason to fear God and to keep his commandments; to be conscientiously just, kind, affectionate, charitable, and forgiving; to preserve, on all occasions, and under all circumstances, the most sacred regard for truth; and to relieve the distresses and supply the wants of the poor and unfortunate. She aimed, at a very early period, to enlighten his conscience, to make him afraid of sin, and to teach him to hope for pardon only through Christ. The impressions thus made upon his mind in infancy, were never effaced. A great proportion of the instruction which he received before he arrived at the age of six years, was at home with his mother. His school room was the nursery. Here he had his regular hours for study, as in a school; and twice every day she heard him repeat his lesson. Here, in addition to his stated task, he watched the cradle of his younger brother. When his lesson was recited, he was permitted to read such books as he chose, until the limited period was expired. During these intervals, he often read over the historical parts of the Bible, and gave an account of them to his mother. So deep and distinct was the impression which these narrations made upon his mind, that their minutest incidents were indelibly fixed upon his memory. His relish for reading was thus early formed, and was strengthened by the conversation and example of his mother. His early knowledge of the Bible led to that ready, accurate, and extensive acquaintance with Scripture, which is so evident in his sermons and other writings."*

* Mothers of the Wise and Good, p. 142

It is easy to see, in this picture, who it was that laid the foundation of that character which sanctified genius, and caused it to shine with transcendent lustre, for more than twenty years, at the head of Yale college. The mother of President Dwight was well repaid, even in this life, for the pains she took to rear this son for the glory of God; for, while he never disobeyed a command of hers or omitted a filial duty, he was kind and generous to her in her old age, and smoothed her path to a Christian's grave. But her true and great reward for her maternal faithfulness, is in another world, whither she went to receive it about the year 1807.

HAPPY RESULTS OF MATERNAL FIDELITY.

Lift the heart and bend the knee.
MRS. HEMANS.

The superior influence of the mother in forming the character of the child, is generally conceded. Biographical literature abounds with illustrations of this fact, and renders it incontrovertible. As examples, in Great Britain, we are often, with propriety, pointed to the mothers of Isaac and John Newton, Doddridge, the Wesleys, Richard Cecil, Legh Richmond and many others; but it is needless for any people to search in foreign lands for such examples.

In the notices of the mothers of Washington, Jackson, Randolph, Dwight and some others, on preceding pages of this volume, the truth of the same proposition is endeavored to be substantiated: and, as facts most forcibly illustrate argument, and wholesome hints are often easiest given by example, we will add two or three more anecdotes having a bearing on this point.

The mother of Jonathan Edwards, it is well known, began to pray for him as soon as he was born; and probably no mother ever strove harder than she to rear a child "in the nurture and admonition of the Lord." The result of her efforts is known to the world.

The late Professor Knowles, of the Newton theological institution, received much pious instruction from his mother in his infant years; and, as he lost his father at the age of twelve, at that period she assumed wholly the guidance of his steps and his studies. She early discovered his love of books and his promising talents; and while she admonished him, and led him to the Saviour, she also sympathized with him in his literary taste and encouraged him in his scientific pursuits. The zealous minister, the learned biblical instructor, the polished writer and biographer of the first Mrs. Judson, owed very much to the moral training and the literary encouragement of his faithful mother.

Nearly half a century ago, the mother of the celebrated Beecher family, made the following record: "This morning I rose very early to pray for my children; and especially that my sons may be ministers and missionaries of Jesus Christ." The "fervent" prayers of the good woman were "effectual:" her five sons became "ministers and missionaries of Jesus Christ," and all her children—eight in number—are connected with the "household of God"—several on earth and one,* at least, in heaven.

---

* The late George Beecher.

WONDERFUL ENDURANCE AND PERSEVERANCE OF MRS. SCOTT.

——— Mute
The camel labors with the heaviest load,
And the wolf dies in silence; not bestowed
In vain should such examples be; if they,
Things of ignoble or of savage mood,
Endure and shrink not, we of nobler clay,
May temper it to bear — it is but for a day.

BYRON.

Mrs. Scott, a resident of Washington county, Virginia, was taken captive by Indians on the night of the twenty-ninth of June, 1785. Her husband and all her children were slain; and before morning she was forced to commence her march through the wilderness.

On the eleventh day of her captivity, while in charge of four Indians, provision becoming scarce, a halt was made, and three of the number went on a hunting excursion. Being left in the care of an old man, she made him believe she was reconciled to her condition, and thus threw him off his guard. Anxious to escape, and having matured her plans, she asked him, in the most disinterested manner possible, to let her go to a small stream, near by, and wash her apron, which was besmeared with the blood of one of her children. He gave her leave, and while he was busy in "graining a deer-skin," she started off. Arriving at the stream, without a moment's hesitation, she pushed on in the direction of a mountain. Traveling till late at night, she came into a valley where she hoped to find the track along which she had been taken by her captors, and thereby be able to retrace her steps. Hurrying across the valley to the margin of a river, which she supposed must be the eastern branch of the Kentucky, she discovered in the sand the tracks of two men who had followed the stream upwards and returned. Thinking them to be the prints of pursuers, and that they had returned from the search, she took courage, thanked God, and was prepared to continue her flight.

On the third day she came very near falling into the hands of savages, a company whom she supposed had been sent to Clinch river on a pilfering excursion. Hearing their approach before they came in sight, she concealed herself, and they passed without noticing her. She now became greatly alarmed, and was so bewildered as to lose her way and to wander at random for several days.

At length, coming to a stream that seemed to flow from the east, she concluded it must be Sandy river; and resolving to trace it to its source, which was near a settlement where she was acquainted, she pushed on for several days, till she came into mountainous regions and to craggy steeps. There, in the vicinity of a "prodigious waterfall," she was forced to leap from a precipice, upon some rocks, and was so stunned as to be obliged to make a short delay in her journey.

Soon after passing through the mountain,* she was bitten by a snake which she supposed was venomous. She killed it, and expected her turn to die would come next; but the only injury she received was some pain and the slight swelling of one foot. A writer, whose narration we follow and whose facts are more reliable than his philosophy, thinks that, being "reduced to a mere skeleton, with fatigue, hunger and grief," she was probably, on that account, "saved from the effects of the poisonous fangs."

Leaving the river, Mrs. Scott came to a forked valley, and watching the flight of birds, took the branch they did, and in two days came in sight of New Garden, the settlement on Clinch river, before referred to. Thus, after wandering in the wilderness for six long weeks, almost destitute of clothing, without a weapon of defence or instrument for obtaining provision; exposed to wild beasts and merciless savages; subsisting a full month on the juice of young cane stalks, sassafras leaves and similar food; looking to God in prayer for guidance by day, and for protection by night; shielded from serious harm, and led by an unseen Hand, on the eleventh of August, the wanderings of the widowed and childless captive were brought to a close.

---

* Laurel mountain.

SUCCESS OF BOLDNESS.

"Courage, prove thy chance once more."

While Colonel Tarleton was marching through North Carolina, near the close of the Revolution, he passed two nights in Halifax county. From malice or because of a scarcity of provision, he caused his troops to catch all the horses, cattle, hogs, fowls, etc., that could be found, most of which were destroyed. The inhabitants generally fled and concealed themselves in the neighboring swamps and thickets. One young lady, however, in the upper part of the county, where they spent the second night, refused to retire. Remaining on the premises alone, when the marauders came for the horses and cattle thereon, Miss Bishop* ordered them off; but they did not obey. Among the animals they drove to camp, was a favorite pony of hers, which she resolved to recover. When night come on, she went unarmed to the camp, about a mile distant, and boldly made known her errand to Tarleton. "Your roguish men in red coats," she said to him, "came to my father's house about sundown and stole my pony, and I have walked here

* Afterwards Mrs. Powell. She died in 1840.

alone and unprotected, to claim and demand him; and, sir, I must and I will have him. I fear not your men. They are base and unprincipled enough to dare to offer insult to an unprotected female; but their cowardly hearts will prevent them from doing her any bodily injury." While thus speaking, her eye happened to fall on her favorite animal, upon which the camp fire flung its light, and she added, "There, sir, is my horse. I shall mount him and ride peacefully home; and if you have any gentlemanly feeling within you, of which your men are totally destitute, or, if you have any regard for their safety, you will see, sir, that I am not interrupted. But, before I go, I wish to say to you that he who can, and will not, prevent this base and cowardly stealing from hen-roosts, stables and barn-yards, is no better, in my estimation, than the mean, good-for-nothing, guilty wretches who do the dirty work with their own hands! Good night, sir."

Tarleton took the hint; ordered his soldiers not to molest her; and she was suffered to take the pony and gallop peacefully home.

MARY KNIGHT.

———The office
Becomes a woman best; I'll take it upon me.
SHAKSPEARE.

The subject of this brief notice was a sister of General Isaac Worrell. She died two or three years since, in Philadelphia. The following tribute to her patriotism and humanity, was paid by a New Jersey newspaper, in July, 1849:

"The deceased was one of those devoted women who aided to relieve the horrible sufferings of Washington's army at Valley Forge—cooking and carrying provisions to them alone, through the depth of winter, even passing through the outposts of the British army in the disguise of a market woman. And when Washington was compelled to retreat before a superior force, she concealed her brother, General Worrell, —when the British set a price on his head—in a cider hogshead in the cellar for three days, and fed him through the bunghole; the house being ransacked four different times by the troops in search of him, without success. She was over ninety years of age at the time of her death."

THE WIFE OF WILLIAM GRAY.

——— Our lives
In acts exemplary, not only win
Ourselves good names, but do to others give
Matter for virtuous deeds, by which we live.

CHAPMAN.

Elizabeth Chipman was born in Essex county, Massachusetts, in May, 1756. She was the daughter of a talented and eminent lawyer of Marblehead, and inherited a highly respectable share of his mental endowments. Her intellectual faculties and moral feelings were early and highly developed; and when, in 1782, she was married to William Gray, the celebrated millionaire, of Salem, in her native county, she was prepared, in all respects, to command the highest influence in society. But, although the wife of the richest man in Massachusetts and probably in New England, she never rose above her duties as a housekeeper, a mother and a Christian. She managed her domestic affairs personally and economically; and inculcated in the minds of her six children, by example as well as precept, the best habits and the noblest principles. "She divided her time between reading, household affairs, and duties to society, in such a manner as never for a moment to be in a hurry."* She was as well known by the poor as the rich: her virtues irradiated every sphere. She was anxious to exalt as much as possible the Christian profession; hence she rode in a plain carriage, and avoided all unnecessary display, "that no evil precedents of expense could arise from her example."

The latter years of this excellent woman were passed in Boston, whither the family had removed, and where she died on the twenty-fourth of September, 1823. In her benevolent acts and cheerful life, is beautifully exemplified the truth of the poet's assertion:

> On piety humanity is built,
> And on humanity, much happiness.

---

* Knapp's Female Biography, p. 235

ANECDOTE OF MRS. HUNTINGTON.

> Earthly power doth then show likest gods,
> When mercy seasons justice.
>
> SHAKSPEARE.

Susan Mansfield was the daughter of the Rev Achilles Mansfield, of Killingworth, Connecticut, and was born on the twenty-seventh of January, 1791. At the age of eighteen or nineteen, she was married to Joshua Huntington, pastor of the Old South church, Boston. She died in 1823. Her memoirs, written by her husband's pastoral successor, B. B. Wisner, was, at one time, a very popular work. It passed through five editions in Scotland, in a very few years.

Her husband preceded her to the grave four years. While a widow, she was robbed of several articles of jewelry by a young woman; and the articles were recovered, and the thief arrested and tried. During the examination, Mrs. Huntington was called into court to identify the property; and having done this, she was asked their value. Knowing that the degree of punishment depended somewhat on the apprisal of the property, and pitying the poor girl, she hinted that she never used much jewelry, and was not a good judge of its value. A person was then called upon to prize the several articles; and she told him to bear in mind that they had been used for many years, were consequently damaged, and out of fashion. In this way she secured a low and, to herself, a satisfactory valuation. She then addressed the judge, stating that she had herself taken the jewelry from a trunk; had carelessly left it exposed on a table; had thus thrown temptation in the way of the girl, and suggested that her own heedlessness might possibly have been the cause of the offence. She did not, she assured the judge, wish to interfere with his duties, or wrongly bias his decisions, but she would, nevertheless, esteem it a favor, if the punishment inflicted on the unfortunate transgressor, could be the lightest that would not dishonor the law. Hoping the ignorant girl would repent and reform, she left the stand with tears in her eyes, which greatly affected the judge. In his sentence he reminded the culprit, that the person whom she had most offended, was the first to plead for a mitigation of her punishment, and had saved her from the extreme rigors of a broken law.

HOSPITALITY OF MRS. BIDDLE.

——All were welcome and feasted.
LONGFELLOW.

In the summer of 1777, while Washington was encamped near Brandywine, a large party of foragers came into the neighborhood, and the General gave orders to a company of his troops, to go in pursuit of them early the next morning, and, if possible, cut off their retreat. As an engagement might ensue, he also gave orders that the women should leave the camp. Receiving intelligence of the latter order, and unwilling to be included in it, the wife of Colonel Clement Biddle, an intimate associate of Mrs. Washington in the camp, went to the General and told him that the officers, who had gone on the expedition, would be likely to return hungry, and she would consider it a favor to be allowed to remain and prepare some refreshment for them. Washington complied with her request, and her servant was immediately posted off in search of provision.

Receiving information that a band of "rebels" was in pursuit of them, the foragers took a quick step out of the neighborhood. The pursuers returne at a late dinner hour exceedingly fatigued and ripe for attacking the "good things" prepared by Mrs. Biddle. Notified of her generosity, the officers forthwith repaired to her quarters, each saying, on his entrance, "Madam, we hear that you feed the army to-day." It is said that at least a hundred officers enjoyed her hospitalities on that occasion.

They ate like Famine, fast and well,
  Piling their plates with turkeys slain;
They conquered — bones alone could tell
  Of fowls late bled at every vein.

KINDNESS OF SOME CONVICTS

———When your head did but ache,
I knit my handkerchief about your brows,
* * * * * *
And with my hand at midnight held your head;
And, like the watchful minutes to the hour,
Still and anon cheered up the heavy time.

SHAKSPEARE.

When the yellow fever broke out in Philadelphia, several years ago, it was extremely difficult to obtain help at the hospital; application was consequently made to the female convicts in the prison. Braving the danger of becoming nurses for the sick under such circumstances, as many as were needed readily profered their aid, and remained as long as desired. There was a scarcity of bedsteads, and these females were asked for theirs. Willing to sacrifice the meagre comforts of a convict for the sake of alleviating the condition of the sick and the dying, they not only gave up their bedsteads, but bedding also. Such humane conduct, coming from whom it may, is deserving of praise and worthy of record.

MARGARET PRIOR.

—— If a soul thou wouldst redeem,
  And lead a lost one back to God;
Wouldst thou a guardian angel seem
  To one who long in guilt hath trod;
Go kindly to him — take his hand,
  With gentlest words, within thine own,
And by his side a brother stand,
  Till all the demon thou dethrone.

Mrs. C. M. Sawyer.

The subject of this notice was a native of Fredericksburgh, Virginia. She was born in 1773. Her maiden name was Barrett. She was married to William Allen, a merchant of Baltimore, at the age of sixteen; resided in that city for several years, and became the mother of seven children. All but one of them died in infancy. Her husband was lost at sea, in 1808, when her only surviving child was about eighteen months old.

Soon after becoming a widow she removed to the city of New York. There, in 1814, she was united in marriage with William Prior, a benevolent and public-spirited member of the Society of Friends. She was herself at that time in communion with the Baptists, she having united with them before the death of her first husband. In 1819 she joined the Methodists, with whom she remained in church-fellowship the residue of her life.

When the New York Orphan Asylum was instituted, she was appointed one of the managers and was, thenceforward, incessantly engaged in benevolent operations. We first find her in the more conspicuous "walks of usefulness," in the severe winter of 1818 and '19. There being, at that time, no public fund for meeting the wants of the poor, she made arrangements with her nearest neighbor—herself a kind-hearted, humane woman—to prepare soup three times a week for the destitute in the ninth ward. She had previously visited that part of the city and made herself acquainted with many suffering individuals. All who applied for soup, if not known, she accompanied to their homes, and presented them with tickets entitling them to further supplies, if found to be true objects of charity. Many, it is thought, were saved from starvation by her humane exertions. "These, and similar deeds of mercy, tended to enlarge her heart: while she watered others, she was watered also herself, and felt continually the truth of the assertion, 'It is more blessed to give than to receive.'" *

Notwithstanding her arduous, public duties, Mrs. Prior managed her household affairs with care, neatness and regularity. It has been appropiately said of her that she had "a place for every thing and

* Walks of Usefulness; or, Reminiscences of Margaret Prior, p. 17

every thing in its place." The time that some spend in fashionable and heartless calls, she devoted to industry and humanity. By rising early, working late, observing the strictest rules of economy, and subjecting herself, at times, to self-denial, she was able to visit the suffering, and to make daily ap propriations from her own table for their relief.

Numerous instances of her self-denial have been related, and one of them we will repeat. She usually obtained assistance to do her washing, and limited herself to a dollar a week to meet that expense. Sometimes the amount she wished to devote to some particular object fell short, and in such instances she would do the washing herself, and thereby save the dollar. She felt, in such cases, as has been remarked, that "the personal effort was made a blessing to herself of greater value than the sum saved."

In the year 1822, Mrs. Prior visited the families on Bowery hill, where she had resided the three previous years; thoroughly acquainted herself with their moral condition and necessities; established a school for poor children; commenced her long-continued weekly visits for conversation and prayer with the pupils, and secured the sympathies and pecuniary assistance of several Christians to aid in supporting the school from year to year. She herself contributed one hundred dollars annually for its maintenance.

On the fourteenth of September, 1829, this good woman again became a widow. Previous to this date she had lost her seventh child, and an adopted one. She had also taken a second motherless child into her family. About the year her second husband died, Bowery hill was dug away, and she changed her residence.

When, in the early part of 1833, the Moral Reform society was organized, she became a prominent member of its board of managers, and, four years afterwards, commenced, under its patronage, her memorable labors as a city missionary. These she continued till 1842, in which year, on the seventh of April, her earthly work was finished.

Two or three incidents connected with her labors as a missionary, will show, in part, at least, the character of her work and the philanthropic spirit by which she was ever actuated.

As she was once passing through the streets, she was accosted by a lady who inquired her name, and wished to know if she did not belong to the society which had opened a register of direction for the accommodation of respectable females. Ascertaining that she was not mistaken in the person, the stranger told Mrs. Prior that two female acquaintances of hers were out of work, had become reduced to want, and were so wretched as to threaten to drown themselves, unless they soon found a situation. They had been working for houses connected with the southern trade which had failed, and thus thrown them out of employment. Learning their residence, Mrs. Prior visited them immediately; told them of the enormity of the crime they had threatened to commit; that she would try to secure work for them, and that it was their duty to seek the grace of God to sustain them in such trying seasons. The next day she found situations for them in pious families, and thus, while she probably saved them from committing suicide, she was, perhaps, the instrument, in the hands of God, of saving them from infamy and eternal ruin.

Passing through the suburbs of the city one day, her attention was arrested by the chime of youthful voices. Seeing that the music proceeded from some little beggar-girls, who were sitting in the sun beside the fence and singing a Sabbath school hymn, she inquired of them what they were doing, when the following dialogue occurred: "We were cold, ma'am, and are getting warm in the sun." "Where do you live?" "In Twentieth street, ma'am." "Why have you come so far away from your homes?" "To get some food and some things to make a fire." "Why were you singing?" "To praise God: we go to the Sunday school, and our teacher says if we are good children God will never let us want." Pleased with the modest and artless answers to her questions, the good woman took them across the street, procured each of them a loaf of bread, gave them some pious counsel, and left them with smiles on their faces and gratitude in their hearts.

Mrs. Prior frequently visited the city prison, and on occasion * went to Sing Sing. She made a record of her visit to the latter place, from which we make an extract: "In visiting the female convicts at their

* June, 1840.

cells on Sabbath morning, after Sabbath school, which, under the customary regulations, we were permitted to do, we found nearly all employed in reading their Bibles. We conversed with them respecting the welfare of their souls, and as we knelt with them at the throne of grace, they on one side of the grated door and we on the other, we felt that He who healed a Mary Magdalene, is still the same compassionate Saviour, and our faith, we trust, apprehended him as the atoning sacrifice, who bore our sins in his own body on the tree, and opened a way for the salvation of even the chief of sinners."

Being on an errand of mercy in G——— street one day, she stepped into a house of infamy to leave a certain tract. As soon as she had entered and made known her mission, the door was closed and locked by one of the female inmates, who told her that she was their prisoner. "For a moment," writes Mrs. Prior, in her journal, "my heart was tremulous; I said nothing till the risings of fear were quelled, and then replied pleasantly, 'Well, if I'm a prisoner, I shall pray here, and would sing praises to God if I were not so hoarse. Yes, bless the Lord! his presence can make me happy here or any where, and you can have no power to harm me unless he gives it. This is a dreadful place, to be sure, but it is not so bad as hell; for there, there is no hope. The smoke of their torment ascendeth up for ever and ever! What a mercy that we are not all there! what compassion in the blessed Jesus that he spares us, when our sins are every day so great.' I talked to them in this manner till they were glad to open the door as a signal for my release."

Such were the doings, such was the character, of Margaret Prior. We see her organizing week-day and Sabbath schools, industrial associations and temperance societies; establishing soup houses and orphan asylums; visiting the sick, the poor, the idle, the culprit, the outcast; pointing the dying to a risen Saviour, leading the destitute by the hand to the place of relief, the idle to houses of industry, and warning the outlaw and the corrupt of the certain and terrible doom that would attend persistency in their downward course. With the sweetness, gentleness, simplicity, and delicacy, so becoming in woman under all circumstances, were blended in her character, energy that was unconquerable, courage that danger could not blench, and firmness that human power could not bend. The contemplation of such a character is superficial, if it does not prompt benevolent feelings, re-affirm virtuous resolutions, and revive and strengthen drooping piety.

NOBLE ACTS OF KINDNESS.

We are to relieve the distressed, to put the wanderer in the way, and divide our bread with the hungry.—SENECA.

The Rev. Thomas Andros, of Berkley, Massachusetts, was a firm patriot and a keen sufferer in the strife for freedom. He was captured whilst on board a privateer, and transferred to the Jersey prison ship. In the autumn of 1781, he escaped; and, skulking through the east end of Long Island, received at the hands of females such marks of pity and kindness as were thought worthy of noting in his journal. The following are extracts:

"I came to a respectable dwelling-house and entered it. Among the inmates were a decent woman and a tailor. To the woman I expressed my want of something to nourish my feeble frame, telling her if she would give me a morsel, it would be a mere act of charity. She made no objection, asked no questions, but promptly furnished me with the dish of light food I desired. Expressing my obligations to her, I rose to depart. But going round through another room, she met me in the front entry, placed a hat on my head, put an apple pie in my hand, and said, 'you will want this before you get through the woods.' I opened my mouth to give vent to the grateful feelings with which my heart was filled. But she would not tarry to hear a word, and instantly vanished. The mystery of her conduct I suppose was this: she was satisfied that I had escaped from prison, and if she granted me any succor, knowing me to be such, it might cost her family the confiscation of their estate. She did not therefore wish to ask me any questions or hear me explain who I was in the hearing of the tailor, who might turn informer. This mark of kindness was more than I could well bear, and as I went on the tears flowed copiously! The recollection of her humanity and pity revives in my breast even now the same feeling of gratitude.

"Some time after, in Suffolk county, being repulsed from one dwelling, I entered another, and informed the mistress of the house of my wants. By the cheerfulness and good-nature depicted in her countenance and first movements, I knew my suit was granted, and I had nothing more to say than to apprise her I was penniless. In a few moments she placed on the table a bowl of bread and milk, a dried bluefish roasted, and a mug of cider, and said, 'sit down and eat.'

"It was now growing dark, so I went but a short distance further, entered a house, and begged the privilege of lodging by the fire. My request was granted. There was no one in the house but the man and his wife. They appeared to be cordial friends to each other—it was indeed one of the few happy matches. Before it became late in the evening the man took his Bible and read a chapter. He then arose and offered up his grateful acknowledgments and supplications to God through the Mediator. I now began to think I had got into a safe and hospitable retreat. They had before made many inquiries such as indicated that they felt tenderly and took an interest in my welfare. I now confessed my situation to them. All was silence. It took some time to recover themselves from a flood of tears. At last the kind woman said, 'Let us go and bake his clothes.' No sooner said than the man seized a brand of fire and threw it into the oven. The woman provided a clean suit of clothes to supply the place of mine till they had purified them by fire. The work done, a clean bed was laid down on which I was to rest, and rest I did as in a new world; for I had got rid of a swarm of cannibals who were eating me up alive! In the morning I took my leave of this dear family with a gratitude that for fifty years has suffered no abatement."*

* Mr. Andros thus describes the old Jersey: "Her dark and filthy exterior corresponded with the death and despair reigning within. It is supposed that eleven thousand American seamen perished in her. None came to relieve their woes. Once or twice, by order of a stranger on the quarter-deck, a bag of apples was hurled promiscuously into the midst of hundreds of prisoners, crowded as thick as they could stand —and life and limbs were endangered in the struggle. The prisoners were secured between the decks by iron gratings; and when the ship was to be cleared of water, an armed guard forced them up to the winches, amid a roar of execrations and reproaches—the dim light adding to the horrors of the scene. Thousands died whose names have never been known; perishing when no eye could witness their fortitude, nor praise their devotion to their country."

THE WIFE OF DR. RAMSAY.

Unrivalled as thy merit, be thy fame.

TICKELL.

Few women of modern times have more charmingly exhibited "the beauties of holiness" than Martha Laurens Ramsay, the wife of the historian of South Carolina. In his interesting series of lectures on the Christian graces, the Rev. Dr. Williams very happily refers to her habit of prayer, to illustrate the spirit of brotherly kindness as shown in the mutual intercession of brethren in the same church. "It is animating," he writes, "and yet, as contrasted with our present remissness, humiliating, to read how Baxter and his people held days of fasting and prayer for each other; or to turn to the pages which describe a Christian matron of the South, the wife of Ramsay and the daughter of Henry Laurens, President of the Continental Congress, praying over a list of her fellow-members, name by name, and remembering, to the best of her knowledge, the cares and wants of each before the throne of grace.*

* Religious Progress, pp. 200-1.

Prior to her marriage, and whilst residing in France with her father, she received from him the handsome present of five hundred guineas. Appropriating a very small portion of this sum to her own use, with the bulk she purchased one hundred French Testaments—all to be found in the market— and distributed them amongst the destitute in Vigan and its vicinity, and organized a school there for the instruction of youth, constituting a fund sufficient to oblite rate its annual charges.

Mrs. Ramsay was remarkably economical of time, rising early and devoting every hour to some useful service; and of money, never indulging herself in any needless expenditure. This principle of economy was observed even at her funeral. She directed that it should be at her own private house; and that her coffin should be plain and without a plate. She died on the tenth of June, 1811.

COURAGE AND PRESENCE OF MIND OF MARGARET SCHUYLER.

—Courage mounteth with occasion.
SHAKSPEARE.

In August, 1781, when the abduction of General Schuyler from his house in the suburbs of Albany, was projected, and John Waltermeyer, the bold partizan of Joseph Bettys, led a motley and blood-thirsty band—tories, Canadians and Indians—in the daring undertaking, a daughter of the General acted so courageous and wise a part as to justify us in giving on outline sketch of the unsuccessful enterprise.

As the family sat in an open door, in the evening of a very sultry day, receiving information that a stranger was waiting at the back gate to see him, General Schuyler mistrusted, at once, that something was wrong; and, instead of repairing to the gate, he instantly closed and fastened the doors, and ran to his bed chamber for his arms. He then hurried his family into the third story, where he immediately discharged a pistol to arouse the careless guards, and afterwards others, to alarm, if possible, the inhabitants of the city. In hurrying up stairs, his wife overlooked her infant, which was asleep in the cradle; and she was about to descend, when the General warned her of the danger, and held her back. Seeing her mother's agony, a daughter named Margaret, rushed down stairs into the nursery, caught the child, and was about ascending, when a tomahawk flew past her, simply grazing her dress and slightly injuring it. Hurrying up a private stairway, she was met by Waltermeyer, who roughly exclaimed, "Wench! where is your master?" With remarkable presence of mind, she answered, "Gone to alarm the town." Fearing that such might be the case, Waltermeyer called his pilfering men, who were bagging plate in the dining hall, and began a consultation. Meanwhile the General was also thinking, and devising a stratagem by which to frighten away the kidnappers. He soon threw up a window, and, in the voice of an experienced commander, cried out, "Come on, my brave fellows; surround the house and secure the villains who are plundering." As he anticipated, the gang, hearing these words, snapped the thread of their consultation, and tested the nimbleness of their feet. The reports of the General's arms had alarmed the people of the city, and they came to the rescue just in season to be unneeded.

NOBLE TREATMENT OF ENEMIES.

—— True religion
Is always mild, propitious and humble,
Plays not the tyrant, plants no faith in blood;
Nor bears destruction on her chariot wheels;
Buts stoops to polish, succor, and redress,
And builds her grandeur on the public good.
MILLER'S MAHOMET.

Among the early converts to Christianity in the Cherokee tribe, were a few women, who formed themselves into a society for propagating the Gospel. They felt its expanding power, and, though poor, were anxious to do something for those who were not sharing in the same blessing. The proceeds of their first year's efforts, were about ten dollars; and while deliberating on the manner of its appropriation, one of the members suggested that it be devoted to the promotion of religion among the Osages, giving as a reason that they were the greatest enemies of the Cherokees, and that the Bible teaches Christians to do good to such.

HUMANITY REWARDED.

——I should some kindness show them.
SHAKSPEARE.

Among the early settlements of New Hampshire, were several on the Piscataqua river, in the neighborhood of the present town of Dover. For awhile the aborigines and whites were on amicable terms, and the former not unfrequently paid the latter a friendly visit. On one of those occasions, a pappoos was suddenly seized with illness, and its mother was obliged to remain several days. She found shelter and accommodations with a widow, who received her cordially, and nursed the feeble infant as her own. Such kindness would not be forgotten, even by savages; and when, after the lapse of years, the bow was bent and the hatchet raised against the settlement where the widow resided, the Indians placed a strong guard around her house; and, though the butchery was terrible, she and her family were unharmed.

MARGARET WINTHROI

——When meet now
Such pairs, in love and honor joined?
MILTON.

Governor Winthrop, the father of the Massach. setts' colony, married Margaret, the daughter of Si John Tindal, in April, 1618. She was his third wife, and a woman of rare qualities both of mind and heart. Previous to their emigration to New England, it was not an uncommon occurrence for them to be separated, and their correspondence on such occasions savors of the purest affection. Who does not see the image of a devoted wife and an exalted spirit in the following letter, written about the year 1627:

"MY MOST SWEET HUSBAND,—How dearly welcome thy kind letter was to me, I am not able to express. The sweetness of it did much refresh me. What can be more pleasing to a wife, than to hear of the welfare of her best beloved, and how he is pleased with her poor endeavors! I blush to hear myself commended, knowing my own wants. But it is your love that conceives the best, and makes all things seem better than they are. I wish that I may be always pleasing to thee, and that those comforts we have in each other may be daily increased, as far as they may be pleasing to God. I will use that speech to thee, that Abigail did to David: 'I will be a servant to wash the feet of my lord.' I will do any service wherein I may please my good husband. I confess I cannot do enough for thee; but thou art pleased to accept the will for the deed, and rest contented.

"I have many reasons to make me love thee, whereof I will name two: first, because thou lovest God; and secondly, because thou lovest me. If these two were wanting, all the rest would be eclipsed. But I must leave this discourse, and go about my household affairs. I am a bad housewife to be so long from them; but I must needs borrow a little time to talk with thee, my sweet heart. I hope thy business draws to an end. It will be but two or three weeks before I see thee, though they be long ones. God will bring us together in his good time; for which I shall pray.

Farewell, my good husband; the Lord keep thee.

Your obedient wife,

MARGARET WINTHROP."

Below is another letter from the pen of this good woman, written after her husband had decided to come to Massachusetts, and just before his embarkation:

"MY MOST DEAR HUSBAND,—I should not now omit any opportunity of writing to thee, considering I shall not long have thee to write unto. But, by reason of my unfitness at this time, I must entreat thee to accept of a few lines from me, and not impute it to any want of love, or neglect of duty to thee, to whom I owe more than I ever shall be able to express.

"My request now shall be to the Lord to prosper thee in thy voyage, and enable thee and fit thee for it, and give all graces and gifts for such employments as he shall call thee to. I trust God will once more bring us together before you go, that we may see each other with gladness, and take a solemn leave, till we, through the goodness of our God, shall meet in New England, which will be a joyful day to us. With my best wishes to God for thy health and welfare, I take my leave and rest, thy faithful, obedient wife, MARGARET WINTHROP."*

Governor Winthrop landed on these shores in June, 1630, and his wife followed him in about a year. She lived till June, 1647, and was perhaps as

---

* The following extract from a letter written by the Governor in March, 1629, shows that he was not unconscious of the excellence of the gift he possessed in his "yokefellow." Addressing her as "MINE OWN DEAR HEART," he proceeds:

"I must confess thou hast overcome me with thy exceeding great love, and those abundant expressions of it in thy sweet letters, which savor of more than an ordinary spirit of love and piety. Blessed be the Lord our God, that gives strength and comfort to thee to undergo this great trial, which, I must confess, would be too heavy for thee, if the Lord did not put under his hand in so gracious a measure. Let this experience of his faithfulness to thee in this first trial, be a ground to establish thy heart to believe and expect his help in all that may follow. It grieveth me much, that I want time and freedom of mind to discourse with thee, my faithful yokefellow, in those things which thy sweet letters offer me so plentiful occasion for. I beseech the Lord, I may have liberty to supply it, ere I depart; for I cannot thus leave thee."

useful in her more private, as her husband in his public and highly honorable, sphere. "A woman of singular virtue, prudence, modesty and piety;" though dignified, she was condescending; and knowing her place, she kept, and filled, and honored it. With undimmed and steady lustre, she shone for sixteen years amid the shadows of night that overhung and threatened the infant colony.

A PIONEER SETTLER'S ADVENTURE.

——Screw your courage up to the sticking place,
And we 'll not fail.

SHAKSPEARE.

The first settler in Hollis, New Hampshire, was Captain Peter Powers. He removed thither in 1731. His nearest neighbor, for a time, was ten miles distant; and in order to exchange courtesies it was necessary for the families to cross the Nashua river. It had but one convenient and safe fording place in that vicinity, and that one only when the river was low.

Having occasion, on a pleasant August morning, to visit her neighbor, Mrs. Powers mounted a Narraganset, hastened away, and reached the place of destination long before noon. Early in the after part of the day a fearful thunderstorm came up, and continued for several hours. Just at sunset the clouds began to break away, and Mrs. Powers immediately started on her return. She did not reach the river until some time after dark; and coming to the ford, she found the bank full and the water — as a narrator of the incident has it—"pressing on it with great rapidity." Added to this alarming circumstance, the wind had shifted and rolled the clouds up the sky again, so that the rain was descending in torrents, and drowning the threatening voice of the waves. Trusting to the experienced animal to keep the ford, and giving a slack rein, without realizing the danger, the courageous woman plunged into the black stream. The steed almost instantly lost its foothold, and "rolling in the waves at a full swim," made for the opposite shore. Missing the ford, and striking a forefoot on a rock in the bed of the stream, the animal was raised momentarily half way out of the water. Then plunging forward, it sank so deep that Mrs. Powers was raised from the pommel; but seizing the horse's mane as it rose, she held her grasp till they were safely on shore. The faithful animal soon found the right track, and in a brief hour Mrs. Powers was under the shelter of her cabin.

MRS. McKENNY.

More can I bear than you dare execute.
SHAKSPEARE.

"Not a great way from Steel's and Taylor's forts was a settlement consisting of a few families, among which were those of William McKenny and his brother James. These lived near Fishing creek. In the summer of 1761, sixteen Indians, with some squaws of the Cherokee tribe, took up their abode for several weeks near what is called Simpson's shoals, for the purpose of hunting and fishing during the hot months. In August, the two McKennys being absent on a journey to Camden, William's wife, Barbara, was left alone with several young children. One day she saw the Indian women running towards her house in great haste, followed by the men. She had no time to offer resistance; the squaws seized her and the children, pulled them into the house, and shoved them behind the door, where they immediately placed themselves on guard, pushing back the Indians as fast as they tried to force their way in, and uttering the most fearful outcries. Mrs. McKenny concluded it was their intention to kill her, and expected her fate every moment. The assistance rendered by the squaws, whether given out of compassion for a lonely mother, or in return for kindness shown them,—proved effectual for her protection until the arrival of one of the chiefs, who drew his long knife and drove off the savages. The mother, apprehending another attack, went to some of her neighbors and entreated them to come and stay with her. Robert Brown and Joanna his wife, Sarah Ferguson, her daughter Sarah and two sons, and a young man named Michael Melbury, came, in compliance with her request, and took up their quarters in the house. The next morning Mrs. McKenny ventured out alone to milk her cows. It had been her practice heretofore to take some of the children with her, and she could not explain why she went alone this time, though she was not free from apprehension; it seemed to be so by a special ordering of Providence. While she was milking, the Indians crept towards her on their hands and knees; she heard not their approach, nor knew any thing till they seized her. Sensible at once of all the horroı of her situation, she made no effort to escape, but promised to go quietly with them. They then set off towards the house, holding her fast by the arm. She had the presence of mind to walk as far off as possible from the Indian who held her, expecting Melbury to fire as they approached her dwelling. As they came up, he fired, wounding the one who held Mrs. McKenny; she broke from his hold and ran, and another Indian pursued and seized her. At this moment she was just at her own door, which John Ferguson imprudently opening that she might enter, the Indians without shot him dead as he presented himself. His mother ran to him and received another shot in her thigh, of which she died in a few days. Melbury, who saw that all their lives depended on prompt action, dragged them from the door, fastened it, and repairing to the loft, prepared for a vigorous defence. There were in all five guns; Sarah Ferguson loaded for him, while he kept up a continual fire, aiming at the Indians wherever one could be seen. Determined to effect their object of forcing an entrance, some of the savages came very near the house, keeping under cover of an outhouse in which Brown and his wife had taken refuge, not being able, on the alarm, to get into the house. They had crept into a corner and were crouched there close to the boarding. One of the Indians, coming up, leaned against the outside, separated from them only by a few boards, the crevices between which probably enabled them to see him. Mrs. Brown proposed to take a sword that lay by them and run the savage through the body, but her husband refused; he expected death, he said, every moment, and did not wish to go out of the world having his hands crimsoned with the blood of any fellow creature. 'Let me die in peace,' were his words, 'with all the world.' Joanna, though in the same peril, could not respond to the charitable feeling. 'If I am to die,' she said, 'I should like first to send some of the redskins on the journey. But we are not so sure we have to die; don't you hear the crack of Melbury's rifle? He holds the house. I warrant you that redskin looked awfully scared as he leaned against the corner here. We could have done it in a moment.'

"Mrs. McKenny, meanwhile, having failed to get into her house, had been again seized by the Indians, and, desperately regardless of her own safety, was doing all in her power to help her besieged friends. She would knock the priming out of the guns carried by the savages, and when they presented them to fire, would throw them up, so that the discharge might prove harmless. She was often heard to say, afterwards, that all fear had left her, and she thought only of those within the building, for she expected for herself neither deliverance nor mercy. Melbury continued to fire whenever one of the enemy appeared; they kept themselves, however, concealed, for the most part, behind trees or the outhouse. Several were wounded by his cool and well-directed shots, and at length, tired of the contest, the Indians retreated, carrying Mrs. McKenny with them. She now resisted with all her strength, preferring instant death to the more terrible fate of a captive in the hands of the fierce Cherokees. Her refusal to go forward irritated her captors, and when they had dragged her about half a mile, near a rock upon the plantation now occupied by John Culp, she received a second blow with the tomahawk which stretched her insensible upon the ground. When after some time consciousness returned, she found herself lying upon the rock, to which she had been dragged from the spot where she fell. She was stripped naked, and her scalp had been taken off. By degrees the knowledge of her condition, and the desire of obtaining help came upon her. She lifted up her head, and looking around, saw the wretches who had so cruelly mangled her, pulling ears of corn from a field near, to roast for their meal. She laid her head quickly down again, well knowing that if they saw her alive, they would not be slack in coming to finish the work of death. Thus she lay motionless till all was silent, and she found they were gone; then, with great pain and difficulty, she dragged herself back to the house. It may be imagined with what feelings the unfortunate woman was received by her friends and children, and how she met the bereaved mother, wounded unto death, who had suffered for her attempt to save others. One of the blows received by Mrs. McKenny had made a deep wound in her back; the others were upon her head. . . . .

"The wounds in Mrs. McKenny's head never healed entirely; but continued to break out occasionally, so that the blood flowing from them stained the bed at night, and sometimes fragments of bone came off; nevertheless, she lived many years afterwards and bore several children. She was at the time with child, and in about three months gave birth to a daughter — Hannah, afterwards married to John Stedman — and living in

Tennessee in 1827. This child was plainly marked with a tomahawk and drops of blood, as if running down the side of her face. The families of McKenny and McFadden, residing on Fishing creek, are descended from this Barbara McKenny; but most of her descendants have emigrated to the West. The above mentioned occurrence is narrated in a manuscript in the hand-writing of her grandson, Robert McFadden."*

* Women of the Revolution, vol. 3.

THE FISHERMAN'S HEROIC WIFE

Strong affection
Contends with all things, and o'ercometh all things.
JOANNA BAILLIE

"One of the small islands in Boston bay was inhabited by a single poor family. The father was taken suddenly ill. There was no physician. The wife, on whom every labor for the household devolved, was sleepless in care and tenderness by the bedside of her suffering husband. Every remedy in her power to procure was administered, but the disease was acute, and he died.

"Seven young children mourned around the lifeless corpse. They were the sole beings upon that desolate spot. Did the mother indulge the grief of her spirit, and sit down in despair? No: she entered upon the arduous and sacred duties of her station. She felt that there was no hand to assist her in burying her dead. Providing, as far as possible, for the comfort of her little ones, she put her babe into the arms of the oldest, and charged the two next in age to watch the corpse of their father. She unmoored her husband's fishing boat, which, but two days before, he had guided over the seas, to obtain food for his family. She dared not yield to those tender recollections, which might have unnerved her arm. The nearest island was at the distance of three miles. Strong winds lashed the waters to foam. Over the loud billows, that wearied and sorrowful woman rowed, and was preserved. She reached the next island, and obtained the necessary aid. With such energy did her duty to her desolate babes inspire her, that the voyage which depended on her individual effort, was performed in a shorter time than the returning one, when the oars were managed by two men, who went to assist in the last offices to the dead."

MRS. JAMES K. POLK.

A fault doth never with remorse
  Our minds so deeply move,
As when another's guiltless life
  Our error doth reprove.

BRANDON.

Sarah Childress Polk is the daughter of an enterprising and wealthy merchant of Rutherford county, Tennessee. She was married on the first of January, 1824.

Fitted to dignify and adorn any station appropriate for woman, while presiding at the White house she was universally esteemed, and retired as honorably as any woman since the days of Washington. She is intelligent, refined, unaffected, affable, courteous, hospitable, and, above all, pious, and exemplary as a Christian. She has been for years in communion with the Presbyterians; and while at the Capital, and the eyes of the whole nation were upon her, she forbade, in the President's mansion, any amusement not in keeping with the Christian profession. In this respect, it may be said of her, in the language of Shakspeare,

Thou art not for the fashion of these times.

The following poetical tribute, from the pen and heart of Mrs. Stephens, is well merited:

LADY! had I the wealth of earth
  To offer freely at thy shrine,
Bright gold, and buds of dewy birth,
  Or gems from out the teeming mine,
A thousand things most beautiful,
  All sparkling, precious, rich, and rare,
These hands would render up to thee—
  Thou noble lady, good and fair!

For, as I write, sweet thoughts arise
  Of times when all thy kindness lent
A thousand hues of Paradise
  To the fleet moments as they went;
Then all thy thoughts were winged with light,
  And every smile was calm and sweet,
And thy low tones and gentle words
  Made the warm heart's blood thrill and beat.

There, standing in our nation's home,
  My memory ever pictures thee
As some bright dame of ancient Rome,
  Modest, yet all a queen should be.
I love to keep thee in my mind,
  Thus mated with the pure of old,
When love with lofty deeds combined,
  Made women great and warriors bold.

When first I saw thee standing there,
  And felt the pressure of thy hand,
I scarcely thought if thou wert fair,
  Or of the highest in the land;
I knew thee gentle, pure as great;
  All that was lovely, meek and good;
And so I half forgot thy state
  In love of thy bright womanhood.

And many a sweet sensation came
  That lingers in my bosom yet,
Like that celestial, holy flame
  That vestals tremble to forget·

And on the earth, or in the sky,
  There's not a thought more true and free
Than that which beats within my heart,
  In pleasant memory of thee.

Lady, I gladly would have brought
  Some gem that on thy heart may live;
But this poor wreath of woven thought
  Is all the wealth I have to give.
All wet with heart-dew, fresh with love,
  I lay the garland at thy feet,
Praying the angel forms above
  To weave thee one more pure and sweet.

THE WIDOW JENKINS.

> In humblest vales the patriot heart may glow.
>
> J. T. FIELDS.

At the time Colonel Watson, the commander of a corps of regulars and tories, was making inroads upon the Pedee, he pitched his tent one night near the house of a widow named Jenkins, and took up his own quarters under her roof. Learning, in the course of the evening, that she had three sons fighting under General Marion, he commenced the following conversation with her:

"So, madam, they tell me you have several sons in General Marion's camp; I hope it is not true."

She said it was very true, and was only sorry that it was not a thousand times truer.

"A thousand times truer, madam!" replied he, with great surprise, "pray what can be your meaning in that?"

"Why, sir, I am only sorry that in place of three, I have not three thousand sons with General Marion."

"Aye, indeed! well then, madam, begging your pardon, you had better send for them immediately to come in and join his majesty's troops under my command: for as they are rebels now in arms against their king, should they be taken, they will be hung as sure as ever they were born."

"Why, sir, you are very considerate of my sons; for which, at any rate, I thank you. But, as you have begged my pardon for giving me this advice, I must beg yours for not taking it. My sons, sir, are of age, and must and will act for themselves. And as to their being in a state of rebellion against their king, I must take the liberty, sir, to deny that."

"What, madam! not in rebellion against their king? Shooting at and killing his majesty's subjects like wolves! don't you call that rebellion against their king, madam?"

"No, sir, they are only doing their duty, as God and nature commanded them, sir."

"The d——l they are, madam!"

"Yes, sir, and what you and every man in England would glory to do against the king, were he to dare to tax you contrary to your own consent and the constitution of the realm. 'T is the king, sir, who is in rebellion against my sons, and not they against him. And could right prevail against might, he would as certainly lose his head as ever king Charles the First did." *

---

* Weems' Marion, pp. 182-3.

A FAITHFUL LITTLE GIRL.

> Labor in the path of duty
> Beam'd up like a thing of beauty.
>
> C. P. CRANCH

"A very profane and profligate sailor, who belonged to a vessel lying in the port of New York, went out one day from his ship into the streets, bent on folly and wickedness. He met a pious little girl, whose feelings he tried to wound by using vile and sinful language. The little girl looked him earnestly in the face, warned him of his danger, and, with a solemn tone, told him to remember that he must meet her shortly at the bar of God. This unexpected reproof greatly affected him. To use his own language, 'it was like a broadside, raking him fore and aft, and sweeping by the board every sail and spar prepared for a wicked cruise.' Abashed and confounded, he returned to his ship. He could not banish from his mind the reproof of this little girl. Her look was present to his mind; her solemn declaration, 'You must meet me at the bar of God,' deeply affected his heart. The more he reflected upon it, the more uncomfortable he felt. In a few days his hard heart was subdued, and he submitted to the Saviour."

HOSPITALITY OF CALIFORNIA WOMEN

> Blest that abode where want and pain repair,
> And every stranger finds a ready chair.
>
> GOLDSMITH.

In his Three Years in California, the Rev. Walter Colton speaks as follows of the native women:

Their hospitality knows no bounds; they are always glad to see you, come when you may; take a pleasure in entertaining you while you remain; and only regret that your business calls you away. If you are sick, there is nothing which sympathy and care can devise or perform, which is not done for you. No sister ever hung over the throbbing brain or fluttering pulse of a brother with more tenderness and fidelity. This is as true of the lady whose hand has only figured her embroidery or swept her guitar, as of the cottage-girl wringing from her laundry the foam of the mountain stream; and all this from the *heart!* If I must be cast, in sickness or destitution, on the care of a stranger, let it be in California; but let it be before avarice has hardened the heart and made a god of gold.

SARAH LANMAN SMITH.

> Where'er the path of duty led,
> With an unquestioning faith she trod.
>
> T. W. Renne.

Among the many names endeared to the friends of missions, is that of Sarah L. Smith, a native of Norwich, Connecticut. Her maiden name was Huntington. She was born in 1802; made a profession of religion in youth; became the wife of the Rev. Eli Smith in July, 1833; embarked with him for Palestine the September following; and died at Boojah, near Smyrna, the last day of September, 1836.

Her work as a foreign missionary was quickly finished. She labored longer as a home missionary among the Moheagans, who live in the neighborhood of Norwich, and there displayed most conspicuously the moral heroism of her nature. In conjunction with Sarah Breed, she commenced her philanthropic operations in the year 1827. "The first object that drew them from the sphere of their own church, was the project of opening a Sabbath school for the poor Indian children of Moheagan. Satisfied that this was a work which Heaven would approve, they marked out their plans, and pursued them with untiring energy. Boldly they went forth, and, guided by the rising smoke or sounding axe, visited the Moheagans from field to field, and from hut to hut, till they had thoroughly informed themselves of their numbers, condition, and prospects. The opposition they encountered, the ridicule and opprobrium showered upon them from some quarters, the sullenness of the natives, the bluster of the white tenants, the brush wood and dry branches thrown across their pathway, could not discourage them. They saw no 'lions in the way,' while mercy, with pleading looks, beckoned them forward."

The Moheagans then numbered a little more than one hundred, only one of whom was a professor of religion. She was ninety-seven years of age. In her hut the first prayer meeting and the first Sabbath school gathered by these young ladies, were held.

Miss Breed soon removed from that part of the country, and Miss Huntington continued her labors for awhile alone. She was at that time very active in securing the formation of a society and the circulation of a subscription, having for their object the erection of a chapel. She found, ere long, a faithful co-worker in Miss Elizabeth Raymond. They taught a school in conjunction, and aside from their duties as teachers, were, at times, "advisers, counsellors, lawgivers, milliners, mantuamakers, tailoresses and almoners." *

* Missionary Offering, p. 86. We are indebted to the same source for most of the particulars embraced in this article.

"The school was kept in a house on Fort Hill, leased to a respectable farmer in whose family the young teachers boarded by alternate weeks, each going to the scene of labor every other Sabbath morning and remaining till the evening of the succeeding Sabbath, so that both were present in the Sabbath school, which was twice as large as the other. A single incident will serve to show the dauntless resolution which Miss Huntington carried into her pursuits. Just at the expiration of one of her terms of service during the winter, a heavy and tempestuous fall of snow blocked up the roads with such high drifts, that a friend who had been accustomed to go for her and convey her home in bad weather, and had started for this purpose in his sleigh, turned back, discouraged. No path had been broken, and the undertaking was so hazardous that he conceived no female would venture forth at such a time. He therefore called at her father's house to say that he should delay going for her till the morrow. What was his surprise to be met at the door by the young lady herself, who had reached home just before, having walked the whole distance on the hard crust of snow, *alone*, and some of the way over banks of snow that entirely obliterated the walls and fences by the roadside."

While at Moheagan, Miss Huntington corresponded with the Hon. Lewis Cass, then Secretary of War, and secured his influence and the aid of that department. In 1832, a grant of nine hundred dollars was made from the fund devoted to the Indian depart ment, five hundred being appropriated towards the erection of missionary buildings and four for the support of a teacher. Before leaving the Moheagan, for a wider field, this devoted and heroic missionary had the happiness of seeing a chapel, parsonage and school house, standing on "the sequestered land"* of her forest friends, and had thus partially repaid the debt of social and moral obligation to a tribe who fed the first and famishing settlers in Connecticut, and strove to protect them against the tomahawk of inimical tribes, and whose whoop was friendly to freedom when British aggressors were overriding American rights.

* That was its original name. It is a reserved tract; contains between two and three thousand acres, and a considerable part is now occupied by white tenants. Its situation is on the Thames between New London and Norwich.

A BROTHER SAVED BY HIS SISTER.

Brave spirits are a balsam to themselves.

CARTWRIGHT.

During the invasion of the Mohawk valley by Sir John Johnson, Samson Sammons, of Johnstown, and his three sons, were taken captive early one morning in May. The females were not made prisoners. While a soldier was standing sentinel over the youngest son, named Thomas, who was about eighteen, the latter, who was not more than half dressed, said he was not going to Canada in such a plight; that he should need his shoes especially; and asked permission to go to his chamber and get his clothes. The favor was not granted; but Thomas, resolving to have his shoes, stepped towards the door, when the barbarous soldier pointed a bayonet at his back, and made a plunge. At that moment a sister, who had watched every movement with breathless anxiety, sprang forward, seized the gun, threw herself across its barrel, bore it to the ground, and thus saved her brother's life. After a brief struggle, the soldier disengaged his weapon, but before he had time to make another plunge, an officer rushed forward and asked what was the trouble. The heroic girl stated the case, when the soldier was severely rebuked, and her brother permitted to obtain his shoes and all the raiment he desired.*

---

* It may be interesting to the reader to know that Thomas Sammons did not go to Canada. He was released in the afternoon of the same day, with some other persons who had been taken prisoners during the forenoon. Feigning extreme lameness in one foot, he attracted the attention and excited the sympathy of the widow of a British officer: she had resided in the neighborhood, knew many of the captives, and as some were her personal friends, she asked Sir John to permit their release. He did so; and on going into the field to select them, writes Colonel Stone, "she adroitly smuggled young Sammons into the group, and led him away in safety."

PATRIOTIC SACRIFICE OF MRS. BORDEN

They love their land because it is their own.
HALLECK.

At the darkest period of the Revolution, New Jersey was, for a short time, full of British soldiers, and Lord Cornwallis was stationed at Bordentown.* He visited Mrs. Borden one day, at her elegant mansion, and made an effort to intimidate her. He told her that if she would persuade her husband and son, who were then in the American army, to join his forces, none of her property should be destroyed; but if she refused to make such exertions, he would burn her house, and lay waste her whole estate. Unintimidated and patriotic, she made the following bold reply, which caused the execution of the threat: "The sight of my house in flames would be a treat to me, for I have seen enough to know that you never injure what you have power to keep and enjoy. The application of a torch to my dwelling I should regard as the signal for your departure." And such it was.

* Major Garden.

MARGARET CORBIN.

Where cannon boomed, where bayonets clashed,
There was thy fiery way.

SARA J. CLARKE.

An act similar to that recorded of Mrs. Pitcher at the battle of Monmouth, was performed by Mrs. Margaret Corbin at the attack on Fort Washington. Her husband belonged to the artillery; and, standing by his side and seeing him fall, she unhesitatingly took his place and heroically performed his duties. Her services were appreciated by the officers of the army, and honorably noticed by Congress. This body passed the following resolution in July, 1779:

"Resolved,—That Margaret Corbin, wounded and disabled at the battle of Fort Washington, while she heroically filled the post of her husband, who was killed by her side serving a piece of artillery, do receive during her natural life, or continuance of said disability, one-half the monthly pay drawn by a soldier in service of these States; and that she now receive out of public stores, one suit of clothes or value thereof in money."

BRAVERY OF MRS. CHANNING.

——The truly brave,
When they behold the brave oppressed with odds,
Are touched with a desire to shield or save.

BYRON.

Soon after the commencement of the Revolutionary war, the family of Dr. Channing,* being in England, removed to France, and shortly afterwards sailed for the United States. The vessel, said to be stout and well-armed, was attacked on the voyage by a privateer, and a fierce engagement ensued. During its continuance, Mrs. Channing stood on the deck, exhorting the crew not to give up, encouraging them with words of cheer, handing them cartridges, and aiding such of them as were disabled by wounds. When, at length, the colors of the vessel were struck, she seized her husband's pistols and side arms, and flung them into the sea, declaring that she would prefer death to the witnessing of their surrender into the hands of the foe.

* This anecdote, which is recorded in several works, cannot refer to the late William Ellery Channing, as he was not born at the commencement of the Revolution.

COMMENDABLE COURAGE.

Have chivalry's bold days
A deed of wilder bravery
In all their stirring lays?
SARA J. CLARKE

An incident which occurred at one of the forts in the Mohawk valley, might have been mentioned in connection with the heroism of Schoharie women. It is briefly related by the author of Border Wars of the American Revolution. "An interesting young woman," he writes, "whose name yet lives in story among her own mountains, perceiving, as she thought, symptoms of fear in a soldier who had been ordered to a well without the works, and within range of the enemy's fire, for water, snatched the bucket from his hands, and ran forth for it herself. Without changing color, or giving the slightest evidence of fear, she drew and brought back bucket after bucket to the thirsty soldiers, and providentially escaped without injury."

THE HEROINE OF SHELL'S BUSH.

> I dare do all that may become a man.
> Who dares do more, is none.
>
> SHAKSPEARE.

For three-fourths of a century, there has been a wealthy settlement of Germans four or five miles north of the village of Herkimer, in the upper part of the Mohawk valley, called Shell's Bush. Among the early settlers, was John Christian Shell, who had a family of six brave sons and a no less brave wife. When, on the sixth of August, 1781, a Scotch refugee named Donald McDonald, at the head of sixty-six tories and Indians, attacked that settlement, Mrs. Shell acted the part of an heroic dame. The house was built for border emergencies, and when the enemy approached, the husband and older boys * fled from the fields, entered their castle, and strongly barricaded the doors. From two o'clock in the afternoon until twilight, the besieged kept up an almost incessant firing, Mrs. Shell loading the guns for her

* The two youngest boys, who were twins and about eight years old, were captured; and when the enemy fled, they were carried away as prisoners.

husband and older sons to discharge. During the siege, McDonald attempted to force the door with a crow bar, and was shot in the leg, seized by Shell and drawn within doors. Exasperated at this bold feat, the enemy soon attempted to carry the fortress by assault, five of them leaping upon the walls and thrusting their guns through the loopholes. At that moment the cool and courageous woman seized an axe, smote the barrels and bent and spoiled them. Her husband then resorted to stratagem to drive the besiegers away: running up stairs and calling to Mrs. Shell in a very loud voice, he said that Captain Small was approaching with help from Fort Dayton. Then raising his voice to its highest pitch, he exclaimed, "Captain Small, march your company round upon this side of the house. Captain Getman, you had better wheel your men off to the left, and come up upon that side." * Fearing the phantom troops whom Mr. Shell's imagination had conjured, the enemy shouldered their guns—crooked barreled and all—and quickly buried themselves in the dense forest.

* Border Wars of the American Revolution, vol. 2, p. 153.

FATHER TAYLOR'S WIDOWED FRIEND

Humble toil and heavenward duty.
MRS. HALE.

"A pious widow, who resided among ignorant and vicious neighbors in the suburbs of B———, Massachusetts, determined to do what she could for their spiritual benefit; and so she opened her little front room for weekly prayer meetings, and engaged some pious Methodists to aid in conducting them. Much of the seed thus scattered on a seemingly arid soil, produced fruit. One instance deserves special notice.

"Among others who attended, was a young sailor of intelligent and prepossessing countenance. A slight acquaintance with him discovered him to be very ignorant of even the rudiments of education; but, at the same time, he had such manifestly superior abilities, that the widow became much interested in his spiritual welfare, and could not but hope that God would in some way provide for his further instruction, convert him and render him useful. But in the midst of her anticipations, he was suddenly summoned away to sea. He had been out but a short time when the vessel was seized by a British privateer and carried into Halifax, where the crew suffered by a long and wretched imprisonment.

"A year had passed away, during which the good woman had heard nothing of the young sailor. Still she remembered and prayed for him with the solicitude of a mother. About this time, she received a letter from her relations, who resided in Halifax, on business which required her to go to that town. While there, her habitual disposition to be useful, led her with a few friends to visit the prison with Bibles and tracts. In one apartment were the American prisoners. As she approached the grated door, a voice shouted her name, calling her mother, and a youth appeared and leaped for joy at the grate. It was the lost sailor boy! They wept and conversed like mother and son, and when she left she gave him a Bible—his future guide and comfort. During her stay at Halifax, she constantly visited the prison, supplying the youth with tracts, religious books, and clothing, and endeavoring by her conversation to secure the religious impression made on his mind at the prayer meetings in B———. After many months she removed to a distant part of the provinces; and for years she heard nothing more of the young sailor.

"We pass over a period of many years, and introduce the reader to Father T———, the distinguished mariners' preacher in the city of B———. In a spacious and substantial chapel, crowded about by the worst habitations in the city, this distinguished man delivered every Sabbath, discourses as extraordinary, perhaps, as are to be found in the Christian world. In the centre column of seats, guarded sacredly against all other intrusion, sat a dense mass of mariners—a strange medley of white, black, and olive; Protestant, Catholic, and Pagan. On the other seats in the galleries, the aisles, the altar, and on the pulpit stairs, were crowded, week after week, and year after year—the families of sailors, and the poor who had no other temple—the elite of the city—the learned professor—the student—the popular writer—the actor—groups of clergymen, and the votaries of gayety and fashion, listening with throbbing hearts and wet eyes, to a man whose only school had been the forecastle, and whose only endowments were those of grace and nature.

"In the year 183—, an aged English local preacher moved into the city of B——— from the British provinces.

"The old local preacher was mingling in a public throng one day with a friend, when they met 'Father T———.' A few words of introduction led to a free conversation, in which the former residence of his wife in the city was mentioned, and allusion was made to her prayer meeting—her former name was asked by 'Father T———;' he seemed seized by an impulse—inquired their residence, hastened away, and in a short time arrived in a carriage, with all his family, at the home of the aged pair. There a scene ensued which must be left to the imagination of the reader. 'Father T———' was the sailor boy of the prayer meeting and the prison. The old lady was the widow who had first cared for his soul."

PICTURE OF A REVOLUTIONARY MOTHER.

This is my own, my native land.
SCOTT.

True wit is nature to advantage dressed.
POPE.

Mrs. Eliza Wilkinson resided during the Revolution on Yonge's island, thirty miles south of Charleston, South Carolina. She was a cheerful, witty and accomplished young widow, and a keen sufferer on account of her whig principles. Her letters, arranged by Mrs. Gilman, and published several years ago, afford a panoramic view of many dark scenes at the gloomiest period of American history, and beautifully daguerreotype her own pure and patriotic heart. A single extract will show her character. She visited the city of Charleston soon after its surrender, and witnessed the departure of her exiled friends. Referring to matters about that period, she writes:

"Once I was asked by a British officer to play the guitar.

"'I cannot play; I am very dull.'

"'How long do you intend to continue so, Mrs. Wilkinson?'

"'Until my countrymen return, sir!'

"'Return as what, madam?—prisoners or subjects?'

"'As conquerors, sir.'

"He affected a laugh. 'You will never see that, madam!'

"'I live in hopes, sir, of seeing the thirteen stripes hoisted once more on the bastions of this garrison.'

"'Do not hope so; but come, give us a tune on the guitar.'

"'I can play nothing but rebel songs.'

"'Well, let us have one of them.'

"'Not to-day—I cannot play—I will not play; besides, I suppose I should be put into the Provost for such a heinous crime.'

"I have often wondered since, I was not packed off, too; for I was very saucy, and never disguised my sentiments.

"One day Kitty and I were going to take a walk on the Bay, to get something we wanted. Just as we had got our hats on, up ran one of the Billets into the dining-room, where we were.

"'Your servant, ladies.'

"'Your servant, sir.'

"'Going out, ladies?'

"'Only to take a little walk.'

"He immediately turned about and ran down stairs. I guessed for what. . . . He offered me his hand, or rather arm, to lean upon.

"'Excuse me, sir,' said I; 'I will support myself if you please.'

"'No, madam, the pavements are very uneven; you may get a fall; do accept my arm.'

"'Pardon me, I cannot.'

"'Come, you do not know what your condescension may do. I will turn rebel!'

"'Will you?' said I, laughingly —'Turn rebel first, and then offer your arm.'

"We stopped in another store, where were several British officers. After asking for the articles I wanted, I saw a broad roll of ribbon, which appeared to be of black and white stripes.

"'Go,' said I to the officer who was with us, 'and reckon the stripes of that ribbon; see if they are *thirteen!*' (with an emphasis I spoke the word) — and he went, too!

"'Yes, they are thirteen, upon my word, madam.'

"'Do hand it me.' He did so; I took it, and found that it was narrow black ribbon, carefully wound round a broad white. I returned it to its place on the shelf.

"'Madam,' said the merchant, 'you can buy the black and white too, and tack them in stripes.'

"By no means, sir; I would not have them *slightly tacked*, but *firmly united*.' The above mentioned officers sat on the counter kicking their heels. How they gaped at me when I said this! But the merchant laughed heartily."

SUCCESSFUL DARING.

———He stopped the fliers.
SHAKSPEARE'S CORIOLANUS.

Many years ago, while a stage was passing through Temple, New Hampshire, the driver's seat gave way, and himself and a gentleman seated with him, were precipitated to the ground. The latter was killed. The horses took fright at the noise, and ran a mile or more at full speed. Meanwhile, Miss Abigail Brown, the only inside passenger and now the sole occupant of the stage, endeavored, by speaking soothingly, to stop the horses. At length they came to a high hill, when their speed began to slacken, and Miss Brown, having previously opened the door and taken a convenient position to alight, sprang out. Not content to save her own life, but bent on acting the part of a heroine, she rushed forward, seized the leaders, turned them out of the road, and held them fast till persons whom she had passed and who had tried to stop the flying steeds, came to her relief. Had this feat, trifling as it may seem, been performed by the wife of some Roman dignitary, she would have been apotheosized and her biography inserted in Lempriere's Classical Dictionary.

WORTHY EXAMPLE OF FORGIVENESS

They who forgive most shall be most forgiven.—BAILEY.

"A worthy old colored woman in the city of New York, was one day walking along the street, on some errand to a neighboring store, with her tobacco pipe in her mouth, quietly smoking. A jovial sailor, rendered a little mischievous by liquor, came sawing down the street, and when opposite our good Phillis, saucily crowded her aside, and with a pass of his hand knocked her pipe out of her mouth. He then halted to hear her fret at his trick, and enjoy a laugh at her expense. But what was his astonishment, when she meekly picked up the pieces of her broken pipe, without the least resentment in her manner, and giving him a dignified look of mingled sorrow, kindness and pity, said, 'God forgive you, my son, as I do.' It touched a tender cord in the heart of the rude tar. He felt ashamed, condemned and repentant. The tear started in his eye; he must make reparation. He heartily confessed his error, and thrusting both hands into his two full pockets of '*change*,' forced the contents upon her, exclaiming, 'God bless you, kind mother, I'll never do so again.'"

CROOKSHANKS SAVED BY A FEMALE.

——Oh the tender ties,
Close twisted with the fibres of the heart.

YOUNG.

The night before the surprise of Georgetown, Adjutant Crookshanks, one of the enemy's officers, together with some of his commissioned comrades, slept at a public house. The next morning it was surrounded, and the Adjutant would have lost his life, but for the interposition of the landlord's daughter, to whom he was affianced. Awakened and, at first, alarmed by the firing without and the bustle at the door, and hearing her lover's voice, she sprung out of bed and rushed, half dressed, into the piazza. At that moment the swords of her countrymen were raised over his head, and she threw her arms around his neck, exclaiming, "O save! save Major Crookshanks!" Though made a prisoner, he was forthwith paroled, and left, for the time, with the brave and true-hearted maiden.

A PATRIOTIC ARTIST.

Genius, the Pythian of the Beautiful,
Leaves its large truths a riddle to the dull.

BULWER.

"At the commencement of the Revolution, Mrs. Wright, a native of Pennsylvania, a distinguished modeler of likenesses and figures of wax, was exhibiting specimens of her skill in London. The king of Great Britain, pleased with her talents, gave her liberal encouragement, and, finding her a great politician, and an enthusiastic republican, would often enter into discussion relative to passing occurrences, and endeavored to refute her opinion with regard to the probable issue of the war. The frankness with which she delivered her sentiments, seemed rather to please than to offend him; which was a fortunate circumstance, for, when he asked an opinion, she gave it without constraint, or the least regard to consequences. I remember to have heard her say, that on one occasion, the monarch, irritated by some disaster to his troops, where he had prognosticated a triumph, exclaimed with warmth: 'I wish, Mrs. Wright, you would tell me how it will be possible to check the silly infatuation of your countrymen, restore them to reason, and render them good and obedient subjects.' — 'I consider their submission to your majesty's government is now altogether out of the question,' replied Mrs. Wright: 'friends you may make them, but never subjects; for America, before a king can reign there, must become a wilderness, without any other inhabitants than the beasts of the forest. The opponents of the decrees of your parliament, rather than submit, would perish to a man; but if the restoration of peace be seriously the object of your wishes, I am confident that it needs but the striking off of *three heads* to produce it.'—'O, Lord North's and Lord George Germaine's, beyond all question; and where is the third head?' O, sir, politeness forbids me to name *him*. Your majesty could never wish me to forget myself, and be guilty of an incivility.'

"In her exhibition room, one group of figures particularly attracted attention; and by all who knew her sentiments, was believed to be a pointed hint at the results which might follow the wild ambition of the monarch. The busts of the king and queen of Great Britain, were placed on a table, apparently intently gazing on a head, which a figure, an excellent representation of herself, was modeling in its lap. It was the head of the unfortunate Charles the First."

TEMPERANCE MOVEMENT AMONG MOHAWK WOMEN.

Beware the bowl! though rich and bright
Its rubies flash upon the sight,
An adder coils its depths beneath,
Whose lure is woe, whose sting is death.

STREET.

In the years 1801 and 1802, great efforts were made by the chiefs of the Mohawk Indians to prevent the sale of spirituous liquors among their people. In this humane movement the women of the tribe readily joined; and having assembled in council, on the twenty-second of May, 1802, they addressed the chiefs, whom they had summoned, as follows:

"UNCLES,—Some time ago the women of this place spoke to you, but you did not then answer them, as you considered their meeting not sufficient. Now, a considerable number of those from below having met and consulted together, join in sentiment, and lament, as it were with tears in our eyes, the many misfortunes caused by the use of spirituous liquors. We therefore mutually request that you will use your endeavors to have it removed from our neighborhood, that there may be none sold nigher to us than the mountain. We flatter ourselves that this is in your power, and that you will have compassion on our uneasiness, and exert yourselves to have it done." STRINGS OF WAMPUM.

This appeal had a good effect on the chiefs; and received suitable attention, drawing from them the following reply. It was delivered by Captain Brant:

"NIECES,—We are fully convinced of the justice of your request; drinking has caused the many misfortunes in this place, and has been, besides, a great cause of the divisions, by the effect it has upon the people's speech. We assure you, therefore, that we will use our endeavours to effect what you desire. However, it depends in a great measure upon government, as the distance you propose is within their line. We cannot, therefore, absolutely promise that our request will be complied with."

STRINGS.

A FEMALE IN THE REVOLUTIONARY ARMY.

She'll be a soldier too, she'll to the wars.
SHAKSPEARE.

Deborah Samson, the daughter of very poor parents, of Plymouth county, Massachusetts, began, when about twenty years of age, to feel the patriotic zeal which had prompted the sterner sex in her neighborhood to take up arms in their country's defence. She accordingly assumed male attire, and enlisted in the Revolutionary army. We agree with Mrs. Ellet that, while this course cannot be commended, her exemplary conduct, after taking the first step, goes far to plead her excuse, and is worthy of record. Her method of obtaining men's garments, and her military career, are thus narrated by the author just mentioned:

By keeping the district school for a summer term, she had amassed the sum of twelve dollars. She purchased a quantity of coarse fustian, and, working at intervals when she could be secure from observation, made up a suit of men's clothing; each article, as it was finished, being hid in a stack of hay Having completed her preparations, she announced her intention of going where she could obtain better wages for her labor. Her new clothes and such articles as she wished to take with her, were tied in a bundle. The lonely girl departed; but went not far, probably only to the shelter of the nearest wood, before putting on the disguise she was so eager to assume. Although not beautiful, her features were animated and pleasing, and her figure, tall for a woman, was finely proportioned. As a man, she might have been called handsome; her general appearance was extremely prepossessing, and her manner calculated to inspire confidence.

She now pursued her way to the American army, where she presented herself, in October, 1778, as a young man anxious to join his efforts to those of his countrymen, in their endeavors to oppose the common enemy. Her acquaintances, meanwhile, supposed her engaged in service at a distance. Rumors of her elopement with a British soldier, and even of her death, were afterwards current in the neighborhood where she had resided; but none were sufficiently interested to make such search for her as might have led to a discovery.

Distrusting her own constancy, and resolute to continue in the service, notwithstanding any change of her inclination, she enlisted for the whole term of the war. She was received and enrolled in the army by the name of Robert Shirtliffe. She was one of the first volunteers in the company of Captain Nathan

Thayer of Medway, Massachusetts; and as the young recruit appeared to have no home or connections, the Captain gave her a home in his family until his company should be full, when they were to join the main army.

We now find her performing the duties and enduring the fatigues of military life. During the seven weeks she passed in the family of Captain Thayer, she had time both for experience and reflection; but, in after years, her constant declaration was that she never, for one moment, repented or regretted the step she had taken. Accustomed to labor from childhood, upon the farm and in out-door employment, she had acquired unusual vigor of constitution; her frame was robust, and of masculine strength; and having thus gained a degree of hardihood, she was enabled to acquire great expertness and precision in the manual exercise, and to undergo what a female delicately nurtured would have found it impossible to endure. Soon after they had joined the company, the recruits were supplied with uniforms by a kind of lottery. That drawn by Robert did not fit; but, taking needle and scissors, he soon altered it to suit him. To Mrs. Thayer's expression of surprise, at finding a young man so expert in using the implements of feminine industry, the answer was—that his mother having no girl, he had been often obliged to practice the seamstress's art.

While in the house of Captain Thayer, a young girl visiting his wife, was much in the society of Deborah, or, as she was then called, Robert. Coquettish by nature, and perhaps priding herself on the conquest of the "blooming soldier," she suffered her growing partiality to be perceived. Robert, on his part, felt a curiosity to learn by new experience how soon a maiden's fancy might be won; and had no scruples in paying attentions to one so volatile and fond of flirtation, with whom it was not likely the impression would be lasting. This little piece of romance gave some uneasiness to the worthy Mrs. Thayer, who could not help observing that the liking of her fair visitor for Robert was not fully reciprocated. She took an opportunity of remonstrating with the young soldier, and showed what unhappiness might be the consequence of such folly, and how unworthy it was of a brave man to trifle with a girl's feelings. The caution was taken in good part, and it is not known that the "love passage" was continued, though Robert received at parting some tokens of remembrance, which were treasured as relics in after years.

For three years our heroine appeared in the character of a soldier, being part of the time employed as a waiter in the family of Colonel Patterson. During this time, and in both situations, her exemplary conduct, and the fidelity with which her duties were performed, gained the approbation and confidence of the officers. She was a volunteer in several hazardous enterprizes, and was twice wounded, the first time by a sword cut on the left side of the head. Many were the adventures she passed through; as she herself would often say, volumes might be filled with them.

Sometimes placed, unavoidably, in circumstances in which she feared detection, she nevertheless escaped without the least suspicion being awakened among her comrades. The soldiers were in the habit of calling her "Molly," in playful allusion to her want of a beard; but not one of them ever dreamed that the gallant youth fighting by their side, was in reality a female.

About four months after her first wound she received another severe one, being shot through the shoulder. Her first emotion when the ball entered, she described to be a sickening terror at the probability that her sex would be discovered. She felt that death on the battle-field were preferable to the shame that would overwhelm her, and ardently prayed that the wound might close her earthly campaign. But, strange as it may seem, she escaped this time also unsuspected; and soon recovering her strength, was able again to take her place at the post of duty, and in the deadly conflict. Her immunity was not, however, destined long to continue—she was seized with a brain fever, then prevalent among the soldiers. For the few days that reason struggled against the disease, her sufferings were indescribable; and most terrible of all was the dread lest consciousness should desert her, and the secret she had guarded so carefully be revealed to those around her. She was carried to the hospital, and there could only ascribe her escape to the number of patients, and the negligent manner in which they were attended. Her case was considered a hopeless one, and she perhaps received less attention on this account. One day the physician of the hospital, inquiring—"How is Robert?" received from the nurse in attendance the answer—"Poor Bob is gone." The doctor went to the bed, and taking the hand of the youth supposed dead, found that the pulse was still feebly beating; attempting to place his hand on the heart, he perceived that a bandage was fastened tightly around the breast. This was removed, and to his utter astonishment he discovered a female patient where he had least expected one!

This gentleman was Dr. Binney, of Philadelphia. With a prudence, delicacy and generosity, ever afterwards warmly appreciated by the unfortunate sufferer, he said not a word of his discovery, but paid her every attention, and provided every comfort her perilous condition required. As soon as she could be removed with safety, he had her taken to his own house, where she could receive better care. His family wondered not a little at the unusual interest manifested for the poor invalid soldier.

Here occurred another of those romances in real life, which in strangeness surpass fiction. The doctor had a young and lovely niece, an heiress to considerable property, whose compassionate feelings led her to join her uncle in bestowing kindness on the friendless youth. Many censured the uncle's imprudence in permitting them to be so much in each other's society, and to take drives so frequently together. The doctor laughed to himself at the warnings and hints he received, and thought how foolish the censorious would feel when the truth should come out. His knowledge, meanwhile, was buried in his own bosom, nor shared even with the members of his family. The niece was allowed to be as much with the invalid as suited her pleasure. Her gentle heart was touched by the misfortunes she had contributed to alleviate; the pale and melancholy soldier, for whose fate no one seemed to care, who had no possession in the world save his sword, who had suffered so much in the cause of liberty, became dear to her. She saw his gratitude for the benefits and kindness received, yet knew by intuition that he would never dare aspire to the hand of one so gifted by fortune. In the confiding abandonment of woman's love, the fair girl made known her attachment, and offered to provide for the education of its object before marriage. Deborah often declared that the moment in which she learned that she had unwittingly gained the love of a being so guileless, was fraught with the keenest anguish she ever experienced. In return for the hospitality and tender care that had been lavished upon her, she had inflicted pain upon one she would have died to shield. Her former entanglement had caused no uneasiness, but this was a heart of a different mould; no way of amends seemed open, except confession of her real character, and to that, though impelled by remorse and self-reproach, she could not bring herself. She merely said to the generous girl, that they would meet again; and, though ardently desiring the possession of an education, that she could not avail herself of the noble offer. Before her departure, the young lady pressed on her acceptance several articles of needful clothing, such as in those times many of the soldiers received from fair hands. All these were afterwards lost by the upsetting of a boat, except the shirt and vest Robert had on at the time, which are still preserved as relics in the family.

Her health being now nearly restored, the physician had a long conference with the commanding officer of the company in which Robert had served, and this was followed by an order to the youth to carry a letter to General Washington.

Her worst fears were now confirmed. From the time of her removal into the doctor's family, she had cherished a misgiving which sometimes amounted almost to a certainty, that he had discovered her deception. In conversation with him she anxiously watched his countenance, but not a word or look indicated suspicion, and she had again flattered herself that she was safe from detection. When the order came for her to deliver a letter into the hands of the Commander-in-chief, she could no longer deceive herself.

There remained no course but simple obedience. When she presented herself for admission at the head-quarters of Washington, she trembled as she had never done before the enemy's fire. Her heart sunk within her: she strove in vain to collect and compose herself, and, overpowered with dread and uncertainty, was ushered into the presence of the Chief. He noticed her extreme agitation, and, supposing it to proceed from diffidence, kindly endea vored to re-assure her. He then bade her retire with an attendant, who was directed to offer her some refreshment, while he read the communication of which she had been the bearer.

Within a short time she was again summoned into the presence of Washington. He said not a word, but handed her in silence a discharge from the service, putting into her hand at the same time a note containing a few brief words of advice, and a sum of money sufficient to bear her expenses to some place where she might find a home. The delicacy and forbearance thus observed affected her sensibly. "How thankful," she has often said, "was I to that great and good man who so kindly spared my feelings! He saw me ready to sink with shame; one word from him at that moment would have crushed me to the earth. But he spoke no word—and I blessed him for it."

After the termination of the war, she married Benjamin Gannett, of Sharon. When Washington was President, she received a letter inviting Robert Shirtliffe, or rather Mrs. Gannett, to visit the seat of government. Congress was then in session, and during her stay at the capital, a bill was passed granting her a pension in addition to certain lands, which she was to receive as an acknowledgment for her services to the country in a military capacity. She was invited to the houses of several of the officers, and to parties given in the city; attentions which manifested the high estimation in which she was there held.

HOSPITALITY OF ELIZABETH BRANT.

Stranger, whoe'er thou art, securely rest
Affianced in my faith, a friendly guest.

POPE.

At the close of the last war, John and Elizabeth Brant, children of the celebrated warrior, took possession of their father's mansion at the head of lake Ontario, and dispensed his "ancient hospitalities." While making the tour of Canada West with two of his daughters, in 1819, James Buchanan, Esq., British consul for the port of New York, visited the "Brant House," and afterwards published the following interesting account in a small volume of Indian sketches:

"After stopping more than a week under the truly hospitable roof of the Honorable Colonel Clarke, at the Falls of Niagara, I determined to proceed by land, round lake Ontario, to York; and Mrs. Clarke offered to give my daughters a letter of introduction to a Miss Brant, advising us to arrange our time so as to sleep and stop a day or two in the house of that lady, as she was certain we should be much pleased with her and her brother. Our friend did not intimate, still less did we suspect, that the introduction was to an Indian prince and princess. Had we been in the least aware of this, our previous arrangements would all have given way, as there was nothing I was more anxious to obtain than an opportunity such as this was so well calculated to afford, of seeing in what degree the Indian character would be modified by a conformity to the habits and comforts of civilized life.

"Proceeding on our journey, we stopped at an inn, romantically situated, where I determined to remain all night. Among other things, I inquired of the landlord if he knew the distance to Miss Brant's house, and from him I learned that it was about twenty miles farther. He added, that young Mr. Brant had passed that way in the forenoon, and would, no doubt, be returning in the evening, and that, if I wished it, he would be on the lookout for him. This I desired the landlord to do, as it would enable me to intimate our introduction to his sister, and intention of waiting on her the next morning.

"At dusk Mr. Brant returned, and, being introduced into our room, we were unable to distinguish his complexion, and conversed with him, believing him to be a young Canadian gentleman. We did not, however, fail to observe a certain degree of hesitation and reserve in the manner of his speech. He certainly expressed a wish that we would do his sister and himself the favor of spending a few days with them, in order to refresh ourselves and our horses: but we thought his style more laconic than hospitable. Before candles were brought in our new friend departed, leaving us still in error as to his nation.

"By four o'clock in the morning we resumed our journey. On arriving at the magnificent shores of lake Ontario, the driver of our carriage pointed out, at the distance of five miles, the house of Miss Brant, which had a very noble and commanding aspect; and we anticipated much pleasure in our visit. Young Mr. Brant, it appeared, unaware that with our carriage we could have reached his house so soon, had not arrived before us; so that our approach was not announced, and we drove up to the door under the full persuasion that the family would be apprised of our coming. The outer door, leading to a spacious hall, was open. We entered and remained a few minutes, when, seeing no person about, we proceeded into the parlor, which, like the hall, was for the moment unoccupied. We therefore had an opportunity of looking about us at our leisure. It was a room well furnished, with a carpet, pier and chimney glasses, mahogany tables, fashionable chairs, a guitar, a neat hanging bookcase, in which, among other volumes, we perceived a Church of England Prayer Book, translated into the Mohawk tongue. Having sent our note of introduction in by the coachman, and still no person waiting on us, we began to suspect (more especially in the hungry state we were in) that some delay or difficulty about breakfast stood in the way of the young lady's appearance. I can assure my readers that a keen morning's ride on the shores of an American lake is an exercise of all others calculated to make the appetite clamorous, if not insolent. We had already penetrated into the parlor, and were beginning to meditate a farther exploration in search of the pantry, when, to our unspeakable astonishment, in walked a charming, noble-looking Indian girl, dressed partly in the native and partly in the English costume. Her hair was confined on the head in a silk net, but the lower tresses, escaping from thence, flowed down on her shoulders. Under a tunic or morning dress of black silk was a petticoat of the same material and color, which reached very little below the knee. Her silk stockings and kid shoes were, like the rest of her dress, black. The grace and dignity of her movement, the style of her dress and manner, so new, so unexpected, filled us all with astonishment. With great ease, yet by no means in that commonplace mode so generally prevalent on such occasions, she inquired how we found the roads, accommodations, etc. No flutter was at all apparent on account of the delay in getting breakfast; no fidgeting and fuss-making, no running in and out, no idle expressions of regret, such as 'Oh! dear me! had I known of your coming, you would not have been kept in this way!' but, with perfect ease she maintained conversation, until a squaw, wearing a man's hat, brought in a tray with preparations for breakfast. A table-cloth of fine white damask being laid, we were regaled with tea, coffee, hot rolls, butter in water and ice-coolers, eggs, smoked beef, ham, broiled chickens, etc., all served in a truly neat and comfortable style. The delay, we afterwards discovered, arose from the desire of our hostess to supply us with hot rolls, which were actually baked while we were waiting. I have been thus minute in my description of these comforts, as they were so little to be expected in the house of an Indian.

"After breakfast Miss Brant took my daughters out to walk, and look at the picturesque scenery of the country. She and her brother had previously expressed a hope that we would stay all day; but, though I wished of all things to do so, and had determined, in the event of their pressing their invitation, to accept it, yet I declined the proposal at first, and thus forfeited a pleasure which we all of us longed in our hearts to enjoy; for, as I afterward learned, it is not the custom of any uncorrupted Indian to repeat a request if once rejected. They believe that those to whom they offer any mark of friendship, and who give a reason for refusing it, do so in perfect sincerity, and that it would be rudeness to require them to alter their determination or break their word. And as the Indian never makes a show of civility but when prompted by a genuine feeling, so he thinks others are actuated by a similar candor. I really feel ashamed when I consider how severe a rebuke this carries with it to us who boast of civilization, but who are so much carried away by the general insincerity of expression pervading all ranks, that few, indeed, are to be found who speak just what they wish or know. This duplicity is the effect of what is termed a high state of refinement. We are taught so to conduct our language that others cannot discover our real views or intentions. The Indians are not only free from this deceitfulness, but surpass us in another instance of good breeding and decorum, namely, of never interrupting those who converse with them until they have done speaking; and then they reply in the hope of not being themselves interrupted. This was perfectly exemplified by Miss Brant and her brother; and I hope the lesson my daughters were so forcibly taught by the natural politeness of their hostess will never be forgotten by them, and that I also may profit by the example."

Elizabeth was the youngest daughter of Joseph Brant. She was married to William Johnson Kerr, a gentleman who bore a commission in the last war, and fought against the Americans on the Niagara frontier. He is a grandson of Sir William Johnson. The author of American Border Wars, wrote in 1843, as follows: "Mrs. Kerr, as the reader must infer from what has been previously said respecting her, was educated with great care, as well in regard to her mental culture as her personal accomplishments. With her husband and little family, she now occupies the old mansion of her father, at the head of lake Ontario; a noble situation, as the author can certify from personal observation."

BRIEF ANECDOTES.

> The worthy acts of women to repeat.
>
> MIRROR FOR MAGISTRATES.

Immediately after the dreadful massacre of Virginia colonists, on the twenty-second of March, 1622, Governor Wyat issued an order for the remainder of the people to "draw together" into a "narrow compass;"* and most of the eighty plantations were forthwith abandoned. Among the persons who remained at their homes, was Mrs. Proctor, whom Dr. Belknap calls "a gentlewoman of an heroic spirit."† She defended her plantation against the Indians a full month, and would not have abandoned it even then, had not the officers of the colony obliged her to do so.

One of the best women of her times was Experience West, wife of the Rev. Dr. West, who was pastor of a church in New Bedford, Massachusetts, for nearly half a century. Her life abounded in praiseworthy, though unrecorded, deeds. The Doctor

* Belknap. † American Biography, vol. 2, p. 182.

was aware of the worth of his "help-meet," and had a punning way of praising her which must have sounded odd in a Puritan divine a hundred years ago. She was unusually tall, and he sometimes remarked to intimate friends, that he had found, by *long Experience*, that it is good to be married.

The Rev. Dr. Mather Byles, of Boston, a tory of considerable notoriety, paid unsuccessful addresses to a young lady who subsequently gave her hand to a gentleman of the name of Quincy. Meeting her one day, the Doctor remarked: "So, madam, it appears that you prefer a Quincy to Byles." "Yes," she replied, "for if there had been any thing worse than *biles*, God would have afflicted Job with them." *

A married Shawnee woman was once asked by a man who met her in the woods, to look upon and love him: "Oulman, my husband, who is forever before my eyes, hinders me from seeing you or any other person."

* Sabine's American Loyalist. The loyal divine was himself a wicked punster. "Near his house, in wet weather, was a very bad slough. It happened that two of the selectmen who had the care of the streets, driving in a chaise, stuck fast in this hole, and were obliged to get out in the mud to extricate their vehicle. Doctor Byles came out, and making them a respectful bow, said; 'Gentlemen, I have often complained to you of this nuisance without any attention being paid to it, and I am very glad to see you stirring in the matter now.' On the celebrated dark day in 1780, a lady who lived near the Doctor, sent her young son with her compliments, to know if he could account for the uncommon appearance. His answer was: 'My dear, you will give my compliments to your mamma, and tell her that I am as much in the dark as she is.'"

While the husband of Mrs. Dissosway, of Staten island, was in the hands of the British, her brother Nathaniel Randolph, a Captain in the American army, repeatedly and greatly annoyed the tories; and they were anxious to be freed from his incursions Accordingly, one of their colonels promised Mrs. Dissosway to procure her husband's release, if she would prevail upon her brother to leave the army She scornfully replied: "And if I could act so dastardly a part, think you that General Washington has but one Captain Randolph in his army?"

When, by permission of the British authorities, the wife of Daniel Hall was once going to John's island, near Charleston, to see her mother, one of the king's officers stopped her and ordered her to surrender the key of her trunk. On her asking him what he wished to look for, he replied, "For treason, madam." "Then, said she, you may be saved the trouble of search, for you may find enough of it at my tongue's end." *

When a party of Revolutionary patriots left Pleasant River settlement, in Maine, on an expedition, one of the number forgot his powder horn, and his wife, knowing he would greatly need it, ran twenty miles through the woods before she overtook him.

When the village of Buffalo was burnt during the last war, only one dwelling-house was suffered to stand. Its owner, Mrs. St. John, was a woman of

* Major Garden.

wonderful courage and self-possession; and when the Indians came to fire it, and destroy its inmates, she ordered them away in such a dignified, resolute and commanding, yet conciliatory, manner, that they seemed to be awed in her presence, and were kept at bay until some British officers rode up and ordered them to desist from the work of destruction. Saved by her presence of mind and heroic bravery, she who saw her neighbors butchered at their doors and the young village laid in ashes, lived to see a new village spring up, phoenix-like, and expand into a city of thirty-five thousand inhabitants.

Mrs. Beckham, who resided in the neighborhood of Pacolet river, South Carolina, was a true friend of freedom, and a great sufferer on that account. Tarleton, after sharing in her hospitality, pillaged her house, and then ordered its destruction. Her eloquent remonstrance, however, caused him to recall the order. Concealing a guinea in her braided hair, she once went eighty miles to Granby, purchased a bag of salt, and safely returned with it on the saddle under her.*

The house of Captain Charles Sims, who resided on Tyger river, South Carolina, was often plundered by tories; and on one of these occasions, when his wife was alone and all the robbers had departed but one, she ordered *him* away, and he disobeying, she broke his arm with a stick, and drove him from the house.

---

* Vide- -Women of the Revolution, vol. 1, p. 296.

Several years ago, a family, residing on the Colorado, in Texas, were attacked by a party of Camanche Indians, who first fell upon two workmen in the fields and slew them. Seeing one of them fall, the proprietor of the establishment, who was standing near his house, caught two guns and ran towards the field. A daughter hastily put on her brother's hat and surtout, and followed her father. She soon overtook him, and persuaded him to return to the house. She bravely assisted in guarding it until the Indians, tired of the assault, departed.

In the year 1777, when General Burgoyne entered the valley of the Hudson, the wife of General Schuyler hastened to Saratoga, her husband's country seat, to secure her furniture. "Her carriage," writes the biographer of Brant, "was attended by only a single armed man on horseback. When within two miles of her house, she encountered a crowd of panic-stricken people, who recited to her the tragic fate of Miss M'Crea,* and, representing to her the danger of proceeding farther in the face of the enemy, urged her to return. She had yet to pass through a dense forest within which even then some of the savage

* The circumstances in regard to the murder of Jane M'Crea, have been variously stated. The following version of the cruel story is probably correct: "Miss M'Crea belonged to a family of loyalists, and had engaged her hand in marriage to a young refugee named David Jones, a subordinate officer in the British service, who was advancing with Burgoyne. Anxious to possess himself of his bride, he dispatched a small party of Indians to bring her to the British camp. Her family and friends were strongly opposed to her going with such an escort; but her affection overcame her prudence, and she determined upon the

troops might be lurking for prey. But to these prudential counsels she would not listen. 'The General's wife,' said she, 'must not be afraid!' and, pushing forward, she accomplished her purpose."

While Thomas Crittenden, the first Governor of Vermont, was discharging the functions of an executive, he was waited upon one day, in an official capacity, by several gentlemen from Albany. The visitors were of the higher class, and accompanied by their aristocratic wives. At noon the hostess summoned the workmen from the fields, and seated them at the table with her fashionable visitors. When the females had retired from the dinner table to an apartment by themselves, one of the visitors said to the lady of the house, "You do not usually have your hired laborers sit down at the first table

---

hazardous adventure. She set forward with her dusky attendants on horseback. The family resided at the village of Fort Edward, whence they had not proceeded half a mile before her conductors stopped to drink at a spring. Meantime, the impatient lover, who deserved not her embrace for confiding her protection to such hands, instead of going himself, had dispatched a second party of Indians upon the same errand. The Indians met at the spring; and before the march was resumed, they were attacked by a party of the Provincials. At the close of the skirmish, the body of Miss M'Crea was found among the slain, tomahawked, scalped, and tied to a pine-tree, yet standing by the side of the spring, as a monument of the bloody transaction. The ascertained cause of the murder was this: The promised reward for bringing her in safety to her betrothed was a barrel of rum. The chiefs of the two parties sent for her by Mr. Jones quarreled respecting the anticipated compensation. Each claimed it; and, in a moment of passion, to end the controversy, one of them struck her down with his hatchet."

do you?" "Why yes, madam," Mrs. Crittenden replied, "we have thus far done so, but are now thinking of making a different arrangement. The Governor and myself have been talking the matter over a little, lately, and come to the conclusion that the men, who do nearly all the hard work, ought to have the first table,—and that he and I, who do so little, should be content with the second. But, in compliment to you, I thought I would have you sit down with them, to-day, at the first table."*

At the Fair held in Castle Garden, in the autumn of 1850, was exhibited a large Gothic arm-chair, backed and cushioned with beautifully wrought needle work in worsted. The needle work was from the hands of Mrs. Millard Fillmore. It was setting a noble example for the wife of a President to present her handiwork at an industrial exhibition; and, if the decision of the three Roman banqueters in regard to their wives, was correct—they preferring the one who was found with her maidens preparing loom-work,—Mrs. Fillmore must be ranked among the best of wives.

During the last war, Major Kennedy of South Carolina, wished to raise recruits for his troop of

---

* We find the substance of this anecdote in a copy of the Green Mountain Freeman published in March, 1851. The paper is edited by Daniel P. Thompson, Esq., who prefaces the article with the remark that the anecdote was related to him "by the late Mrs. Timothy Hubbard, of Montpelier, who, while a girl, was intimate with the Governor's family, and knowing to the amusing incident at the time of its occurrence."

norse; and accordingly went to Mrs. Jane White, who had several hardy sons, and made known his wants. She was a true patriot, like her husband, who was an active "liberty man" in the war of '76: hence she was ready and anxious to further the Major's plans. Her sons being at work in the field, excepting the youngest, she called the lad, and ordered him, in her broad Scotch-Irish dialect, to "rin awa' ta the fiel' an' tell his brithers ta cum in an' gang an' fight for their counthry, like their father afore them."*

Among the fine sentiments quaintly uttered by the old dramatic poet, Webster, are these:

> The chiefest action of a man of spirit
> Is, never to be out of action; we should think
> The soul was never to be put into the body,
> Which has so many rare and curious pieces
> Of mathematical motion, to stand still.
> Virtue is ever sowing of her seeds.

One of the models in activity and virtue, and one who doubtless secured thereby the prize of healthy and extreme old age, was Mrs. Lydia Gustin, a native of Lyme, Connecticut. She had five children, all of whom were at home to celebrate the hundredth anniversary of her birth day. She died in New Hampshire, on the twentieth of July, 1847, in the hundred and second year of her age. A part of the labor performed during her hundredth year, was the knitting of twenty-four pairs of stockings.

---

* Mrs. Ellet.

Mrs. Elizabeth Ferguson, who resided near Philadelphia, was one of the number who assisted the American prisoners taken at the battle of Germantown. She spun linen and sent it into the city, with orders that it be made into shirts. She was noted for humanity and benevolence. Learning, one time, while visiting her friends in Philadelphia, that a reduced merchant had been imprisoned for debt, and was suffering from destitution, she sent him a bed and other articles of comfort, and, though far from wealthy, put twenty dollars in money into his hands. She refused to give him her name, but was at length identified by a description of her person.

At the battle of the Cowpens, Colonel Washington wounded Colonel Tarleton; and when the latter afterwards, in conversation with Mrs. Wiley Jones, observed to her: "You appear to think very highly of Colonel Washington; and yet I have been told that he is so ignorant a fellow that he can hardly write his own name;" she replied, "It may be the case, but no man better than yourself, Colonel, can testify that he knows how to make his mark."

PHILANTHROPY OF AMERICAN WOMEN: MISS DIX.

> To the blind, the deaf, the lame,
>   To the ignorant and vile,
> Stranger, captive, slave he came,
>   With a welcome and a smile.
> Help to all he did dispense,
>   Gold, instruction, raiment, food;
> Like the gifts of Providence,
>   To the evil and the good.
>
> MONTGOMERY.

It requires the enlightening and expanding influ ence of Christianity to show the full extent of fraternal obligation, and to make one *feel* the wants of his brother's threefold nature. We must, therefore, look for large hearts, whose antennæ stretch through the domain of man's mental and moral, as well as his physical necessities, among a Christian people: there such hearts abound, and the strongest are among the female sex. Nor is this strange: the feelings of woman are more delicate, her constitution is less hardy, than man's. Physically more frail, she feels more sensibly the need of a helper and protector; and, being the greater sufferer, she thinks more of the sufferings of others, and consequently more fully develops the sisterly and sympathetic feelings of her nature.

It is not, therefore, surprising, that in all the humanitary movements of the age, American women are interested; but it *is* surprising to see with what masculine energy, heroic courage and sublime zeal they often prosecute their philanthropic labors. They lead in the distribution of the poor fund; are untiring in their efforts to sustain Sabbath schools in by-places; form and nobly sustain temperance organizations among themselves; establish and conduct infant schools on their own responsibility; manage orphan asylums; pray, and plead, and labor for the comfort of the insane, and for the education of the deaf, dumb and blind; and, with the religious tract in one hand and the Bible in the other, plunge into the darkest dens of vice, and, nerved by divine power, sow the good seed of truth in the most corrupt soil, with courage that seems to palsy the giant arm of Infamy.

Heroines in the philanthropic movements which so beautify the present age, are found in most of the villages and in every city in the land. Isabella Graham, Sarah Hoffman, Margaret Prior, and others whose names are recorded in this work, are representatives of a class whose number is annually increasing and whose philanthropic exertions are manifest wherever human suffering abounds or the current of moral turpitude is strong and appalling. With the delicacy and fragility inherent in their sex, they possess the bravery and perseverance of the ambitious leader in the military campaign, and shrink from no task, however formidable or disheartening.

They visit the abode of sickness, and the pillow is softened and the pain allayed; they enter the hut of penury, and the cry for bread is hushed, they pour the tide of united and sanctified effort through the Augean stables of iniquity, and the cleansing process is astonishing. Such is the work of philanthropic women; they are the "salt" of the community.

A lady is now living in the city of Buffalo, whose benevolent exertions, in her restricted sphere, would compare favorably with those of the celebrated Quakeress whose mission at Newgate justified, for once, at least, the use of angel as an adjective qualifying woman. The person to whom we refer — who would blush to see her name in print — is foremost in all the humane and charitable operations of the day, and has, for years, been in the habit of visiting the jail regularly and usually alone on the Sabbath, to instruct its inmates from the word of God and to lecture before them on all that pertains to human duty. She is married, and has a family — her children being adopted orphans, — hence her opportunities for public usefulness are measurably limited: but her life-long actions seem to say,

> "Give me leave
> To speak my mind, and I will through and through
> Cleanse the foul body of the infected world,
> If they will patiently receive my medicine."

Aside from our female missionaries, whose heroism is elsewhere partially illustrated in this work, the finest example of a living American philanthropist is Miss D. L. Dix, of Massachusetts. Her extreme modesty, learned through her New England friends, with whom we have corresponded, withholds all facts touching her early and private history, and leaves us a paucity of materials out of which to frame even an outline of her public career.

We first hear of her as a teacher in the city of Boston, in which vocation she was faithful and honored. At the same time, she was connected, as instructor, with a Sabbath school — belonging we believe, to Dr. Channing's society — and while searching in by-places for poor children to enlarge her class, she necessarily came in contact with many destitute persons, and saw much suffering. Ere long she became interested more especially in the condition and wants of poor seamen, and endeavored to enlist the sympathies of others in their behalf. As opportunities presented themselves, she visited the hospital and other benevolent institutions in and near Boston, together with the State Prison. Anon we find her in the possession of a small legacy left by her deceased grand-mother; and, having resigned the office of teacher, she is traveling through the state. Having visited all the counties and most if not all the towns in Massachusetts, hunting up the insane and acquainting herself with their condition, visiting the inmates of the poor-houses and jails, and learning the state of things among all the unfortunate and suffering, she went to the Legislature, made a report, and petitioned for reforms where she thought they were needed.

Having thoroughly canvassed one state, feeling her benevolent heart expand, she entered another, and went through the same routine of labors — visiting, reporting, pleading for reforms. She has traveled through all the states but three or four, and has extended her humane mission to Canada.

She overlooks no almshouse; never fails of seeing and learning the history of an insane person; goes through every jail and prison; and usually, if not invariably, has a private interview with each inmate, imparting such counsel as wisdom and Christian sympathy dictate. She has lately petitioned Congress — as yet unsuccessfully — for a large appropriation of the public lands for the benefit of the insane.

Her petitions are usually presented in a very quiet and modest manner. In her travels, she acquaints herself with the leading minds, and among them the state and national legislators; and when the law-making bodies are in session, she obtains an interview with members in the retirement of the parlor or the small social gathering; communicates the facts she has collected; and secures their coöperation in her plans and their aid in effecting her purposes.

She who began the work of reform as a teacher in a Sabbath school, has advanced, step by step, until her capacious heart has embraced the Union, throughout which the benign influence of her philanthropic labors is sensibly felt. Some one has truthfully remarked that "the blessings of thousands, ready to perish, have come down upon her head," and that the institutions which she has caused to be erected or modified in the several states "are monuments more honorable, if not more enduring than the pyramids."

While Miss Dix has brought about important reforms, she has accomplished her labors by great hardship and the most rigid economy. She had not a princely fortune, like Mrs. Fry, to expend in benevolent causes; she could not ride from place to place in her own private and splendid carriage, saying to this servant, do this, and to another, do that; she has been obliged to travel by public, hap-hazard conveyances — often in most uncomfortable vehicles in the most uncomfortable weather. A part of her early labors in the state of New York were performed in the winter, and when in the north eastern and coldest part, she was under the necessity, on one occasion, of traveling all night in the severest part of the season in an open carriage. To show her economy, which has been hinted at, it is necessary merely to say that she purchases the materials for most of her garments in the places which she visits, and makes them up with her own hands, while traveling on steamboats, waiting for stages at public houses, and such odd intervals of leisure.*

The character of Miss Dix is both pleasant and profitable to contemplate. Every thing connected with her public career is noble and worthy to be imitated. Would that the world were full of such

* For the two last mentioned facts, and some others in regard to Miss Dix, we are indebted to the Rev. G. W. Hosmer, pastor of the Unitarian church, Buffalo.

characters: they are needed. Although she has done a great work, much is yet to do. Our country is wide, and enlarging almost every year; the field of benevolence is white to harvest, and where are the reapers, who, like Miss Dix, will make their "lives sublime?"

THE END.

www.ingramcontent.com/pod-product-compliance
Lightning Source LLC
LaVergne TN
LVHW020921110826
845150LV00004B/729

* 9 7 8 1 4 2 5 5 5 4 6 4 4 *